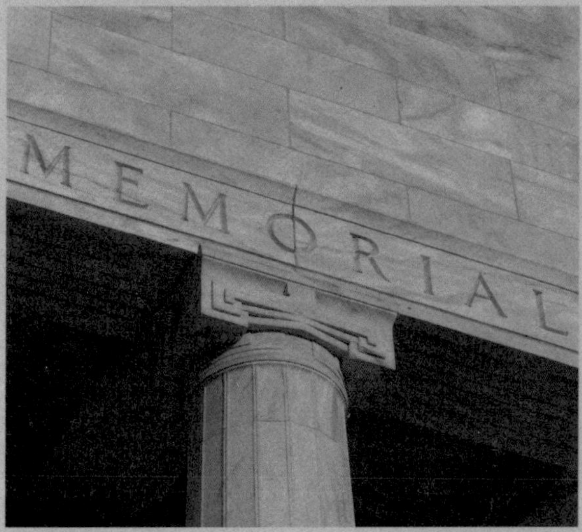
MEMORIAL

JOSLYN ART MUSEUM

a Building History

Graham W. J. Beal

Joslyn Art Museum
Omaha, Nebraska

Joslyn Art Museum: A Building History was published with funds generously provided by Charles W. and Margre H. Durham.

Library of Congress Cataloging-in-Publication Data
Beal, Graham William John.
Joslyn Art Museum : a building history / Graham W.J. Beal.
p. cm.

ISBN 0-936364-25-4
1. Joslyn Art Museum–History. 2. Art deco (Architecture)–Nebraska – Omaha. 3. Architecture, Postmodern–Nebraska–Omaha. 4. McDonald, John, 1861-1956–Criticism and interpretation. 5. McDonald, Alan, 1891-1947–Criticism and interpretation. 6. Foster, Norman, 1935- –Criticism and interpretation. 7. Omaha (Neb.)–Buildings, structures, etc. I. Joslyn Art Museum. II. Title.
N658.B43 1994
708'.182'254–dc20 94-34536
CIP
rev.

Published by Joslyn Art Museum, Omaha, Nebraska.
Designed by Emspace Design + Art Direction.
Film and separations by House of Graphics.
5,000 copies were typeset in Rotis Serif, Rotis Semi Serif, and Rotis Sans Serif and printed by Barnhart Press.

In Memoriam

MICHAEL B. WALSH

GRAHAM W. J. BEAL

Born in Stratford-on-Avon, England, in 1947, Graham W. J. Beal was educated at the University of Manchester and the Courtauld Institute of London University before coming to the United States in 1973. His experience in art museums includes the positions of Chief Curator at the Walker Art Center, Minneapolis, and at the San Francisco Museum of Modern Art. Director of Joslyn Art Museum from 1989 to 1996, he is currently Director of the Los Angeles County Museum of Art.

The archives of Joslyn Art Museum contain numerous historical and pre-renovation photographs, many of which are used in this publication. For images of the completed building and renovation project, the Museum chose Omaha photographer Pat Drickey to portray the visions of both the early and the late twentieth-century architects.

PAT DRICKEY

Pat Drickey has worked in Omaha as a photographer for 25 years. Early in his career Drickey was on the staff of an international architectural firm; he continued as a freelance photographer, specializing in architectural and landscape photography. He probably is best known for his images of the great golf courses and clubhouses around the world. In addition, his panoramic landscape images of the Sandhills in western Nebraska have been featured in a number of national publications. Drickey currently is a director of Stonehouse Publishing Co., which specializes in fine art golf prints.

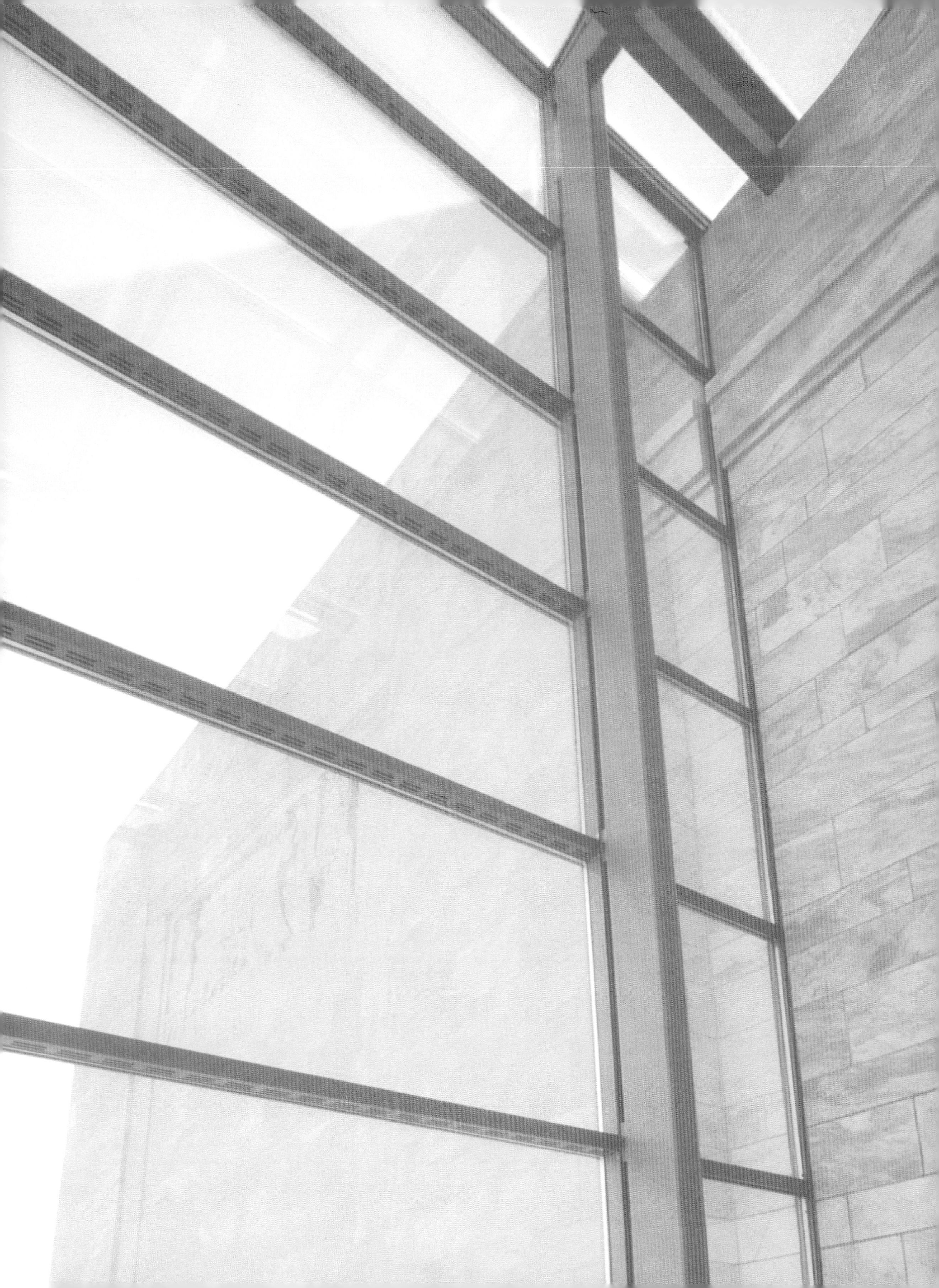

CONTENTS

FOREWORD

From the time of Sarah Joslyn to the present, the story of Joslyn Art Museum is an interesting one. I'm very pleased Graham Beal took on the task of telling that story in this book and adding the latest chapter, the building of the first major addition to the Museum.

Omaha has a number of architectural gems, but few approach the grandeur of Joslyn Art Museum and fewer still have made such major contributions to the life and culture of Omaha. For over sixty-five years, the Museum has fulfilled Sarah Joslyn's vision through its extensive permanent collection, notable special exhibitions, educational programs, and musical performances. It has become, as she wished, an important regional center for the visual and performing arts.

Like Sarah Joslyn, donors to the present-day capital campaign have also given a gift to future generations. Thanks to their collective vision, Joslyn will continue and enhance its mission of excellence for audiences of the twenty-first century.

This keepsake publication chronicles the planning and building of two extraordinary architectural projects which have been combined to form one magnificent museum. We think you'll enjoy Graham's telling of the story and the many historical photos that accompany it.

Walter Scott, Jr.
Chairman, Board of Governors, 1987-1997

PREFACE

In 1928 Sarah Joslyn, widow of the wealthiest man in Nebraska, gave over $3 million in his memory to found an art museum for the city of Omaha. The gift was extremely magnanimous, and the Art Deco building that rose from her gift was extraordinary, receiving national and international attention for its innovative and stunning architecture.

Since its opening in 1931, Joslyn Art Museum has changed dramatically. Already by the 1960s, the building no longer met the needs of a modern museum. It was no easy task, however, for the Joslyn Board to expand the facility, which was constrained by the proximity of two main thoroughfares and neighboring buildings. Also, the original structure was beloved by the community and any addition risked severe criticism. With remarkable restraint, the award-winning English architect Sir Norman Foster, working with HDR, Inc., and Kiewit Construction Company, created in 1994 an elegant "box," perfectly proportioned to match the monumental simplicity of the original building, and sheathed it in the same unusual pink Georgia marble as the 1931 structure. Inside, however, the architect let loose. Spaces soar. Visitors catch their breath in astonishment as they enter the 45-foot-high glass atrium connecting the old and the new buildings, or ascend the great staircase to the new galleries, where curved vaults dramatically float above the rooms like giant seagulls. Besides gaining much-needed gallery space to show the Museum's fine collection and to host national and international traveling exhibitions, the addition has offices, preparation and storage areas, shipping and receiving areas, a security control center, a full-service kitchen, and a 120-seat café. This building campaign added 58,000 square feet. With 213,000 square feet, Joslyn is the largest art museum in the region, and a potent symbol of the renaissance taking place in downtown Omaha.

The Museum today is the result of the benevolence and the persistence of many patrons – first and foremost, that of Sarah Joslyn. But the evolution of the Museum over the decades is due to a great number of dedicated people. Many of them are identified on these pages and on the walls of the Museum. Their names indicate that they wanted to leave the city better than they found it; not simply bigger, or richer, or more imposing, but better. Their generosity and enthusiastic support have enabled us to create the great museum we have today – and will ensure its growth in the future.

The publication of this important book was made possible by Charles W. and Margre H. Durham, long-time Joslyn supporters, to whom we give special thanks. In the following pages, Graham W. J. Beal, former director of Joslyn, tells the story of the two remarkable buildings and the people who created them. His elegantly written text captures the humor and the drama of Joslyn's history in a conversational, easy-to-read tone, making the complicated, simple, and even the mundane, exciting.

As we look to the future, we are planning further renovation of the 1931 galleries in order to make them as up-to-date as the new galleries. This will entail a major reinstallation to heighten visitors' understanding and enjoyment of our collection. Also, the Museum has received funding for refurbishment of the Founder's Room to its original splendor and for the addition of a permanent exhibition on George and Sarah Joslyn.

In the last few years, Joslyn Art Museum has had record-breaking attendance. Additionally, through outreach programs, the Museum serves as an important educational and cultural resource for the entire state and region. When praised for her great gift, Sarah Joslyn said: "I hope it will do some good". It does, Sarah, it does.

John E. Schloder, Ph.D.
Director

INTRODUCTION AND ACKNOWLEDGMENTS

Published after the opening of the 1994 addition to the Joslyn Memorial, this book is an attempt to provide the general reader with an account of the changing life and character of one of Omaha's best-loved buildings. In writing it, I have attempted to kill two birds with one stone: I wanted, generally, to give an indication of the wide variety of considerations that went into the planning of both structures. I also wanted to take the opportunity to describe the unusual sequence of events that transformed the design of the original building from a more or less traditional, classical temple into an unconventional essay in what I have, on occasion, called "Prairie-Egyptian-Deco" architecture.

To many, if not most, people, the art museum represents a distinct phenomenon: aloof, high-minded, and, above all, timeless. These are, I hope, no longer the characteristics that overwhelmingly define Joslyn but, then, art museums have never been quite the static, pickled-in-aspic institutions of popular myth. At their inception in the eighteenth century's Age of Enlightenment, they represented a distinct democratization of the cultural process, making available to the famously growing middle classes art and artifacts hitherto reserved for the aristocracy. A century later, museums in the United States extended this process, attempting to inculcate refinement in its citizens by offering them selected fragments of other historically validated cultures. They were also the first to take an active role in education, providing extensive in-house programs rather than simply making their holdings available to interested individuals.

Later, in the 1920s, two New York institutions were founded with the specific purpose of exhibiting contemporary art, a development expressing a new confidence in its own "ahistorical" culture (although Gertrude Stein, an American living in Paris, was quick to point out that a "museum of modern art" was a contradiction in terms). In the three decades following World War II, American art museums flourished: cities that did not have them built them; those that already possessed them added wings. Record numbers of people crowded in to see "blockbuster" exhibitions, and the idea of the art museum as a place where susceptible individuals could retire to contemplate particular works of art was all but overwhelmed by the notion of the museum as an exhibition hall for coming attractions.

Even so, art museums continue to offer a special kind of environment, and there are few museum-goers today who would not quickly recognize the feelings wittily expressed many years ago by Paul Valéry, poet and friend of the Impressionist painters:

> *At the first step I take toward things of beauty, a hand relieves me of my stick, a notice forbids me to smoke. . . . A soul resigned to torture, I make my way on to the paintings. A strangely organized disorder opens up before me in silence. I am smitten with a sacred horror. My pace grows reverent. My voice alters to a pitch slightly higher than in church, to a tone rather less strong than that of every day. Presently I lose all sense of why I have intruded into this wax-floored solitude, savoring of temple and drawing room, of cemetery and school. . . . Dreariness, boredom, admiration, the fine weather I left outside, my pricks of conscience, and a dreadful sense of how many great artists there are, all walk along with me.*
>
> –Paul Valéry, *The Problem of Museums,* 1923

The need for a facility amenable to activities that are both serious and lively, intellectual and social, underlies much recent museum building. In Joslyn's case, we found ourselves badly in need of basic facilities that would, without destroying its original character, finally convert the sixty-year-old, general-purpose cultural center into a specialist art museum, as well as provide the means to handle the retail and food service operations now common to most art museums of any size.

The origins for Joslyn's needs are to be found in the older part of the story told here: the lives of George and Sarah Joslyn. They were an extraordinary couple, and stories abound of their lives and habits. I myself have told many of them with relish, but the fact is that most of them are caricatures and fanciful exaggerations. I repeat some of the stories in this book, but mainly to establish, in as much as it is possible, the reality behind the fables. It is not always easy to relinquish a juicy anecdote (as the Italian proverb has it: "A good story is preferable to the truth") but, in this case, I hope that the real George and Sarah – individuals who contributed so much to the early social, artistic, and intellectual life of Omaha – come across convincingly. Certainly, they were both "types": he, the hard-driving, hard-drinking, entrepreneurial male, more than a little ruthless; she, high-minded and genteel, occupied in many good works. And, even if many of the exaggerations can be traced back to actual events or genuine personality traits, I came away from my second-hand encounter with them feeling that they were individuals I would very much like to have known. In my mind, especially, the popular image of the stern "Widow Joslyn," seated in her window, ceaselessly on guard against the depredations of children, hobos, and other undesirables, has been replaced by an altogether warmer picture of a highly intelligent, unpretentious yet sensitive woman, who withdrew into a quieter life following the relatively early death of her napoleonic husband.

If the building of the Memorial is a testimony to the devotion of one woman, the rebirth of Joslyn can also be attributed to individual determination. First and foremost, credit must be given to Walter Scott, Jr., who accepted the challenge to address the problems besetting the institution – problems that had, by 1987, reached crisis point. He brought together, in a new Board of Governors, a group of community leaders who contributed time, energy, and considerable resources to provide a thorough analysis of the Museum's needs. Of these, Robert B. Daugherty subsequently led the effort to raise the unprecedented funds required to realize the goals; Michael B. Yanney devised and oversaw the financial strategy that enabled speedy implementation of the capital expansion plans. The process of selecting an architect was given to a special committee of the Board of Governors and involved Harold W. Andersen, Sylvia B. (Babe) Cohn, Margre H. Durham, Willis A. Strauss (Chair 1991-94), and Michael B. Walsh (Chair 1991). I would like to extend my thanks to all committee members for their time, dedication, and support.

For their enthusiasm, diligence, and comradeship in the development and implementation of this exciting project, I owe a great debt of thanks to my colleagues Audrey S . Kauders,

Deputy Director, and Marsha V. Gallagher, Chief Curator. They, in turn, drew on the expertise of other colleagues and, as every single aspect of the Museum's operation was involved, I extend my thanks to all Joslyn staff.

If things went smoothly – and in the great scale of things, I think they did – it is in no small degree due to the early guidance of Bruce Tresslar of Kiewit Construction Company. The team approach that he advocated and initiated set the stage for a stimulating working environment and a genuine "partnership" comprising the design architects Sir Norman Foster, David Nelson, and Nigel Dancey of Sir Norman Foster and Partners; Omaha associate architect Bruce Carpenter and his colleagues in architecture and engineering of HDR, Inc.; and Mark Nienhueser and his colleagues at Kiewit Construction Company. As the representative of Joslyn Art Museum's Board of Governors, it was my pleasure and privilege to work with them in this, the most recent attempt to reinvent the wheel of art museum architecture. (Participants are listed on page 106.)

The self-imposed task of preparing this book turned out to be a little more time-consuming and labor-intensive than I anticipated. In the early stages, I relied heavily upon a manuscript prepared by former Joslyn curator Ellen Simak and, although some of my conclusions and emphases differ slightly from hers, I am extremely grateful for the solid, formative work she did nearly ten years ago. Fletcher Joslyn, George Joslyn's great-great-nephew, gave me valuable advice with regard to the family history and genealogy, and I owe a special debt to Dennis N. Mihelich, Associate Professor of History, Creighton University, whose professional skills, called on very late in the day, quickly revealed that almost every local legend associated with the Joslyns, and much of the material repeated in obituaries and official histories, was a serious distortion of fact, if not downright false. I am only being slightly disingenuous when I claim that I repeat some of them here to give some sense of the spell this Yankee couple held over their adopted city. In pulling the material together for publication (and for keeping my nose to the "pink" grindstone), I owe a great debt of thanks to Ruby C. Hagerbaumer, Curatorial Assistant. Linda Rajcevich, Director of Marketing and Public Relations, coordinated all aspects of this book's production; without her efforts, I doubt it would ever have come off the presses.

In this whole process, I have but one abiding regret. The first Chair of the Joslyn Board of Governors' Architect Selection Committee was Michael B. Walsh, then CEO of Union Pacific Railroad. With his knowledge and conviction, we embarked upon a process designed to bring to Joslyn's building project the best architectural talent possible. Although I was deeply dismayed when, early on in the proceedings, Mike left Omaha for Houston to take over the helm at Tenneco, such feelings were little compared to my sorrow that he did not live to see the fruits of his guidance. This book is dedicated to his memory.

Graham W. J. Beal
Director, 1989-1996

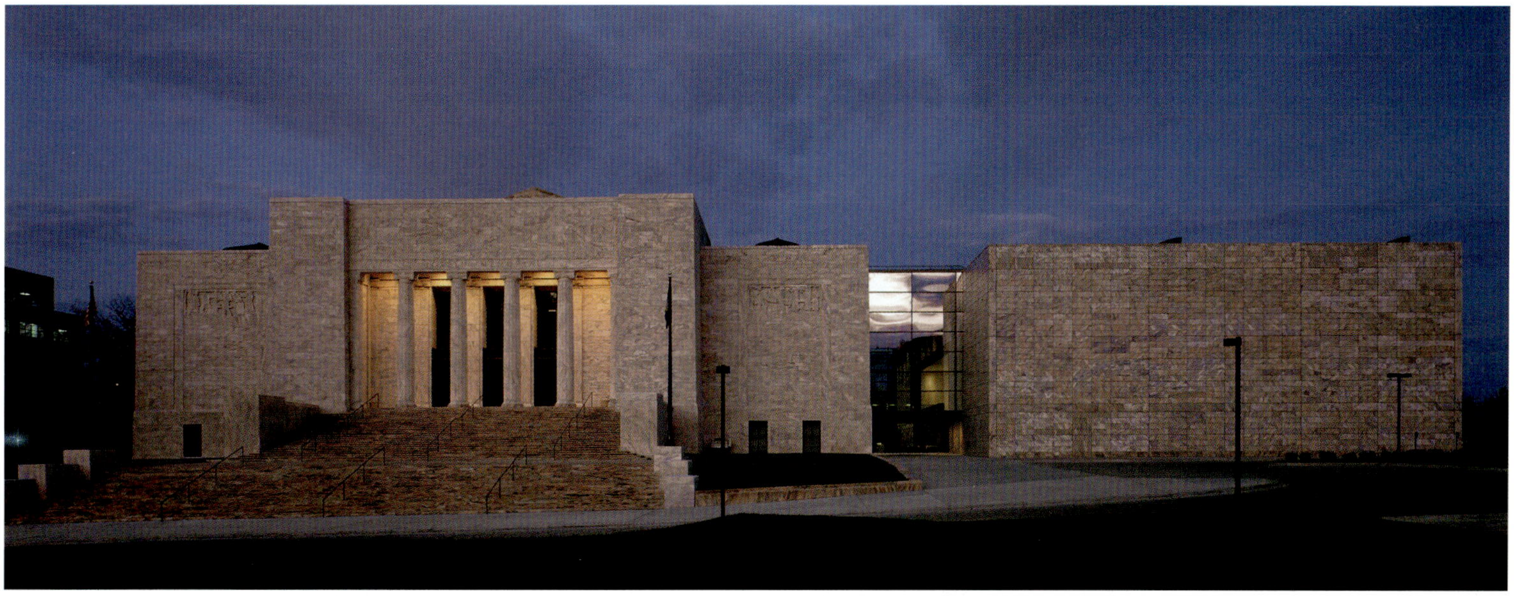

JOSLYN ART MUSEUM

a Building History

i hope it will do some good.

– SARAH JOSLYN in response to fulsome praise for her plan for an arts center

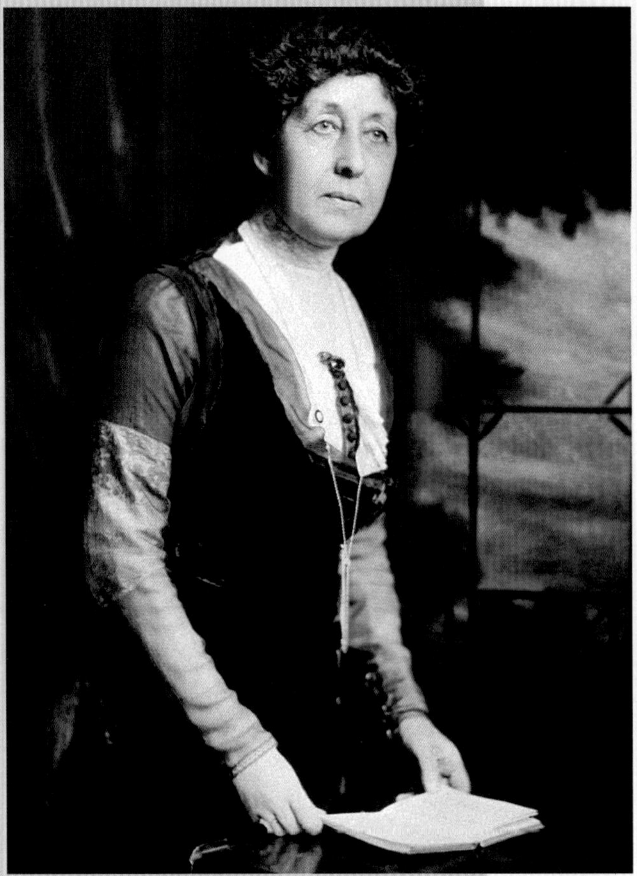

The widow of Nebraska's wealthiest citizen, Sarah Joslyn decided to build a cultural center as a living memorial to her late husband and as a gift of gratitude to the people of Omaha.

Born Sarah Hannah Selleck on April 14, 1851, Mrs. Joslyn (as she was to be known to most) grew up in Waterbury, Vermont, where, by all accounts, she led a lively social life. On September 24, 1872, she married a cousin, George Alfred Joslin, from Waitsfield, Vermont, a town some dozen miles south of Waterbury. Three years older than Sarah, George was one of five children of Alfred Joslin, whose half-sister, Calista, was Sarah's mother. The newly married couple immediately moved to Montreal, where George worked as a bookkeeper for his uncles, George and William Rice, whose company, then producing paper patterns for men's and women's clothing, was expanding into the printing business. It was, as George put it in a speech written many years later, his second attempt to "seek [his] fortune in Canada." It was not successful.

In 1879 they moved to Des Moines, Iowa, where, for $1.25 a day, George began work at the Iowa Printing Company unloading rolls of paper from freight cars. The company's actual business was the supply of "ready-print" to small-town newspapers across the region. In those days, in order to expand coverage while keeping labor costs low, small local newspapers received commentary, serialized novels, special features, and advertisements already printed on one side of the paper. Space was left on the other for each editor to insert the paper's masthead as well as local news and advertising.

George is said to have remarked that, at this time, their worldly possessions consisted of $9.00 and an adequate but limited wardrobe. Before long he advanced to an office position, where his abilities and experience won rapid promotion culminating in the offer, in 1880, to open a branch office of the company in Omaha. The operation, called the Omaha Newspaper Union, was located at 523 South 13th Street. The following year in Des Moines, the expanded company was reincorporated as the Western Newspaper Union with George as the manager in Omaha. Somewhere around this time, George changed the spelling of his surname. According to family legend, he had some business cards printed up, and the printer mistakenly used a "y" instead of an "i." Liking the variant, George adopted it.

George also engaged in a number of business activities unrelated to that of his print company. The most famous involved a patent medicine produced by the Cook Remedy Company, which he owned in Omaha in 1889, moved to Chicago in 1892, and ultimately closed down voluntarily in 1911. In local legend, this obscure operation was renamed and transformed into the center of George Joslyn's fortune. In this story, George won the patent for *Cure-All* (sometimes *Big G*) in a poker game and made his first million

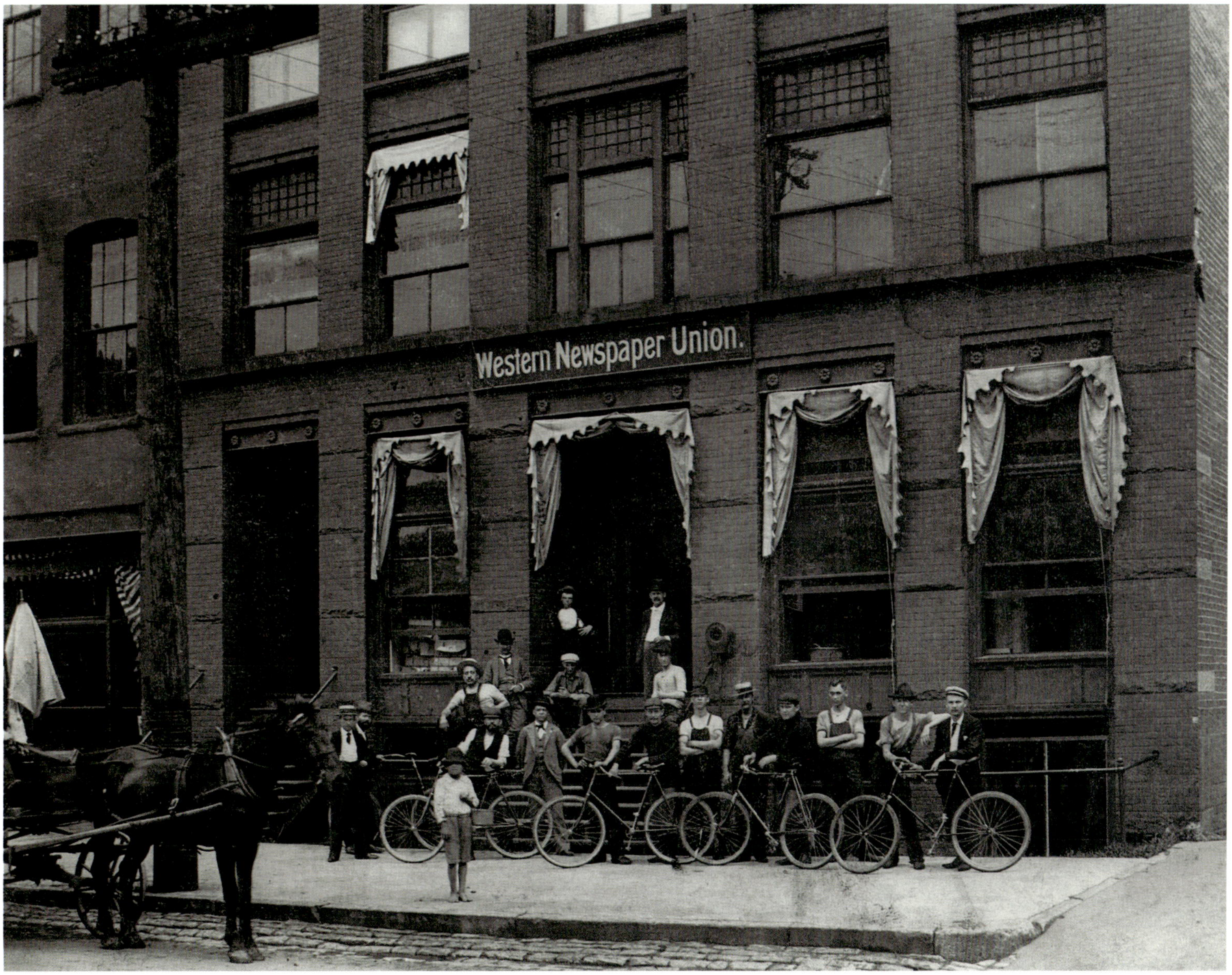

An undated photograph of the Western Newspaper Union building and its staff in the early days.

from it before being obliged, in 1908 (sometimes 1910), to remove it from the market at the suggestion of the Federal Bureau of Chemistry. A good tale, which clearly lost nothing in the telling, it is a complete fabrication that fitted in nicely with the overall legend of George Joslyn as a likable, somewhat roguish figure, prone to high-stakes gambling in business as well as in poker.

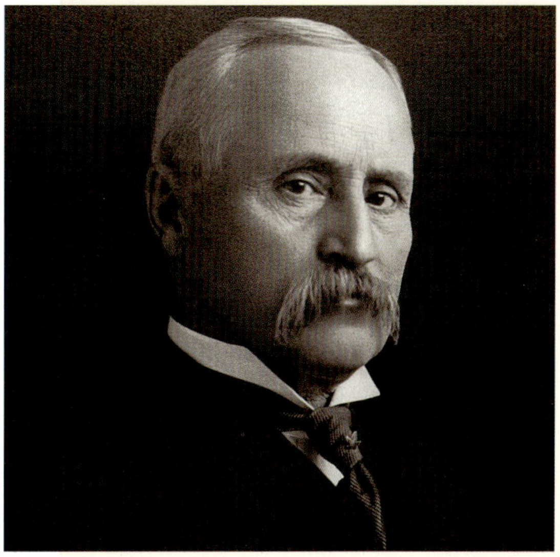

Official histories and other remembrances describe George Joslyn as a "forceful" and "masterful" man whose occasional resort to "rough tactics" was balanced by a lifelong attention to cultural and philanthropic endeavors.

Even George Joslyn's proprietorship of two hotels – the St. Charles and the Metropolitan – became part of the legend. Obituaries and local histories, noting his energy and business acumen, rarely fail to recount as an example of his thoroughness his ploy of arranging meetings with potential newspaper customers in one of his hotels. In this way, the story goes, the customers would be inclined to stay there and give him business of one sort or another. Such accounts give Sarah a role in the management of the hotels, particularly with regard to service in the restaurants. Again, the truth is different. The St. Charles, which George operated from 1883 to 1887, was a residential hotel for 150, mostly single, male blue-collar workers, and it had no dining hall. George operated and resided at the Metropolitan from 1883 to 1885. Also a residential hotel, the Metropolitan

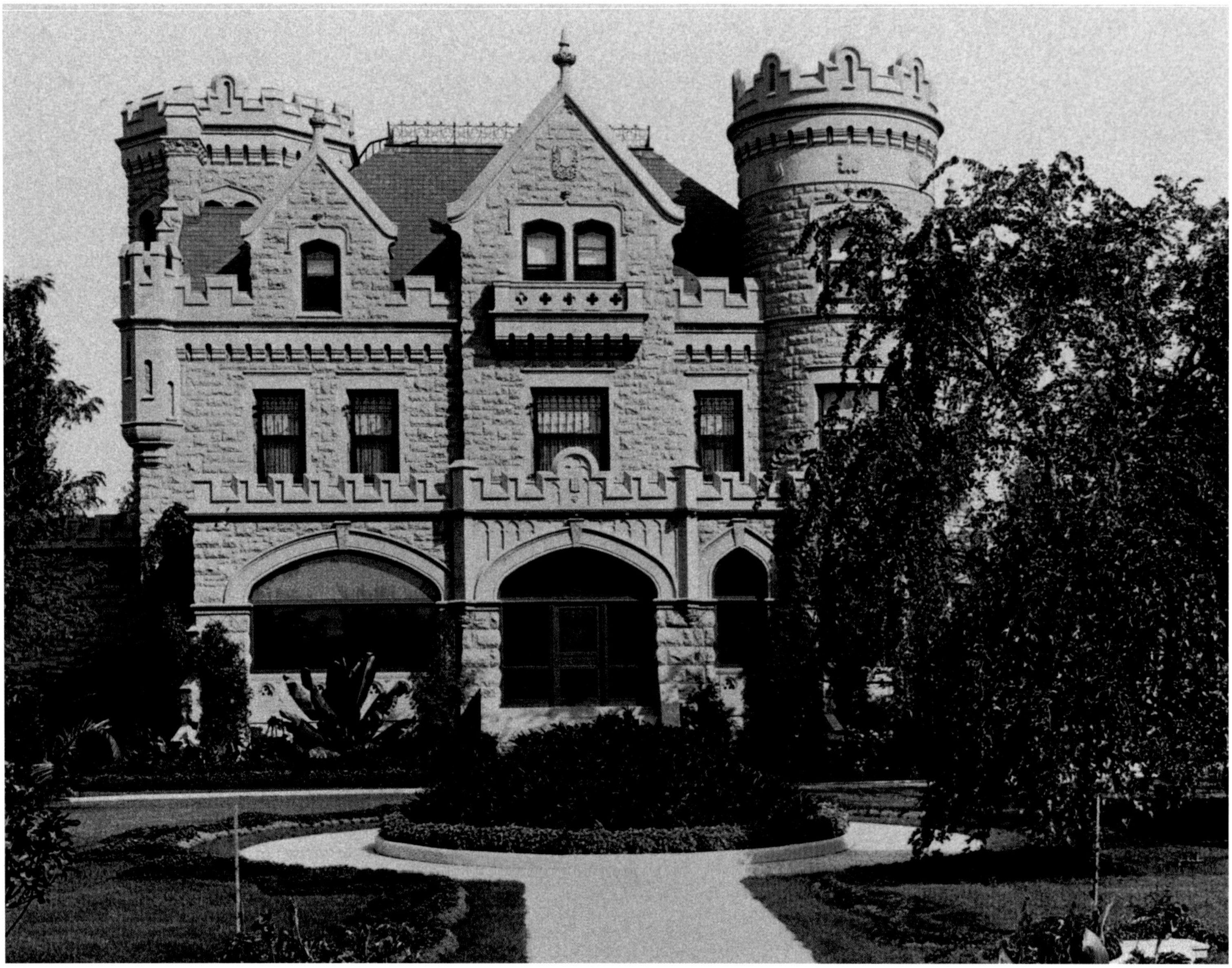

Built in 1903 at a cost of $250,000 and designed by John McDonald in the Scottish Baronial style, their mansion, Lynhurst, was quickly dubbed "the Joslyn Castle" – a sobriquet that George Joslyn cordially disliked. (Photo courtesy Omaha Public Schools.)

catered to middle-class families, among whom numbered George's sister Jessie and her husband, himself a clerk there. Both hotels were indeed managed by a Joslyn relative, cousin Ferdinand Joslin. In 1885 the Metropolitan was sold, and in 1886 George's brother Fred took over at the St. Charles.

Obviously, to have adequate capital to invest so quickly after their arrival in Omaha in two such considerable hotels, the Joslyns could hardly have been penniless immigrants, but George's vision of the crucial importance of local presses across the West was to be amply repaid. By the time of his death in 1916, it could reasonably be claimed that the Western Newspaper Union, with George Joslyn as its president and majority stockholder, was one of the largest newspaper service organizations in the world. With thirty-two offices stretching from Atlanta to Minneapolis and Boston to Salt Lake City, it is estimated that the company serviced 12,000 newspapers across the country. To supply its own ready-print operation with the necessary paper, inks, and equipment, the Western Newspaper Union established the Great Western Type

Foundry in 1888. A decade later George created the Western Paper Company, which eventually had offices in eight cities across the Midwest and West. Also, with the acquisition of the International Press Association, the Western Newspaper Union expanded into the "boilerplate" business: syndicated copy on ready-to-print plates for newspapers.

George repeatedly resisted efforts to persuade him to relocate his headquarters to Chicago on the sentimental grounds that it was Omaha that gave him his real start and so he "intended to stick by it to the last." Commonly held to be the richest man in the state, Joslyn's wealth was estimated at eight to ten million dollars. His only serious relocation from Omaha occurred in 1904, a year after the Joslyns had moved into Lynhurst, their new mansion (George detested it being called a "castle"). The Nebraska legislature had passed a tax on all properties owned by its citizens, even when relevant taxes were paid in other states where such property was located. Incensed by what he, not unreasonably, regarded as an unfair double tax, George boarded up his Omaha residence and moved out of the state. To underline his contempt for the pernicious law, he turned a few cows out to graze on the lawns of his splendid new mansion. The dispute was settled to his satisfaction and the Joslyns returned, happily vindicated, to Omaha.

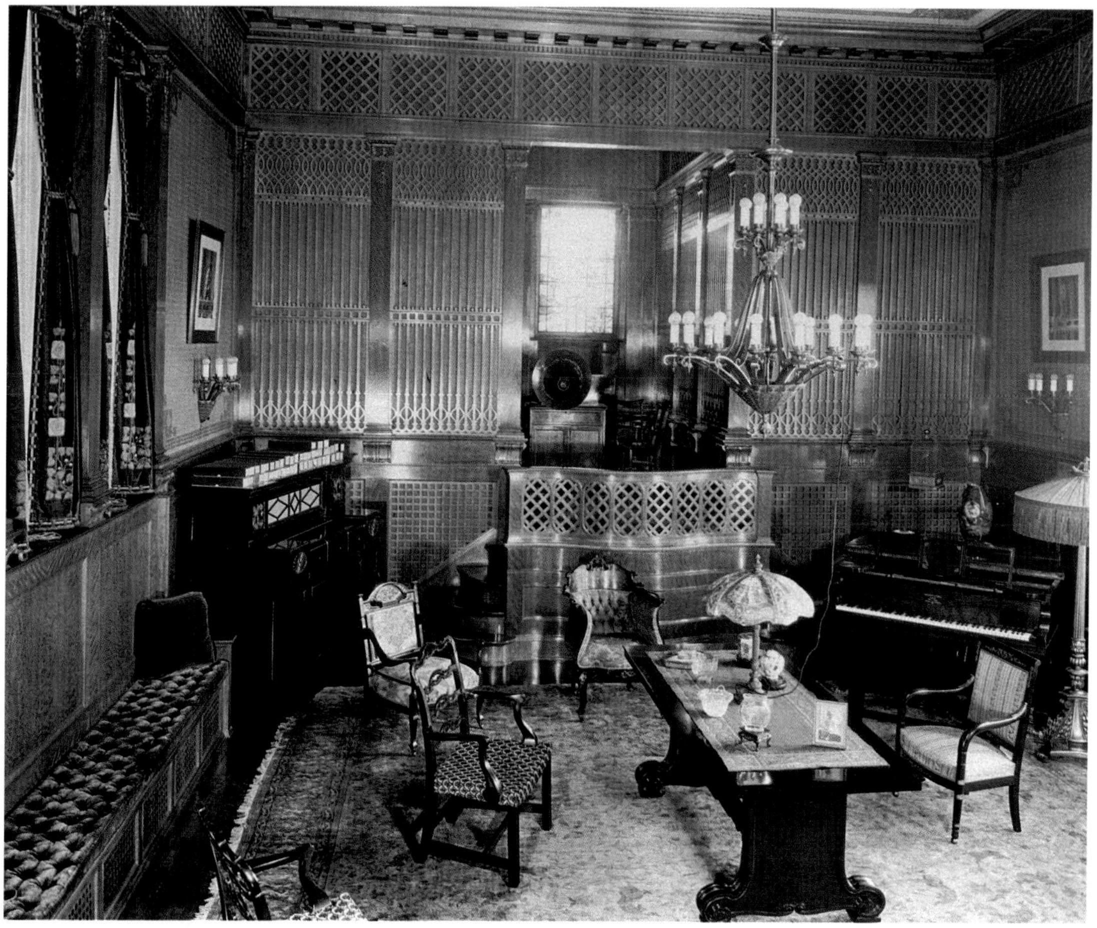

Furniture for the mansion came from the Chicago and St. Louis world expositions, and a special feature was the music room, complete with a hand-built organ that the music-loving Joslyn bought as a gift for his wife. (Photo courtesy Omaha Public Schools.)

Obituaries and official histories of George Joslyn paint a picture of a "forceful" and "masterful" man whose "admirable . . . business qualities" were complemented by qualities "known to few save close personal friends . . . kindly, charitable . . . he gave liberally and often to Omaha and public institutions of other cities, stipulating only that nothing be said of his benefactions." On one hand he is referred to as a man of "rough tactics," on the other he is known to have anonymously supplied provisions to families suffering for no fault of their own. He was also known to enjoy practical jokes – at least inflicting them – a favorite being to leave a musical chair for late-comers to the concerts held in the Joslyns' music room. On sitting down, the unpunctual would have their arrival tunefully proclaimed to the rest of the audience.

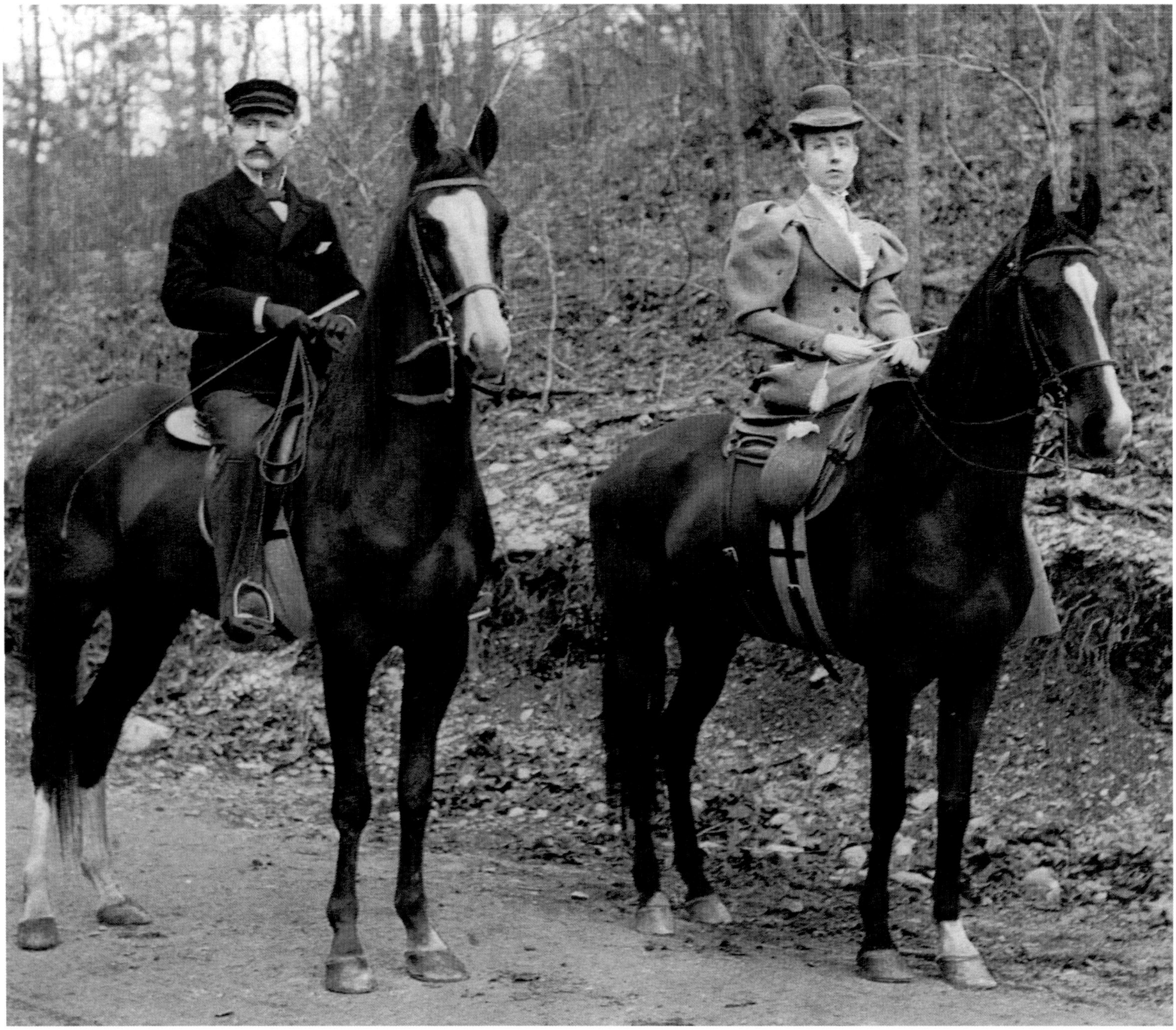

The Joslyns, both avid horseback riders, selected the site of their mansion as a result of their regular rides together.

With the Joslyns' growing wealth and status, Sarah became involved in an increasing number of philanthropic endeavors that were to influence many of her husband's gifts: from support for the Nebraska Humane Society, of which she was a member of the executive board, to $25,000 to the Child Saving Institute for a new building, and a like amount to the University of Omaha, enabling completion of its main building on the original campus at 24th and Pratt. The loss of their only child, an infant son who was born and died in Montreal, may have inspired Sarah's lifelong involvement with child welfare organizations. The couple raised a foster daughter, Violet, who in 1920 moved, with her husband, David Magowan, to Scarsdale, New York, occasionally returning to Omaha with her twin daughters, Joslyn and Sally, and her adopted son, David.

The old local stories about George and Sarah Joslyn paint a picture of two very different individuals. He, driven by ambition, a gambling man and prankster, who invited his drinking buddies to join him secretly in the billiards room at the mansion, reached by way of a tunnel from the carriage house. She, strict, teetotaling, and thrifty, inclining in her late years to near miserliness. The facts suggest a balanced – possibly highly complementary – relationship. Their mansion at 39th and Davenport Streets was the social center of the city, as befits the home of Omaha's wealthiest citizens, and much entertaining went on there. In days when the roles of husband and wife were more strictly defined than today, it was usual for certain social activities to be clearly segregated according to gender; gentlemen retiring to a separate room to enjoy cigars and billiards is perhaps the most famous of these now nearly extinct conventions. Certainly, George Joslyn's billiard table was in full view, and there was no reason for him to have gambled in secret. Rather the opposite: here was a man in control of his destiny, complemented in marriage by an intelligent and strong-minded woman who shared with him a love of such less purely "masculine" activities as horseback riding and the arts. And, while there are plenty of stories illustrating Sarah's highly developed sense of propriety, as well as her concern for economy in household affairs, there are others that amply testify to the dry wit and no-nonsense attitude that comprise such an appealing part of the "Yankee" character. On one hand, she had a special chair situated in a spot in the garden, easily visible from the mansion, so she could make sure that hobos they fed cleaned their plates of the food she gave them. On the other, she attended the opening of the Joslyn Memorial building (as Joslyn Art Museum was first named), along with her foster daughter, as one among the crowd and, on being asked by someone who recognized her from a girls' club project, "Aren't you Mrs. Joslyn?" fired back, "Yes. Who are you?"

Although not a musician himself, George Joslyn had an elaborate music room designed for their mansion, complete with an organ, perhaps the most fashionable instrument of the day. Once again, stories that the couple had a live-in organist for weeks at a time are exaggerated and, in all likelihood, derive from the instance of a well known instrumentalist, Archer Gibbon, once staying with them – probably for less than a month. Sarah Joslyn displayed a lifelong interest in the visual arts and, though by no stretch of the imagination could she be called a collector, she supported the Art Institute of Omaha. Her decision to create a cultural center allowed her to honor the memory of her husband and, at the same time, give back to the people of Omaha no small part of the fortune that had been accumulated in the city.

After her husband's death in 1916, Sarah remained active in community affairs and continued to support their favorite charities, often offering the mansion she and George had built together for fundraising events. She was appointed by the governor to the Child Labor Commission, and, during World War I, was active in the National League of Women's Service. She contributed her time to community groups for such hands-on projects as making "slippers" from carpet remnants to give delivery horses better footing on winter ice in the hilly downtown area (and therefore reduce injuries), and even extended an open invitation to service men stationed at Fort Omaha during the war to visit her home, where they could entertain themselves with its bowling alley, billiard and pool tables, books, and music facilities. After the war, Sarah contributed $30,000 to the University of Omaha for another new building. She served on the board of the Fontenelle Forest Association, and donated some 100 acres of natural habitat to the preserve. Always a strong supporter of the Humane Society (at the 1912 national convention of that organization, held in Omaha, she was elected third vice president, after U.S. President William Howard Taft, first vice president, and Vice President T. R. Marshall, second vice president), in 1924 she financed a new Nebraska headquarters that included the first small animal hospital in Nebraska and Iowa. Her great wealth made her a target for the unscrupulous and, following a death threat from someone outraged at the expenditure of millions of dollars on a lavish cultural center at a time of great social hardship, she spent many of her waking hours in the relative security of her Memorial building, maintaining something of an office in what was called the Lounge or Reception Room (now the Founder's Room). Although she and George had traveled extensively, including a trip to Europe, she ceased such activity after her husband's death, claiming that she had insufficient time for a vacation. Her movements became limited to the Omaha area: for a while in a car that she drove herself; toward the end of her life, on daily drives selected by her chauffeur. Little disposed to nostalgia, she took a very real interest in current events, and she is reported to have told a friend that, while she had no fear of death, she just could not stand the thought of not knowing how things were going to turn out. Each morning during her final illness, when the maid brought in her breakfast tray, Mrs. Joslyn would assert, "Hannah, I'm still here." She died on February 28, 1940; she was 88 years old.

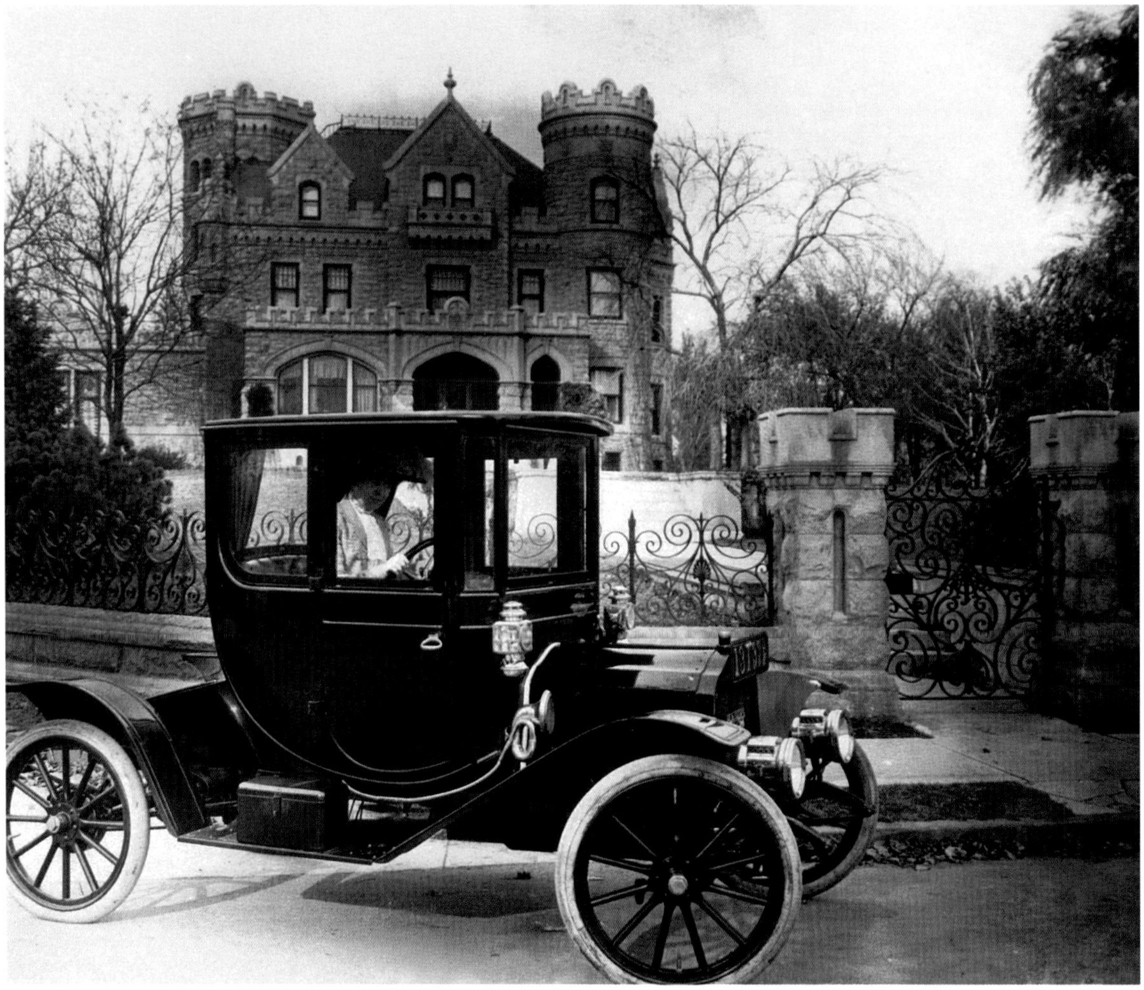

Sarah Joslyn at the wheel of her car outside the gates of Lynhurst, c. 1914. She enjoyed driving, and one of the many, almost certainly apocryphal, tales told of her has it that she drove without regard to the rules of the road. (Photo courtesy Carolyn Lewis.)

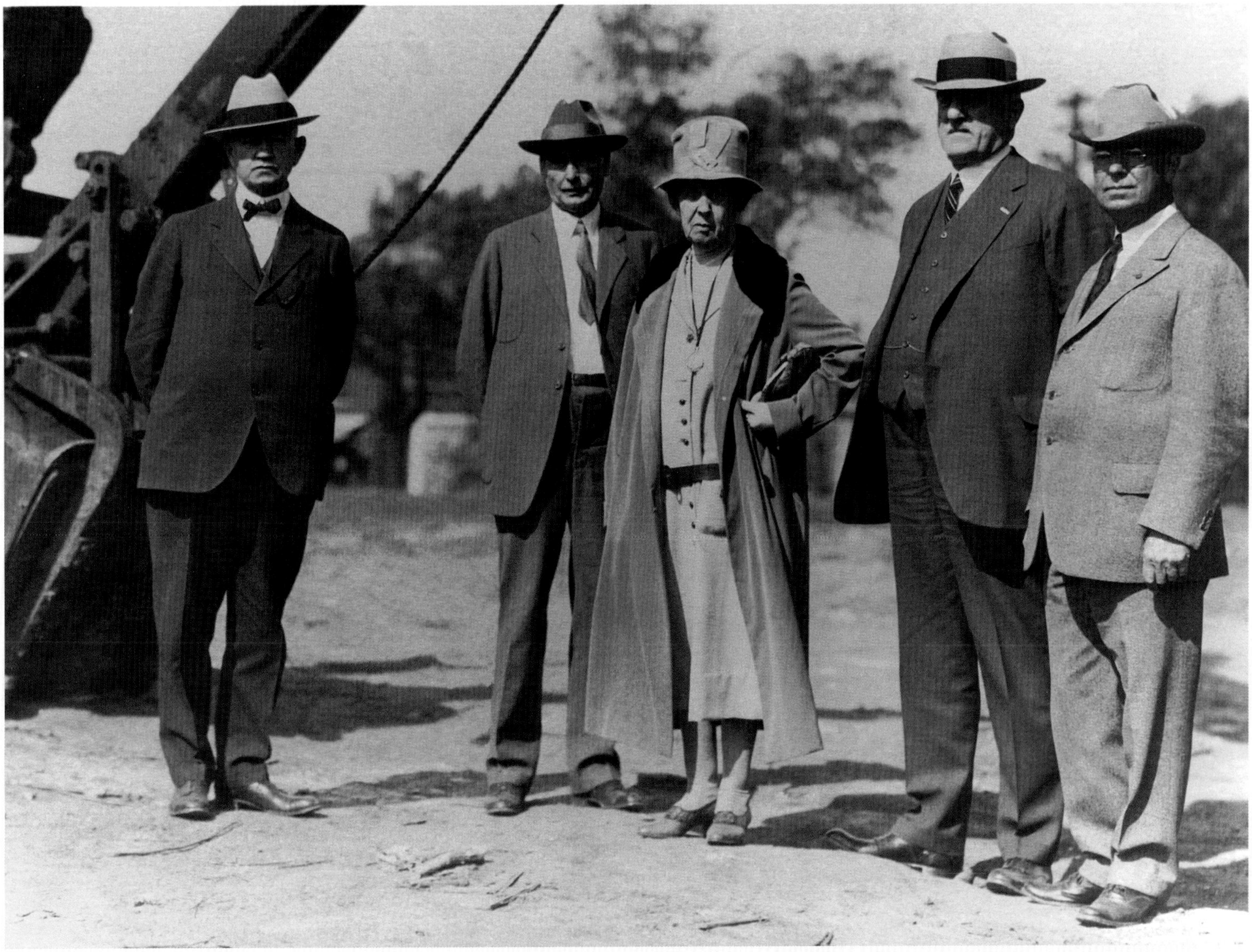

John McDonald, who acted as business manager for the project, is seen with Mrs. Joslyn and other members of the Society of Liberal Arts at the groundbreaking, October 3, 1928. Left to right: C.W. Russell, John McDonald, Sarah Joslyn, H.H. Fish, and C.L. Farnsworth.

The selection of the father-son team of John and Alan McDonald as the architects for Sarah's memorial building was no surprise; John McDonald had worked for the Joslyns on virtually every building they had involved themselves in and had counted George Joslyn among his personal friends. He was a pallbearer at George's funeral and served in an honorary capacity at Sarah's.

Born in 1861 on Prince Edward Island, John McDonald came to Omaha, via Boston, around 1880. Here, he formed a partnership with David Ogilvy – with whom he had studied architecture at McGill University – and the Ogilvy-McDonald company prospered in the city's boom economy. In 1890 Ogilvy moved to Portland, Oregon, to open a branch office of the firm, but the partnership was dissolved the following year. Between 1891 and 1916, John McDonald maintained a flourishing practice and designed over thirty public and residential buildings. Apart from the Joslyn residence

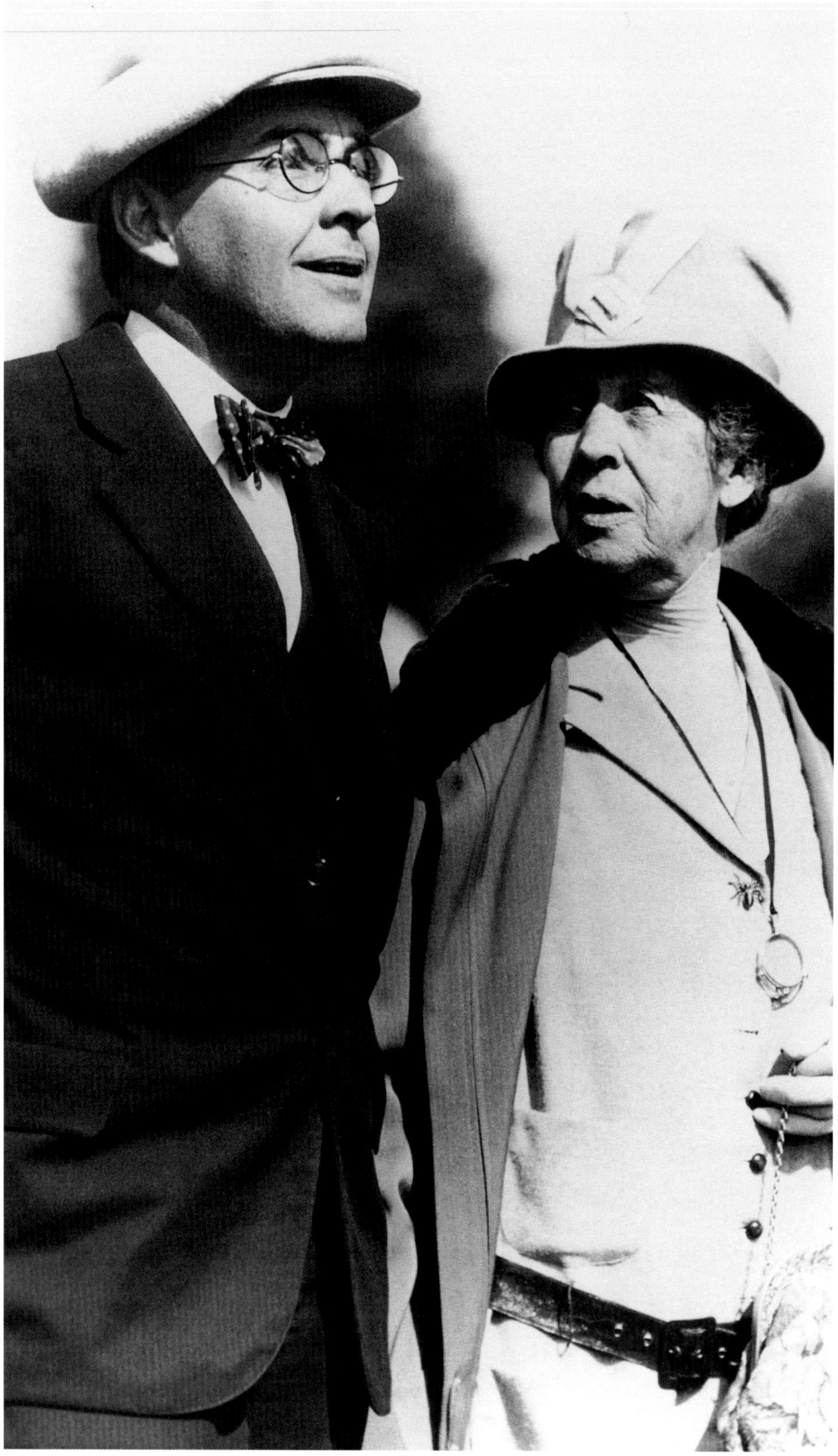

Alan, the younger McDonald, seen here with Sarah Joslyn, took the lead in the Memorial's design.

(1903), his best-known commissions include: First Baptist Church (1903; 421 Park Avenue), Bradford-Pettis residence (1910; 404 South 39th Street), Benson High School (c. 1913; 5148 Maple Street), Yates School (c. 1916; 3252 Davenport Street), and the Muse Theater (1916; 2405-7 Farnam Street). The First Unitarian Church (3114 Harney Street), of which Mrs. Joslyn was a member, was completed in 1918 and straddles the time that Alan joined his father in maintaining one of Omaha's handful of premier architectural firms.

Born in 1891, Alan McDonald received his training from the Harvard School of Architecture, graduating in 1915 and joining his father's firm the following year. Records indicate that, before 1940, they designed twenty-two buildings; among those still standing are the Old People's Home (also called the Fontenelle Home, 1917; 325 Fontenelle Boulevard), the Dundee Theater (c. 1925; 4952 Dodge Street), and Beth-El Synagogue (c. 1940; 210 South 49th Street). Alan McDonald died in 1947; his father in 1956.

As was common for American architects at the turn of the century, the McDonalds worked in a variety of historically based styles, selecting whichever decorative scheme they or their patrons felt appropriate to the type of building: Scottish Baronial for their wealthiest client's home or Collegiate Gothic for Yates School. Left to themselves, they demonstrated a clear preference for the Colonial Revival patterns they both knew and loved from their separate sojourns in New England; a predilection manifested in the exquisitely detailed Unitarian Church and in their design for the Nebraska State Capitol competition in 1921.

John McDonald designed two houses for the Joslyns: the first, at 2111 Emmet Street (now demolished), was a straightforward, comfortable frame house. The second building, on which construction commenced in 1902, fully expressed the substantial position George Joslyn now occupied in the financial world and, much though it irritated the proud owners, it is understandable why the magnificent thirty-two room mansion was dubbed "the Joslyn Castle," an appellation that has stuck over the years to the point of becoming its official name.

Erected on what had been a dairy farm at a location that was then regarded as "way out west," the splendid mansion (page 9) was designed in the Scottish Baronial style, a type of building the Joslyns are said to have seen and admired on their travels in Europe. Rumored to have cost between a quarter and a half million dollars, and the wonder of the city, it was furnished with items acquired at the 1893 Chicago World Columbian Exposition, the 1904 St. Louis World's Fair, and during their frequent travels. At its center was the lavish music room (page 10) with its custom-built pipe organ, commissioned by George as a surprise gift to his wife.

The Joslyn residence is typical of much of the McDonalds' work; finely detailed and sensitively composed, it is a variation on a style that took its impetus from another time and another place. The architects used a flexible and finely shaded vocabulary of forms associated with various historical epochs to provide instant context for contemporaneous social structures. As with the Joslyn mansion and the Unitarian Church, many of the McDonalds' commissions presented a straightforward essay in a particular historical style; they would be judged by their ability to handle well known components with a mixture of restraint and innovation. There is little doubt that they played the game with considerable accomplishment. The design of the Joslyn Memorial building started out this way but, owing to a number of factors – not least of which was the architects' own willingness to embrace a new vocabulary – evolved into something startlingly different.

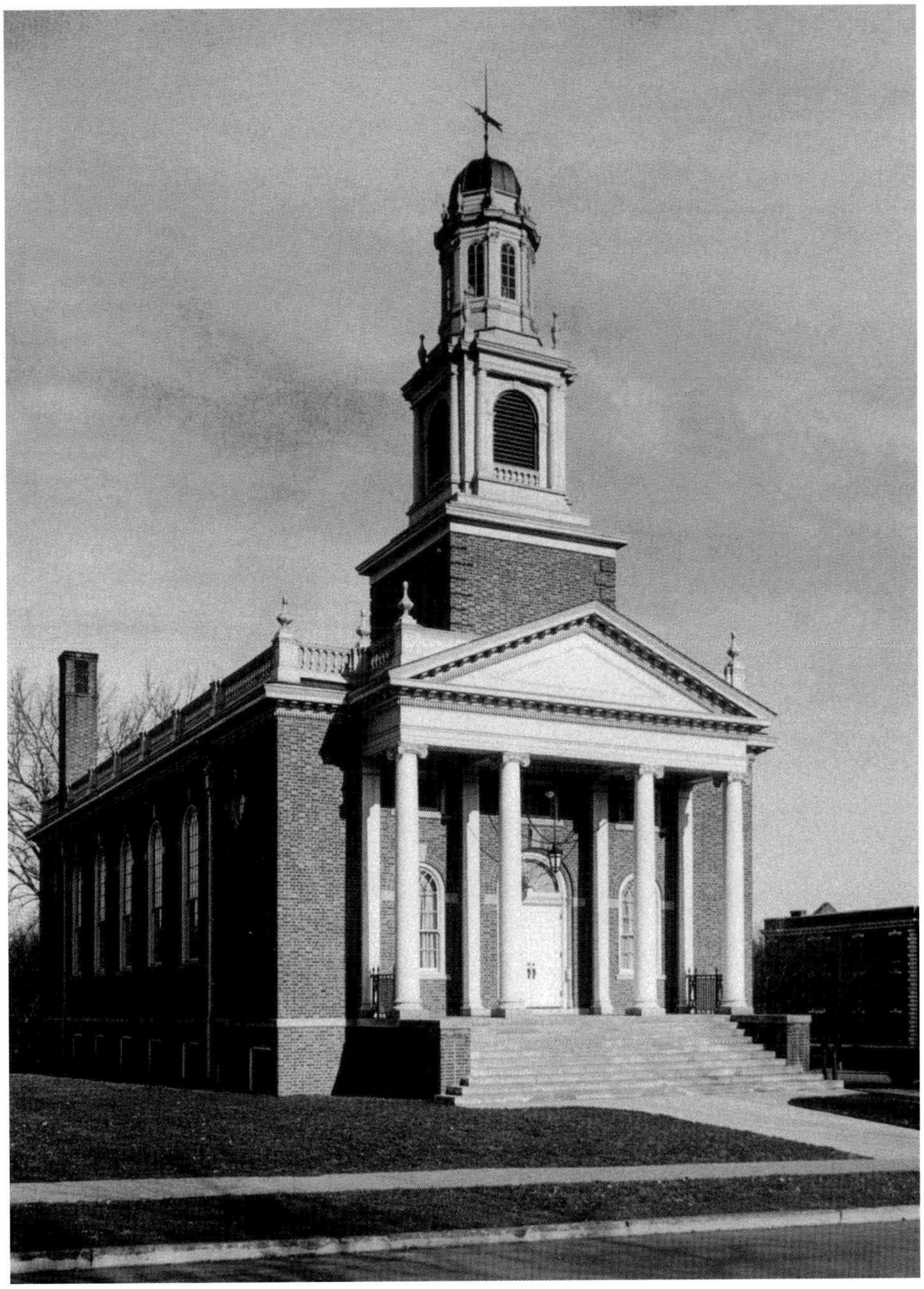

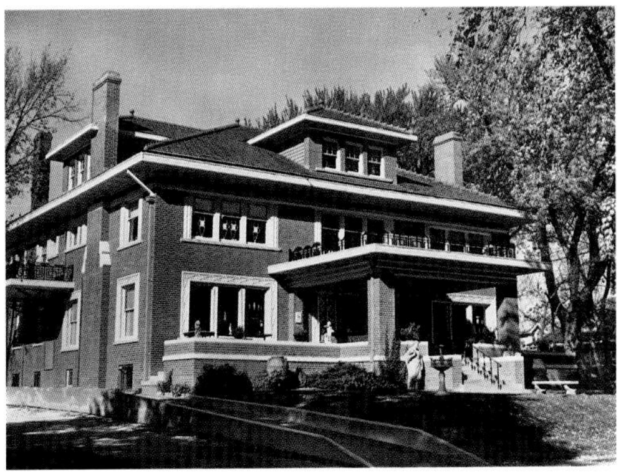

ABOVE: In keeping with their times, the McDonalds were highly accomplished practitioners in a wide variety of architectural styles. For the First Unitarian Church (1918) – of which Mrs. Joslyn was a member – they produced a lovely Colonial essay. (Photo courtesy First Unitarian Church.) RIGHT: The Dana Mansion (c. 1910), by contrast, is a discrete version of Prairie Modernism. For the Joslyn Memorial they were to stretch their own stylistic boundaries and come close to genuine innovation. (Photo courtesy *Omaha World-Herald.*)

GENESIS *of a* CONCEPT

Although the death of her husband caused Sarah Joslyn to withdraw from Omaha's social life, she held fast to his idea that, as their wealth had derived from Omaha, it should, in some form, be returned to the city for the benefit of its citizens.

In an interview with the *Omaha World-Herald* in 1928, she said that the couple had discussed, in desultory fashion, the notion of some sort of public gift, but as "[George] was so very busy with his business, and his illness came so suddenly, . . . nothing like the memorial [had] occurred to him. It didn't to me, for some time after his death." Between 1916 and 1920, Sarah Joslyn methodically considered, and rejected, a number of ideas, including the completion of an up-to-date and luxuriously appointed headquarters for the Western Newspaper Union to be located at 17th and Farnam Streets. George had been working on this project with the McDonalds during the last few years of his life, and it was clearly something dear to his heart, literal testimony to his foresight, energy, and business acumen. Pleasingly symbolic in many ways, the idea failed Mrs. Joslyn's own test that the gift be something that also commemorated her late husband's strong sense of public duty by benefiting the greatest number of people possible. The same condition eliminated more obviously charitable possibilities, notably an orphanage and a new children's hospital. In the end, she returned to their shared love of the arts, particularly music, and decided that a concert hall, with all its connotations of uplift and recreation, would be the most appropriate memorial and, her mind made up, immediately called upon John McDonald, her husband's favorite architect, to design a spacious performing arts center in his name.

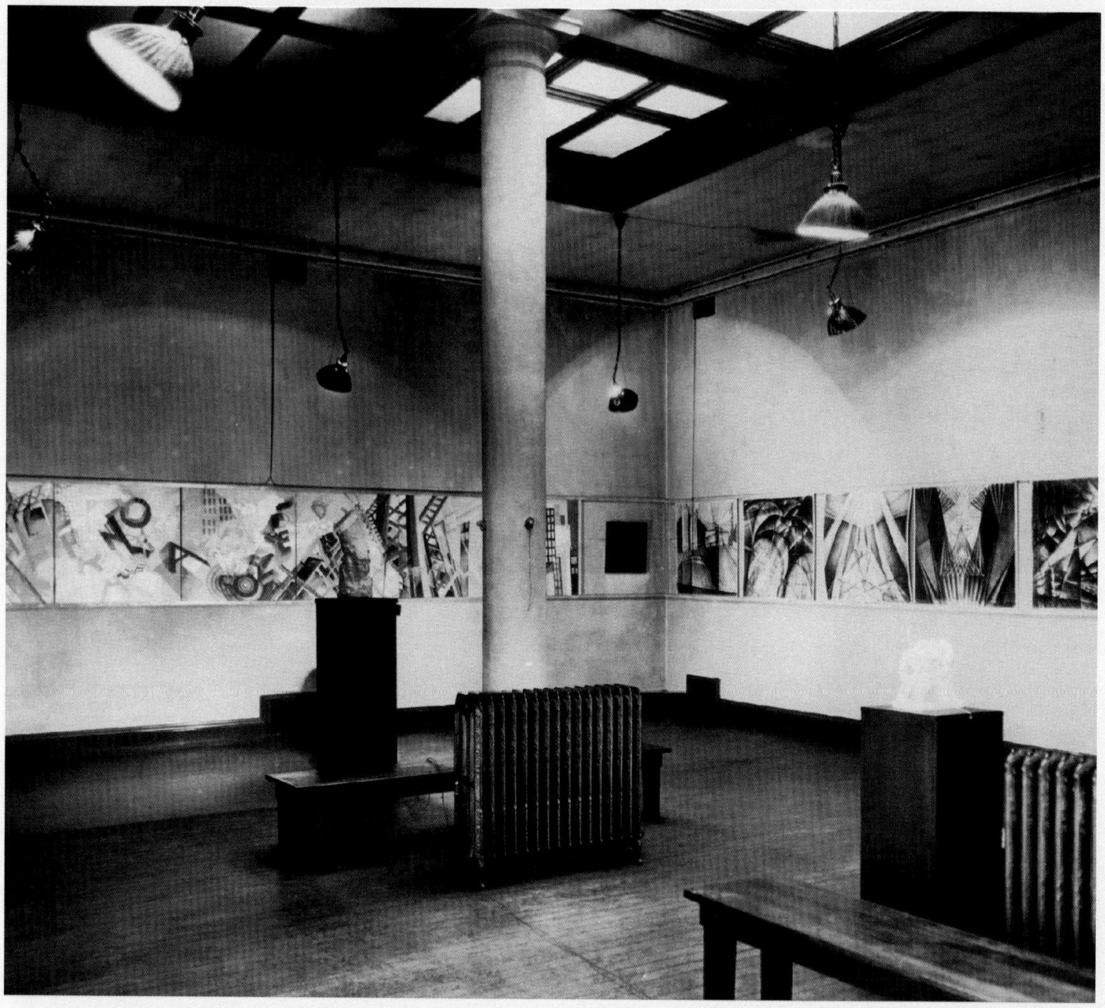

Until the opening of the Joslyn Memorial, leading art societies, such as the Art Institute of Omaha and the Friends of Art, used gallery space in the city library (ABOVE). With the Joslyn Memorial under construction, these groups legally transferred their collections to the Society of Liberal Arts, firmly establishing Joslyn's identity as an art museum.

In 1920, Mrs. Joslyn paid half a million dollars – an enormous sum in those days – for property on Dodge Street, between 22nd and 24th Streets, prime real estate in an old residential area on the bluffs above the busy downtown and immediately accessible to those working or shopping there. In April the following year, a *World-Herald* article entitled "Mrs. Joslyn May Erect Five Million Memorial" described a building containing

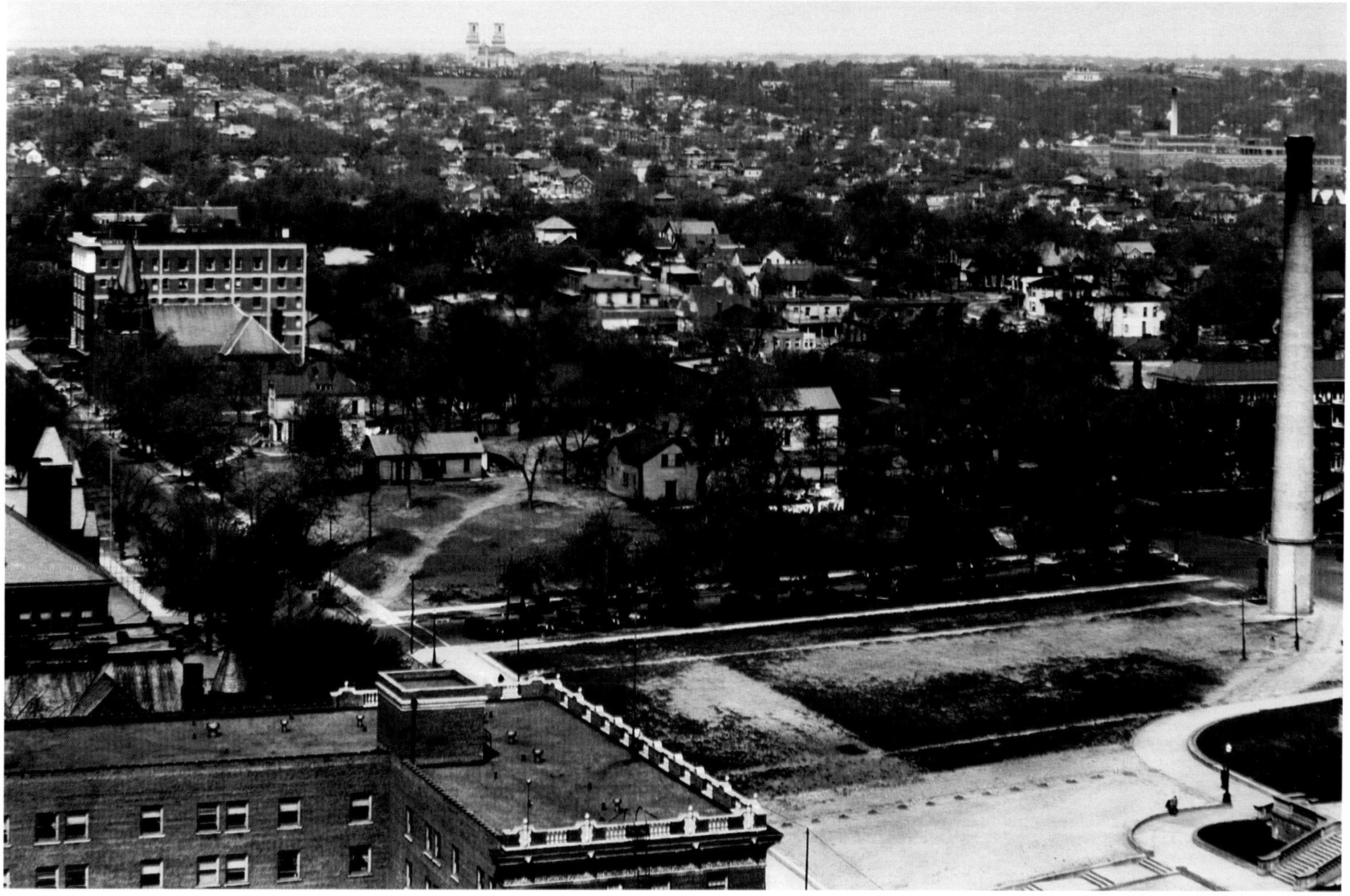

Joslyn Memorial site before construction, viewed from the east, May 7, 1928. Seeking a location for her fine arts center that was convenient, yet not inextricably related to commercial and retail activity, Sarah Joslyn selected a conspicuous site on the bluffs overlooking downtown Omaha and adjacent to the imposing high school – itself occupying the site of the Nebraska Territorial Capitol. She paid almost $500,000 for the four-block property (most of the middle third of this photograph) which, at the time, was dotted with various residential buildings.

two large auditoria, "one of which shall be specifically constructed to house a fine pipe organ, with a view that daily concerts be given." By the end of the year, following a trip east to visit possible prototypes, the architects had submitted several designs, descriptions of which, however, suggest a building with only one auditorium.

The evolution of the design of the memorial is shrouded in mystery. First, Mrs. Joslyn was determined that the building be as much of a surprise to the citizens of Omaha as possible. Second, many of the architects' records have been lost and no preparatory plans have been located. The little that is known has been gleaned from sporadic press reports or inferred from scattered statements.

Less clear is the timing of and the exact motivation behind the decision to include art galleries, although, reading between the lines of the descriptions, it is likely that this was also decided in 1921. One account has the architects themselves petitioning Mrs. Joslyn, on behalf of the art community, to provide much-needed exhibition space for the visual arts, at the time something of an orphan by comparison with the Symphony and the Community Playhouse. Several major collections, it was suggested, would find their way into the right kind of building, most notably that of the city's most important art organization – the Art Institute of Omaha – currently using the public library building. Even without the McDonalds' influence, as a patron of the Art Institute, Mrs. Joslyn must have been only too aware of the need for dignified, purpose-built exhibition space.

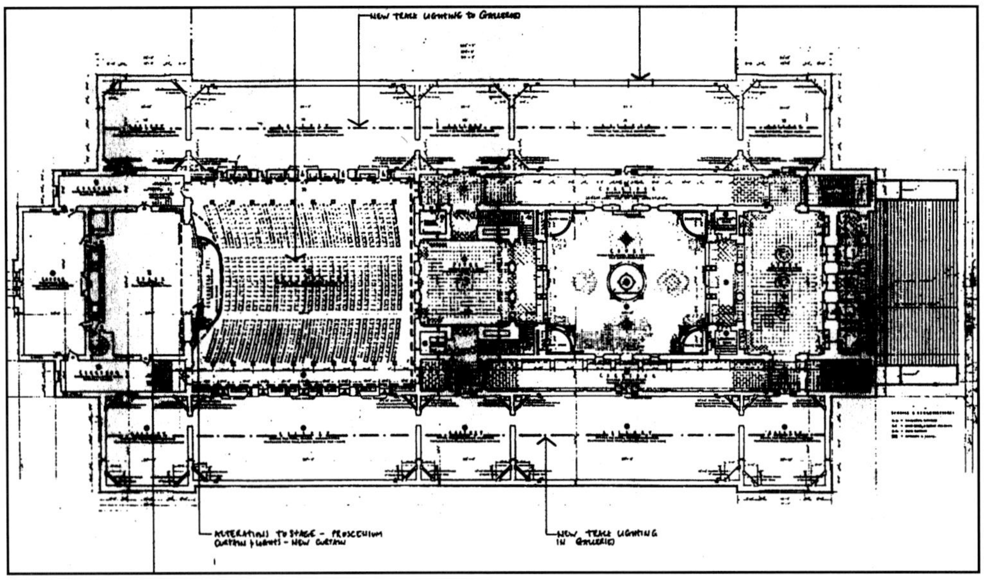

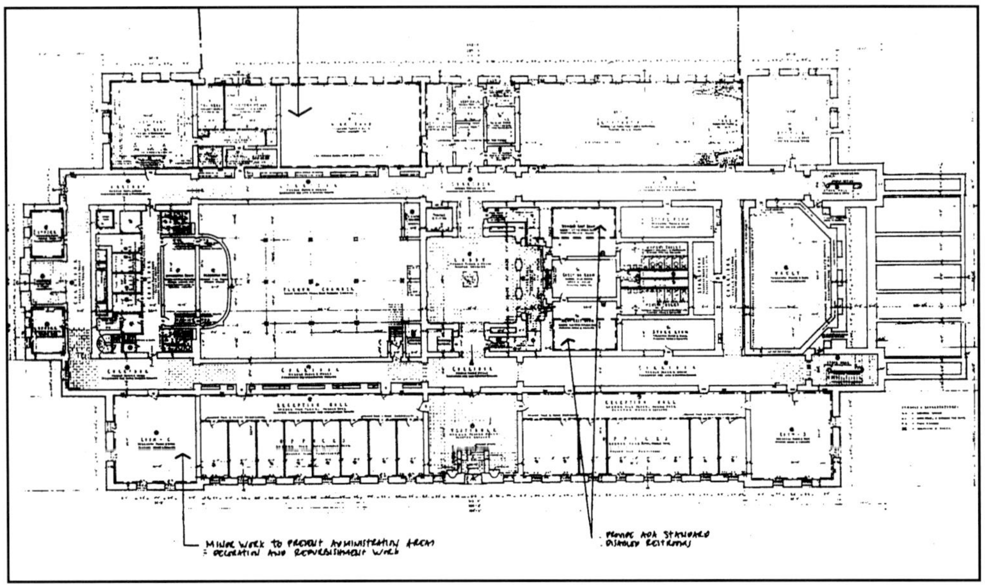

Whatever the impetus, it was probably not too difficult a decision for her to make. She had always been interested in art, and the idea of combining her and her husband's favorite art forms would have had considerable appeal. And, in building a cultural center that embraced both art and music, the Memorial would have even broader appeal to those it was intended to benefit. Galleries were added by the simple expedient of running them down each side of the grand progression of public spaces and the concert hall. Mrs. Joslyn's personal role in the evolution of this design is, again, open to debate. Because reliable accounts have her visiting the McDonalds' offices regularly, it has been inferred that she took a formative role in the plans, but descendants from both families – Joslyn and McDonald – have cast doubt on this, suggesting that she would have been firmly guided by the architect her husband had trusted with all his building projects. Given the distinctive decoration of the finished building, and taking into account Mrs. Joslyn's subsequent exasperated comments about escalating costs and miscalculations of design, it seems likely that, having established the Memorial's basic concept, she left the rest to the architects.

The Memorial was originally conceived of as a concert hall, a reflection of George Joslyn's predilection for music over the other arts. At some time early in the design process, Mrs. Joslyn was persuaded to add galleries and satisfy the long-standing need for suitable exhibition space for Omaha's various art groups. The plan of the main level (TOP) clearly reflects the two-stage development in design. A sequence of grand public spaces, culminating in the concert hall, dominates the core of the building, with art galleries running down each side. The lower level (ABOVE) consists of an extensive array of classrooms, study areas, a library, and offices.

Incorporated in 1928, the original mission of the Society of Liberal Arts – as the governing body of the Memorial was titled – called for the promotion of "education in sculpture, literature, painting, music, drama and kindred branches of art." To accommodate this ambitious program, the McDonalds designed a veritable temple to the arts: a huge, 148,000-square-foot monument complete with concert hall, galleries, lecture hall, classrooms, library, and offices. It was to be situated, Parthenon-like, on the bluffs above Omaha and, in keeping with the building's grand cultural intent, was to be dressed in full imperial attire: an elaborate Greco-Roman costume, in fact, complete with Doric, Ionic, Corinthian, and Composite orders. This, at least, was what the "finished" blueprints of 1928 called for. As built, the Joslyn Memorial was a very different entity and, in many ways, the story of the building only really began in 1929, well after the architects' design had been approved by their client and published to the world, in fact, after ground had been broken and walls and floors already laid.

a decade ago something happened architecturally. Nebraska became the point to which the entire architectural world turned its attention. A building was arising on the plains of Nebraska which was to affect the architecture of the nation. Bertram Grosvenor Goodhue, its architect, must be given the credit for having courageously gathered up the best of all the past ages into what he himself calls the "here and now." . . . Through the state, in every important center one sees buildings rising which for want of a better term we now call modern in style as well as in facilities.

– Alan McDonald, in "Prairie Architecture," the Omaha Chamber of Commerce Journal, June 1930

Thus did the younger McDonald encapsulate his and, presumably, his father's feelings about the extraordinary edifice that Bertram Goodhue, a California architect, had designed for the Nebraska State Capitol. The McDonalds themselves had been finalists in the competition held to select the architect; they had – and here their personal preference in matters of architectural style coincided with tradition – submitted a design based on the old Boston City Hall: a grand, domed structure with a lineage stretching back through Christopher Wren's St. Paul's Cathedral in London to Michelangelo's St. Peter's Basilica in Rome, and held in common by most state capitol buildings across the nation. In a radical departure, Goodhue envisioned a tower rising out of a spreading base. A dramatic form, thrusting up out of the dominant horizontals of the Great Plains, this inspired concept combined references to the ultimate symbol of American modernity, the skyscraper, with distinct local characteristics. As Vincent Scully has written: "Driving across rolling . . . fields, we see the unmistakable shape of grain elevators everywhere on the horizon. All at once, one of them is seen shining gold on top; it is the state capitol with its dome, growing out of the place to become its emblem." (*Architecture: The Natural and the Man-Made,* 1991, p. 171.)

Especially startling was the style the architect used for this modern wonder of the world: stripped down and spare, with flattened, geometrical ornament, it represented the American response to a variety of European tendencies in architecture and design that received its clearest manifestation in the 1925 Paris exhibition *Exposition International des Arts Décoratifs et Industriels Modernes* (hence, the term "Art Deco"). Deriving from a variety of sources that included such art movements as Cubism and Constructivism, as well as machinery and industrial design, Art Deco is characterized by sharp-angled geometry, smooth surfaces, and shimmering color. Skyscrapers like New York's Chrysler Building (1930, William van Alen) epitomize American architectural Art Deco.

In Goodhue's hands, especially in his last projects (which include the Nebraska State Capitol), the more aggressive aspects of modernity were modulated and embedded within a classical framework. The resulting style, monumental and familiar, but without the traditional finery of European culture, had immediate appeal to an audience looking for architecture appropriate to the "American Century." By the time he died in 1925, Goodhue "was considered by many to be the most important modernist, more important even than Frank Lloyd Wright." (Richard Guy Wilson, "Architecture in the Machine Age," *The Machine Age in America, 1918-1941,* 1986, p. 150.)

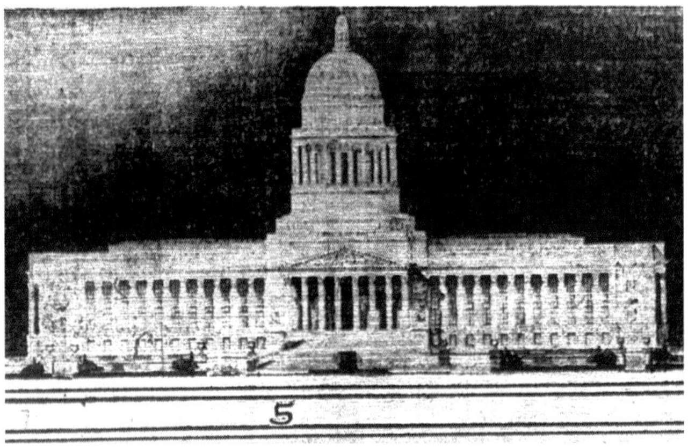

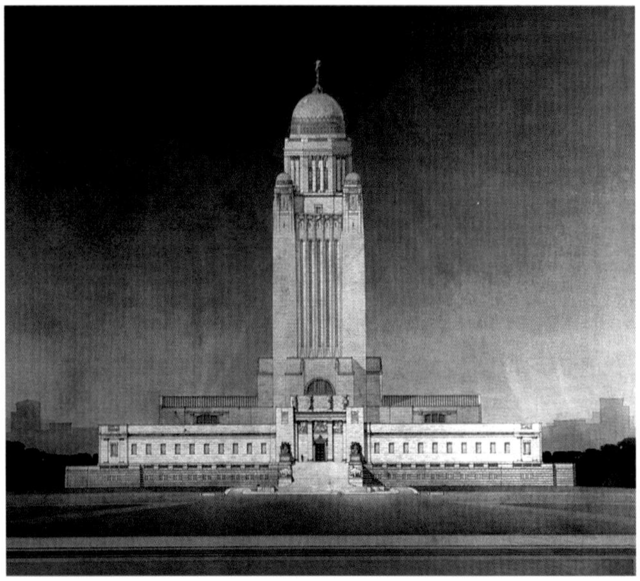

Even so, the McDonalds' conversion to the "Moderne" – as the style is often referred to in its American incarnation – was far from immediate. According to an article in the *Omaha World-Herald* (May 8, 1928), "The [Joslyn] building is not only the result of eight years' planning by architects, but also the result of advice given by others. Alan McDonald said that many changes have been made in the plans before those were adopted. The late Bertram Goodhue, designer of the new Nebraska capitol, examined the plans for the building, and the suggestions of nearly all the architects of Omaha have been considered." As the plans described in 1928 are those of the classical temple, Goodhue's influence in the early stages was felt more in the overall organization of the design and, perhaps, in the limitation of decorative elements to logical points of emphasis – corners, windows, doors. Certainly, the sloping profile and bold use of blank walls on the main floor, sitting atop a row of windows that define the layout of the offices on the lower level, strongly follow the example of the State Capitol design. But for all his innovative decoration, Goodhue was a strong exponent of processional and axial organization in plan, an essentially classical characteristic. One of the most striking features in the plan of the Joslyn Memorial is its thorough-going symmetry, and it is possible that the nationally acclaimed architect also gave his provincial colleagues the benefit of his wider experience in the dramatic organization of space and helped with the fine tuning of the grand sequence of public spaces.

Perhaps, perhaps not; for there is very little in the original approved designs that the McDonalds could not have worked out for themselves from their own training and experience. From this point of view, the Joslyn Memorial can be viewed as a continuation of the same Beaux-Arts Classicism favored by the McDonalds for their Unitarian Church. The decoration of the north, south, and west facades was based on an ornate version of Tuscan and Doric styles: the earliest, most "primitive" of the classical orders, and generally carrying connotations of austerity and purity. The portico on the east facade was articulated in the restrained elegance of the Ionic order, historically the order following Doric. The interiors were far more ornate and called for use of the opulent Corinthian and Composite orders, interspersed with Ionic for secondary layers. Blank spaces were left high on the corners of the exterior for what are described only as "decorative panels"; no program was suggested. This is all very traditional, a text-book approach taught in architecture schools across the Western world and traceable back through the Renaissance to the writings of the ancient Roman commentator, Vitruvius. There is, in fact, little in the McDonalds' original design that would not have been understood – and applauded – by Thomas Jefferson.

TOP: As one of ten firms asked to participate in the competition for the Nebraska State Capitol design, the McDonalds submitted a proposal reflecting their preference for the classical tradition: a grand, domed structure with a lineage stretching back through the nation's Capitol in Washington, D.C., to Wren's St. Paul's Cathedral in London and Michelangelo's St. Peter's Basilica in Rome. (Photo courtesy University of Nebraska Library.)
ABOVE: Bertram Grosvenor Goodhue's innovative and imposing design for the State Capitol was a considerable influence on the Joslyn Memorial: initially in overall plan and massing, but ultimately in all aspects of its appearance. (Photo courtesy Nebraska State Historical Society.)

RIGHT: The brickwork, with the specially sized and cost-saving bricks, that lies behind the marble walls can be seen in this early construction photograph showing parts of the basement and lower level areas.

Goodhue was to exercise far greater influence posthumously, after the Omaha architects had observed, close up, his design actually "arising on the plains." Two related features, in particular, seem to have impressed them. The more they gained familiarity with it, the more they came to appreciate the potential of a design scheme expressing a continuous narrative and philosophical themes inspired by local history and experience; in short, a modern *American* style, referring to but detached from its European antecedents.

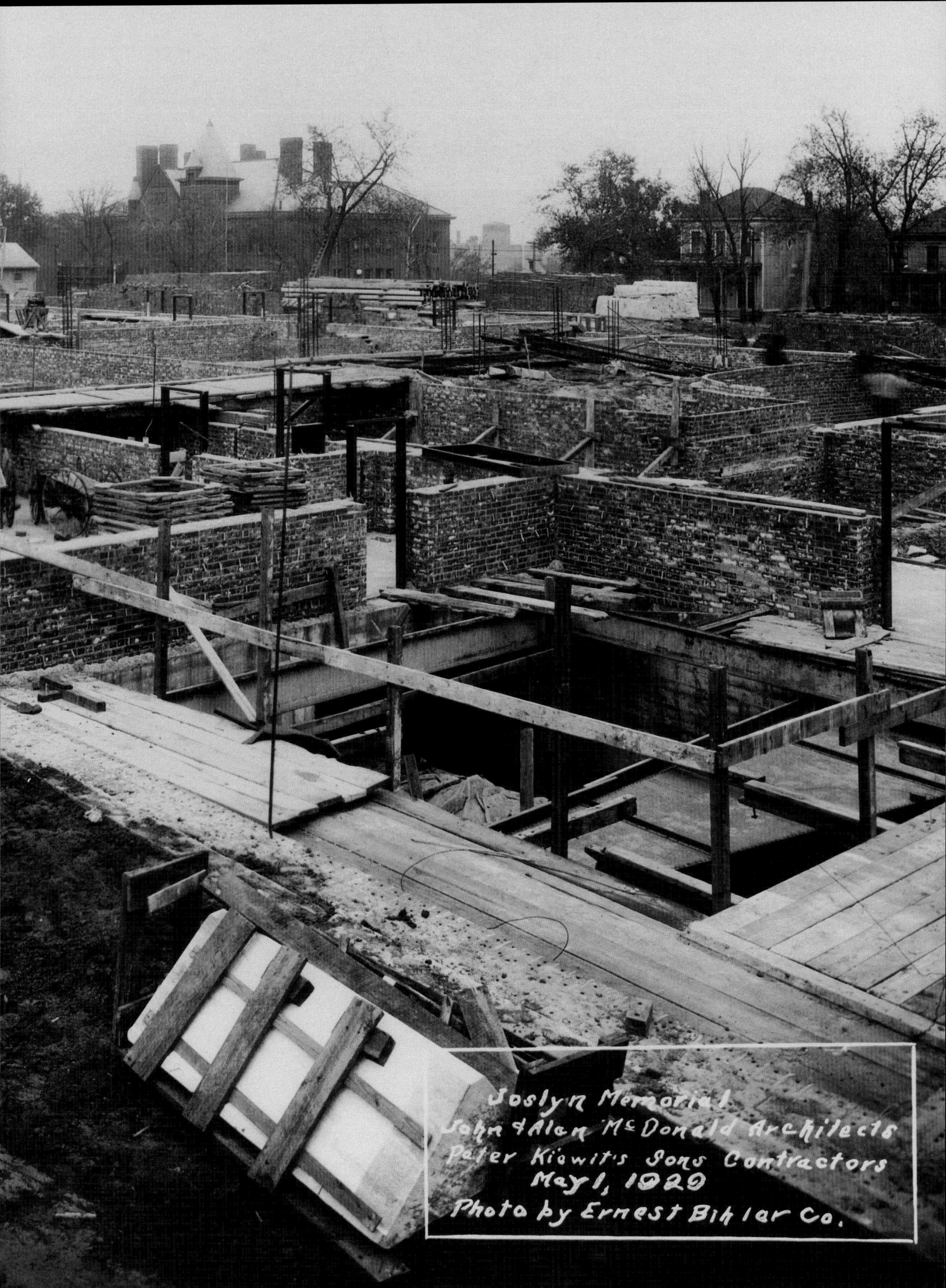
Joslyn Memorial
John & Alan McDonald Architects
Peter Kiewit's Sons Contractors
May 1, 1929
Photo by Ernest Bihler Co.

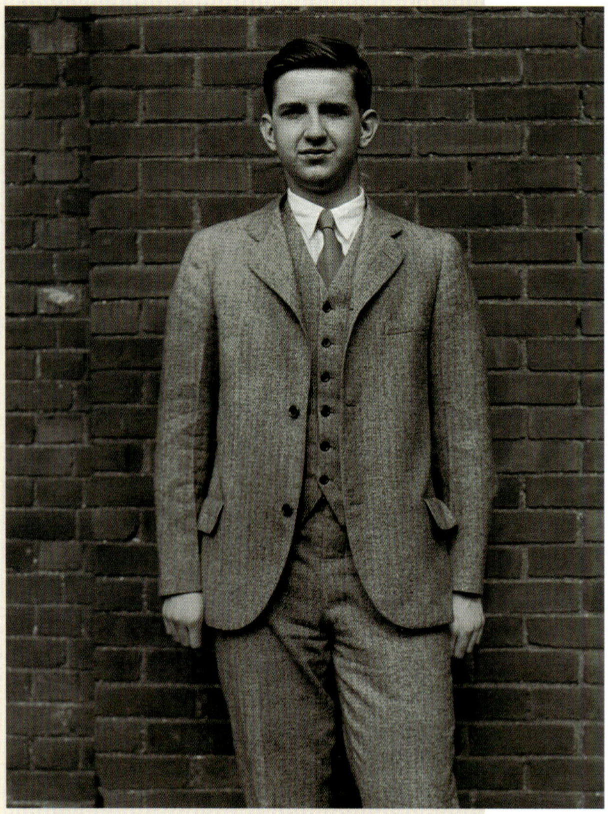

On the recommendation of Thomas Kimball, Omaha's most highly regarded architect, the McDonalds engaged Herschel Elarth, an award-winning graduate from the School of Architecture at the University of Illinois, to carry out the details of recasting the Joslyn Memorial in a Moderne style. A native of Omaha, who was to become head of the College of Architecture at Virginia Polytechnic Institute and State University at Blacksburg, Elarth recalled years later how the thunderbird capitals on the Memorial building resulted from an "endeavor to fuse our Classical traditions with some significant expression of indigenous Indian culture."

Acting on these realizations, the McDonalds must have persuaded Mrs. Joslyn to make the vital changes that were to give the Memorial its notable Art Deco character.

Ground was broken for the Joslyn Memorial on October 3, 1928, at 11:10 a.m. and, as Mrs. Joslyn was determined both to avoid speculation and to maintain the element of maximum surprise for the opening, strictest secrecy was kept about the progress of the building. According to Herschel Elarth, architectural draftsman working in the McDonalds' office, most of the significant changes in ornamentation occurred during the "time-rushed summer of 1929."

When Elarth arrived, he later wrote, "walls and floors . . . were just being laid; so there was an opportunity, when John and Alan McDonald wished, to [translate] the literal, classical design . . . into regional, symbolic forms so well exemplified by the Nebraska State Capitol." Elarth described how "classical details in the exterior elevations . . . were largely stripped away to reveal those severe cubistic shapes symbolically reflecting western Nebraska buttes." In the new "de-classified" treatment, the existing inward tilt of the exterior walls, one degree out of the vertical, is more eloquent and gives added force to the geological allusion. At the same time, the building's architectural massing strongly evokes the time-worn and historically charged forms of ancient Egyptian architecture.

Appearing like a benign *éminence grise* throughout Elarth's recollections is Thomas Kimball. As Nebraska's pre-eminent architect, Kimball coordinated the State Capitol competition and wrote persuasively about Goodhue's design. He seems to have been instrumental in placing the young Elarth with the McDonalds when the father-son team suddenly found themselves in need of a sympathetic spirit to carry out the details of their modernistic redesign. John Nyquist, a long-time associate with the McDonalds, had been working on the Joslyn Memorial but, in mid 1929, "almost without notice," he departed; the proposed updating being, Elarth surmises, too much of a change for an architect trained in pre-World War I Munich. Elarth also credits Kimball with being the most likely source for introducing the McDonalds to Hartley Burr Alexander, whose philosophical and rhetorical skills were to play a large part in the final decorative scheme of the Joslyn Memorial.

Elarth had his work cut out for him in the race to redesign even as the building went up. In some cases it was too late. Many of the doors and grills had already been manufactured, particularly those of the lower level exterior, and they were, by and large, too expensive to discard. On the main level, the same was true for the entry doors for the concert hall, and here, as well as in the north, south, and west doors, the old design peeps through, hinting at the essentially conservative nature of the overall building. Even so, the rest of the decoration was so thoroughly recast that,

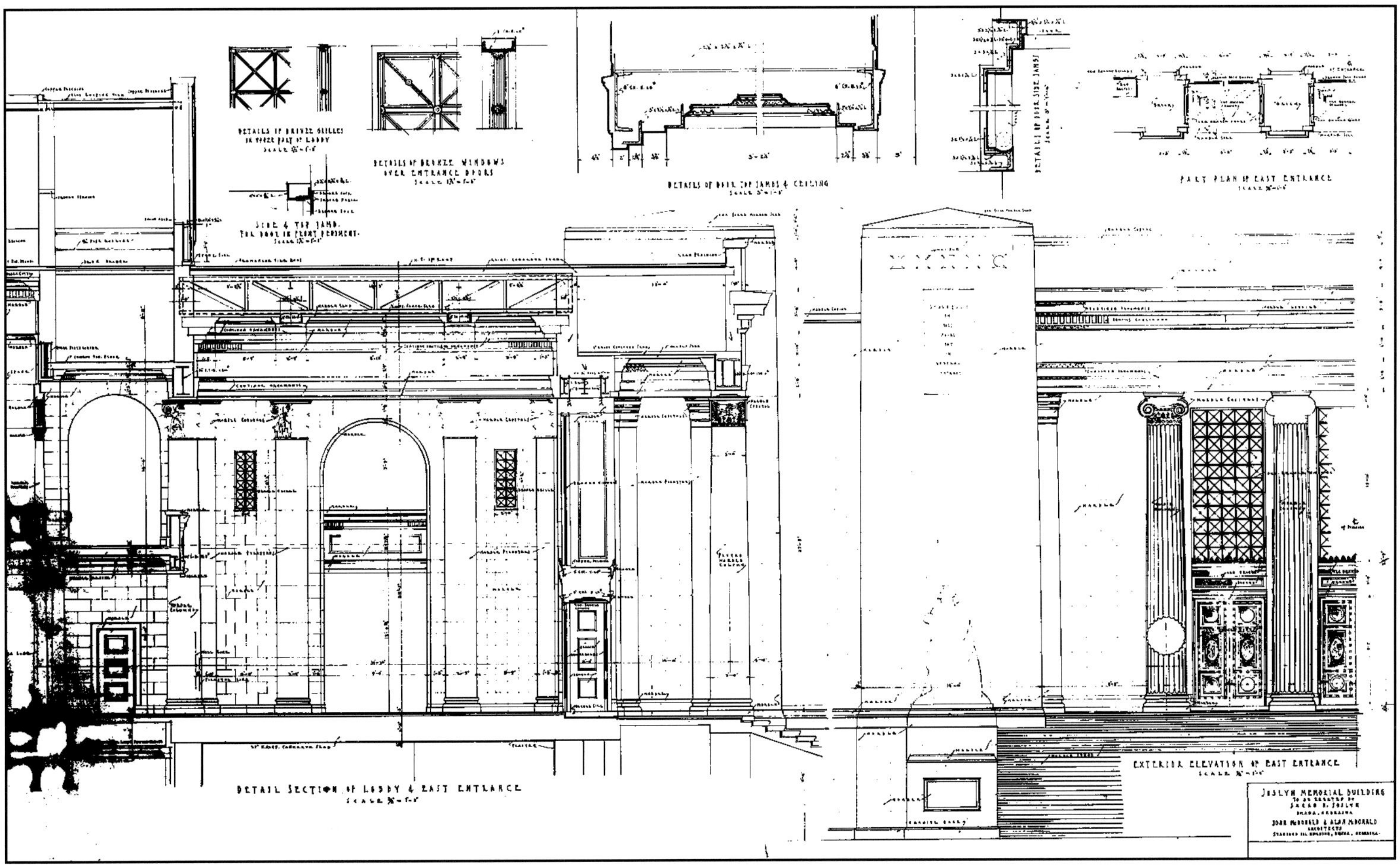

upon opening, the building was immediately hailed as a tour de force of contemporary design and has been recognized as a classic of American Art Deco ever since.

Elarth had studied under Thomas Kimball during the summers of 1927 and 1928, when Kimball became his "patron and critic on programs given out by the Beaux-Arts Institute of Design, New York." Elarth's submission to the Institute's competition for the design of an aqueduct was sponsored by Kimball and garnered the student a "prestigious first place, mentioned." Elarth was already an admirer of Goodhue's work, and Kimball was instrumental not only in giving him "an introduction to the technology of reinforced concrete as used . . . with the problem of [constructing] an aqueduct," but also "to use of indigenous cultural forms, such as the thunderbird motif incorporated into the spandrels of the bridge." With the encouragement of the McDonalds, decorative elements based on the thunderbird became the dominant theme throughout the Joslyn Memorial. "Thunderbird capitals were," Elarth has written, the result of "an endeavor to fuse our Classical tradition with some significant expression of indigenous Indian culture. For the Plains and Northwest Indians, at least, the Thunderbird was thought an important spirit whose great voice meant the beginning of Spring. And further, the Thunderbird was the very image of an eagle, the great predator that carries . . . uplifted feelings . . . in all directions." So it was that a "gradual transformation took place first in the classical Ionic capital" of the entrance portico, spreading to virtually every notable area of the building: from

Though undoubtedly bold in its massing, the detailing of the McDonalds' original design was less radical. The "finished" blueprints of 1928 show a building articulated in the traditional classical orders, predominately Doric outside and Corinthian/Composite within. Their deepening understanding of the thoroughgoing nature of Goodhue's decorative scheme for the State Capitol caused them to completely recast the Memorial in a Moderne style – even though construction had already begun.

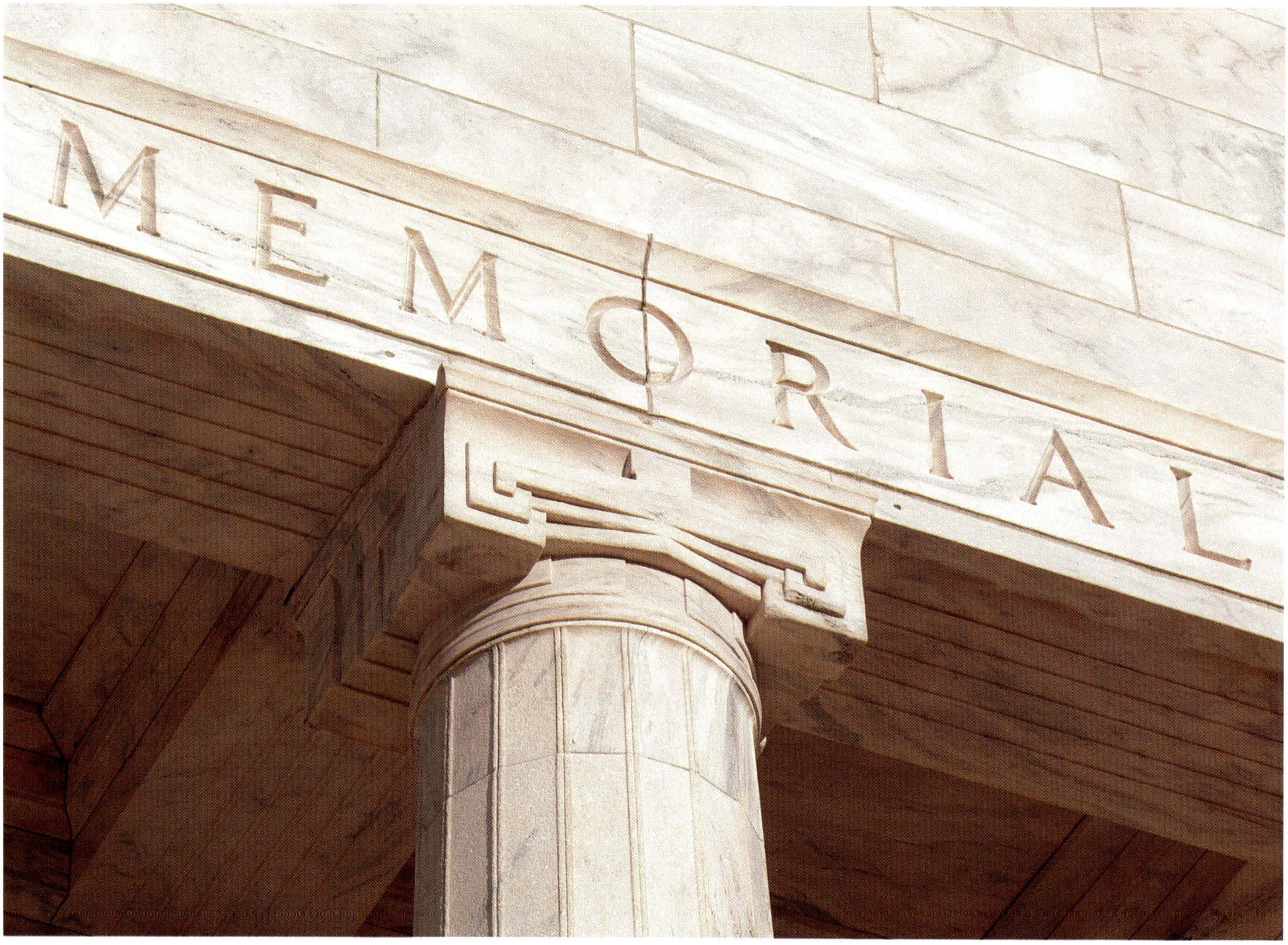

TOP: The original Beaux-Arts designs for the Memorial called for the use of the Ionic order for main columns. With considerable economy, Elarth converted the characteristic curving volutes of the ancient Greek order into rectilinear designs based on the traditional Native American "thunderbird" design.

RIGHT: Not quite one year after groundbreaking the Memorial's walls have reached the main floor level, inner brickwork and marble cladding being laid more or less simultaneously. The basic floor plan of the lower level is already easily discernible.

the first landing on the east steps, through the colorful floral court, to the design of the inlaid wood ceiling in the reception room at the west end.

For all their enthusiasm, the McDonald team could not redesign every element. Some features, such as the stained glass window and the Gothic chimney breast, both in the reception room, remained unchanged – presumably, as both contained mementos of her life with her husband – at Mrs. Joslyn's request. Other components were probably beyond the McDonald office's competence, given the deadlines that confronted them once they had made the decision to modernize their design. "Some areas/details," Elarth concludes in a two-page note, "such as the Batchelder tile, [and] bronze grillework being previously on order, [were] carried over in execution. The wall sconces and ceiling hung lighting fixtures elsewhere in the interior were designed [in] New York – under contract." Making extensive use of aluminum and fluorescent-tube lighting, these fixtures are among the most thoroughgoing Art Deco features of the building. Drawing little or no inspiration from ancient cultures, classical or native, the inventive light designs add a final, emphatically Moderne note to what Alan McDonald himself described as an attempt "to combine the spirit of the modern with the culture of the past."

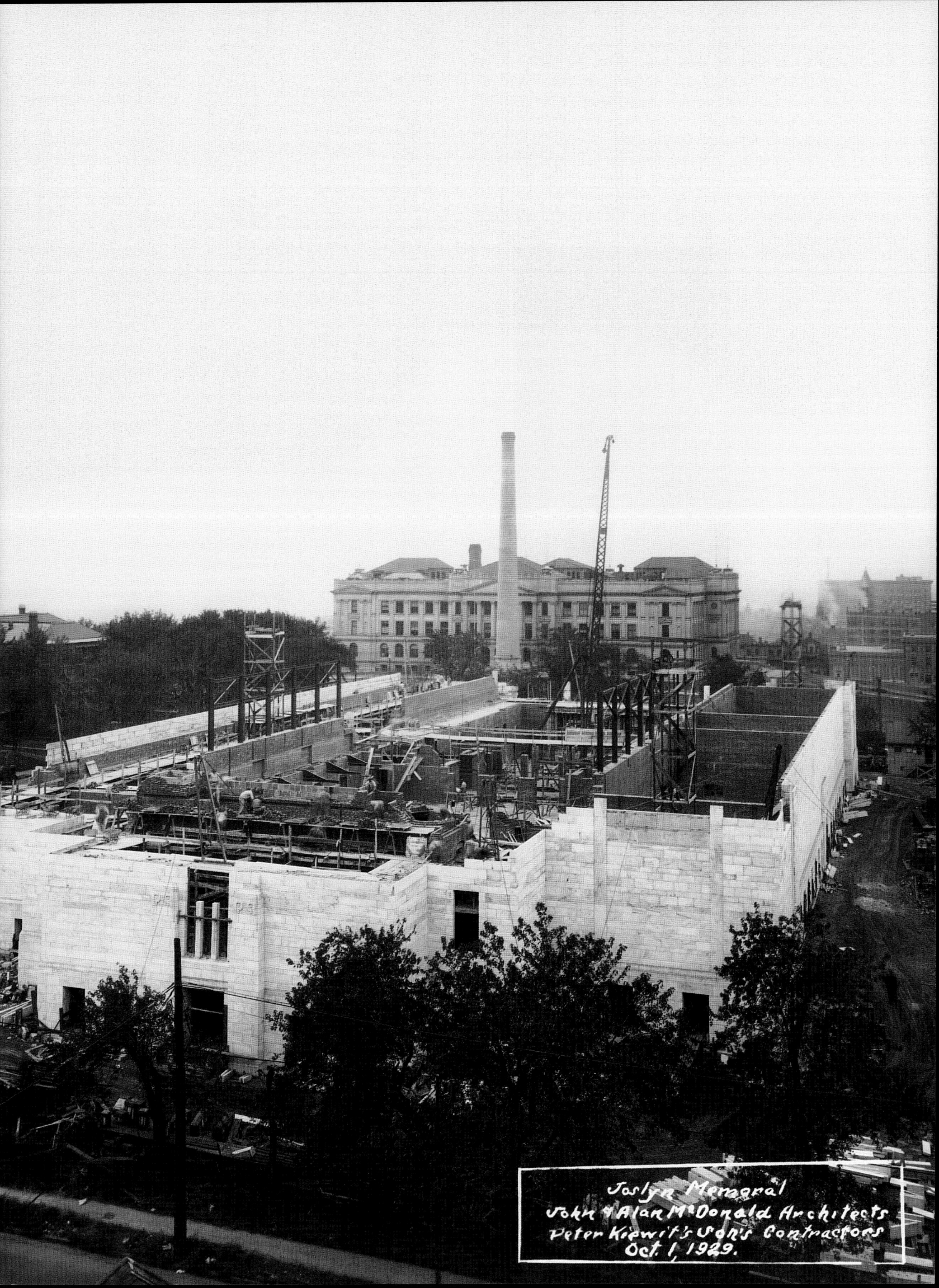
Joslyn Memorial
John & Alan McDonald Architects
Peter Kiewit's Son's Contractors
Oct. 1, 1929.

JOHN DAVID BRCIN
Sculptor

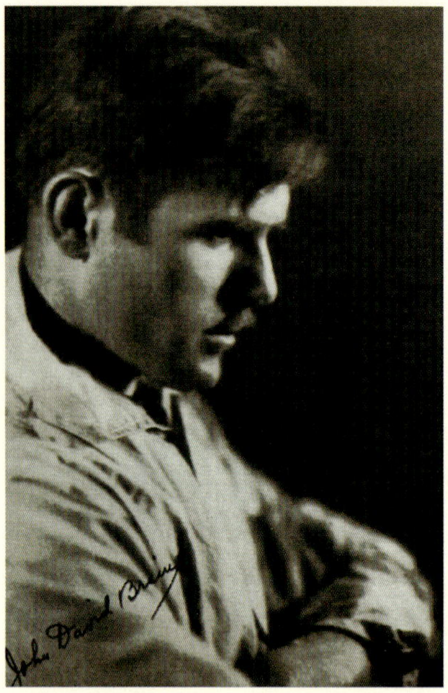

Although a rising star in the U.S. art world, the young Serb-born sculptor, John David Brcin, was a surprisingly bold choice as sole artist for the Memorial's sculptural program. Shown here in a pensive mood, the enthusiastically "Americanizing" immigrant artist was to see his original proposals constantly reshaped – sometimes out of all recognition – by his collaborator, the learned cultural historian, Hartley Burr Alexander.

A Serb, born in Gracac, Croatia, in 1899, John David Brcin (pronounced *Brr-chin*) was raised by his uncle, a farmer, carpenter, and stonemason. At age fourteen he joined his brother in Gary, Indiana, where, in Brcin's own words (writing in the third person singular), "a detailed program was waiting for him in his Americanization." His interest in art sparked by reading about "Giotto, Millet and Mestrovic . . . in the fall of 1917, he found himself enrolled in the sculpture class of the Art Institute of Chicago." Largely forgotten today, in the early years of the twentieth century, the Serbian sculptor Ivan Mestrovic was regarded as a leader in modern figurative sculpture. Of particular interest to Brcin (whose "detailed Americanization" was never as fully realized as his public pronouncements were designed to make it seem), Mestrovic's work was largely based on Slavic history and, in a style combining Rodin and the Romanesque, he gave eloquent voice to ancient Serbian patriotism.

At the Art Institute of Chicago, Brcin studied under Albin Polasek, receiving a number of awards and honors that culminated in a fellowship to study in Europe. He spent 1921 in Serbia (by then part of Yugoslavia), Italy, and France, returning to further study and additional awards at the Institute in 1922 and 1923.

By the time he was awarded the Joslyn Memorial commission in 1929, the young Brcin's star was firmly in the ascendancy. He

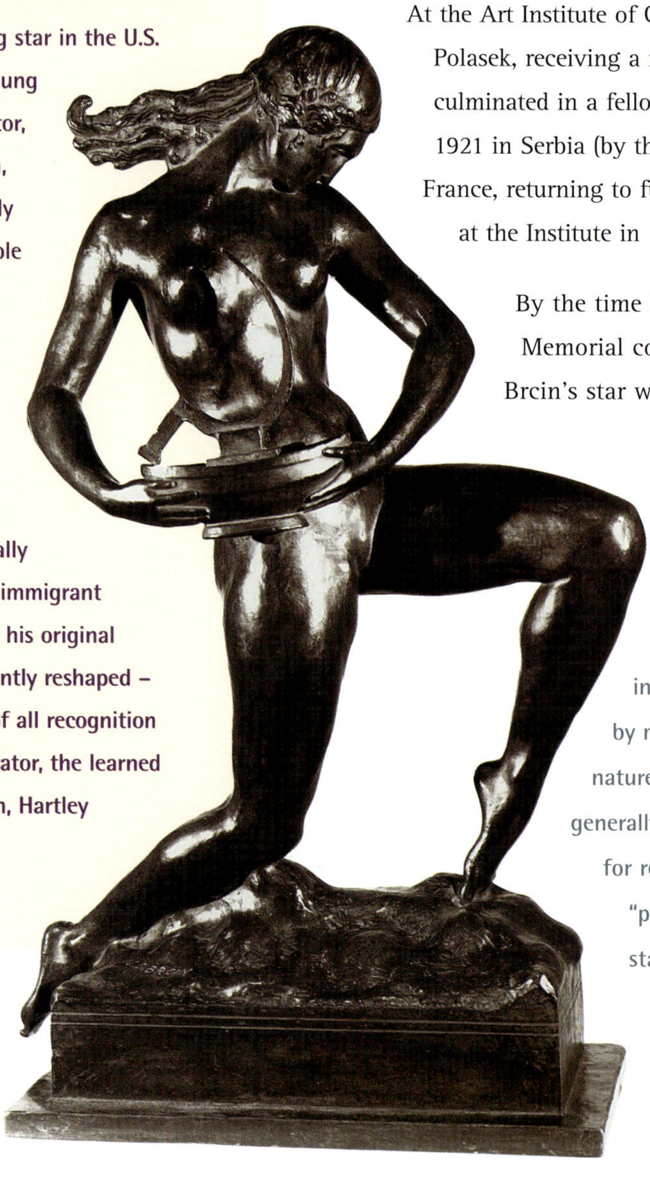

Brcin's sculptures were described as being "a new thing . . . full of dynamic thrust, a smooth sharp-edged symmetry which admirably interprets the spirit of an age governed by machinery." In fact, depending on the nature of the project, Brcin's style varied, generally reserving his "sharp-edged" manner for reliefs and architectural projects. For "pure" sculpture, such as the allegorical statue *Fantasy*, 1924, (LEFT) he employed sleek, flowing forms; for portrait commissions he used a more traditional realism.

had been featured in a number of group exhibitions and, in 1928, been the subject of a one-artist show organized in Chicago and subsequently presented at the Brooks Memorial Gallery in Memphis, the Art Institute of Omaha (April 24 – May 14, 1928), the Museum of Fine Arts in Houston, and the Witte Museum in San Antonio. Once again, there is precious little in the way of documentation, but it seems likely that Brcin's traveling exhibition played no small part in his somewhat surprising selection as sculptor for the Joslyn Memorial.

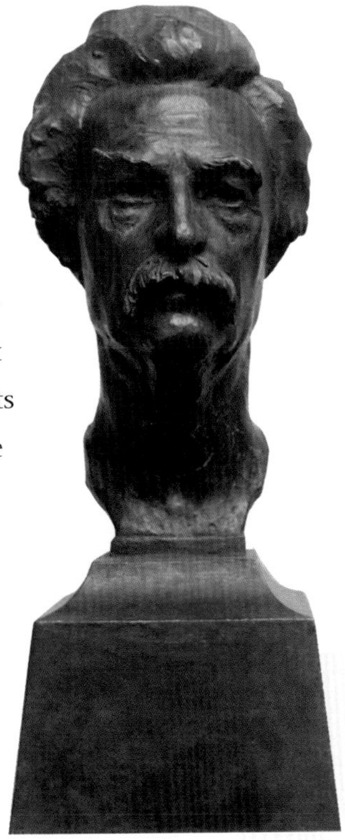

In 1926, Brcin's bust of Mark Twain was seen by the highly regarded sculptor Lorado Taft, who was inspired to write:

My dear Mr. Brcin:
I have been doing a bust which has rather pleased me, but your Mark Twain is so much better . . . that I am inclined to turn to truck gardening. I congratulate you.

Cordially yours,
Lorado Taft

P.S. Do you know anything about chicken farms?

Although not yet thirty, Brcin had already developed three distinct approaches to his medium: traditional portraiture, sleekly stylized statuary, and sharply cut bas-reliefs combining geometric and figurative elements. Taken as a whole, Brcin's stylistic flexibility must have suggested to the McDonalds that here was a rising talent well equipped to execute the sculptural components of Mrs. Joslyn's temple to the arts. Perhaps by way of a trial, they commissioned him to create a memorial plaque for their First Unitarian Church. This carving, a portrait of the church's late minister, Newton Mann, was carried out in Brcin's more traditional style.

The Joslyn commission, which occupied two years of his life and was the cause of equal amounts of elation and frustration, turned out to be the high point of Brcin's career. It established him as a notable representative of his era and, when the Memorial was completed, the critic of the *Chicago Herald-Examiner* declared: "Brcin's carvings are a new thing; they are full of dynamic thrust, a smooth sharp-edged symmetry which admirably interprets the spirit of an age governed by machinery." Ensuing "ages" were less amenable and, although Brcin continued to receive public commissions, the emergence of a home-grown avant-garde, personified by New York's Jackson Pollock and Willem de Kooning, consigned the Serb-born sculptor to the margins of twentieth-century art history. In retrospect, Brcin can be seen, along with such Regionalist painters as Grant Wood and Thomas Hart Benton, as a representative of the conservative swing against European-inspired abstraction that Brcin himself described as following a "mathematically inspired formula which is much to blame for the present day decadence."

Brcin prided himself – and was frequently congratulated – on the peasant Serbian warmth that imbued his art; but when, following World War II, the mood swung to the heated, autographical emotionalism of Abstract Expressionism, Brcin's approach seemed both naive and quaint. His reputation in serious art circles, along with those of Wood and Benton, plummeted. After the mid 1950s, he supported himself by teaching and with portrait commissions; he died in Boulder, Colorado, in 1983.

HARTLEY BURR ALEXANDER
Poet and Philosopher King

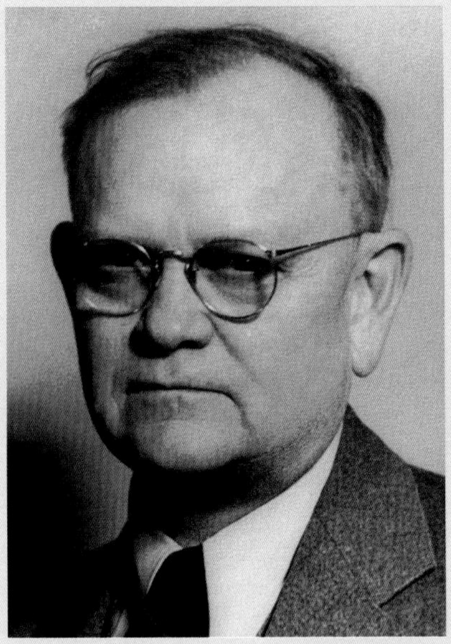

Alexander's diverse knowledge of world cultures, as well as his experience with the decorative scheme for the State Capitol, were perfectly suited to the task of developing a similar program for the Joslyn Memorial. He had to call upon considerable diplomatic skills to mediate between architect and artist in what became an increasingly strained relationship.

Art is a great and dangerous abstraction. It is great because it comes closer to presenting to our minds the universals that form the truth of reality than does any other mode of human thought. It is dangerous because this close similitude is ever persuading us to accept itself as the complete and faithful reproduction of reality.

What Art abstracts from reality is Beauty: it is the business of Art to be beautiful, Art exists for the sake of Beauty, we say. But just because the beauty which the artist gives us is an abstracted beauty, a beauty taken out of its natural context and presented without its natural relations, just because of this, the Beauty with which Art enlightens us is a falsification of natural Beauty. It is static and fictive as are all conceptual universals.

– HARTLEY BURR ALEXANDER, "Beauty and Pain," in *Nature and Human Nature: Essays Metaphysical and Historical,* 1923, p. 200

Born in Lincoln in 1873, Hartley Burr Alexander grew up in Syracuse, some thirty-five miles to the east of Nebraska's capitol. His father, a Methodist minister, and his mother, an artist of local reputation, imbued in their son a high-minded seriousness and thorough appreciation for cultural values. He graduated from the University of Nebraska in 1897 and taught for a year before going on to the University of Pennsylvania and, finally, Columbia University, where he gained his doctorate in 1901. In 1908, after working in New York as an editor on scholarly materials, he returned to the University of Nebraska as a professor of philosophy. A man of wide interests, Alexander combined a love of poetry, philosophy, and anthropology, publishing extensively in the area of Native American culture. His growing reputation and convenient proximity made him an ideal participant in the task of working out the decorative scheme for the State Capitol with its architect, Bertram Goodhue, and sculptor, Lee Lawrie. It is clear that Goodhue had the greatest respect for Alexander's abilities, and the relationship between them was both harmonious and productive. In 1928, his credentials publicly enhanced, Alexander was offered, and accepted, a position at Scripps College in Claremont, California. There he remained until his death in 1939; and from his new home on the Pacific Ocean, Alexander accepted the challenge of devising, at long distance and on short notice, a decorative program for the Joslyn Memorial. This time, things would not go so smoothly.

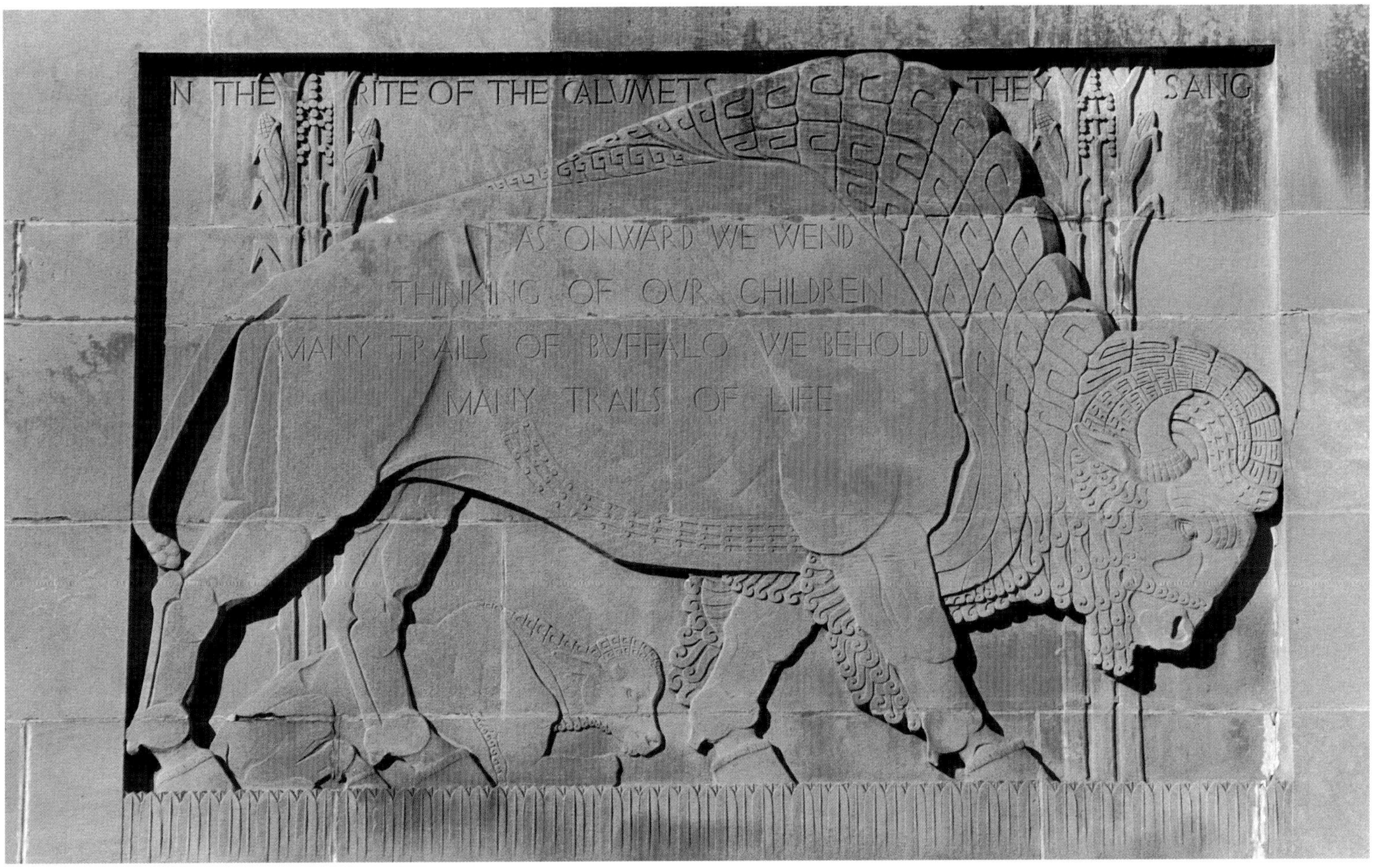

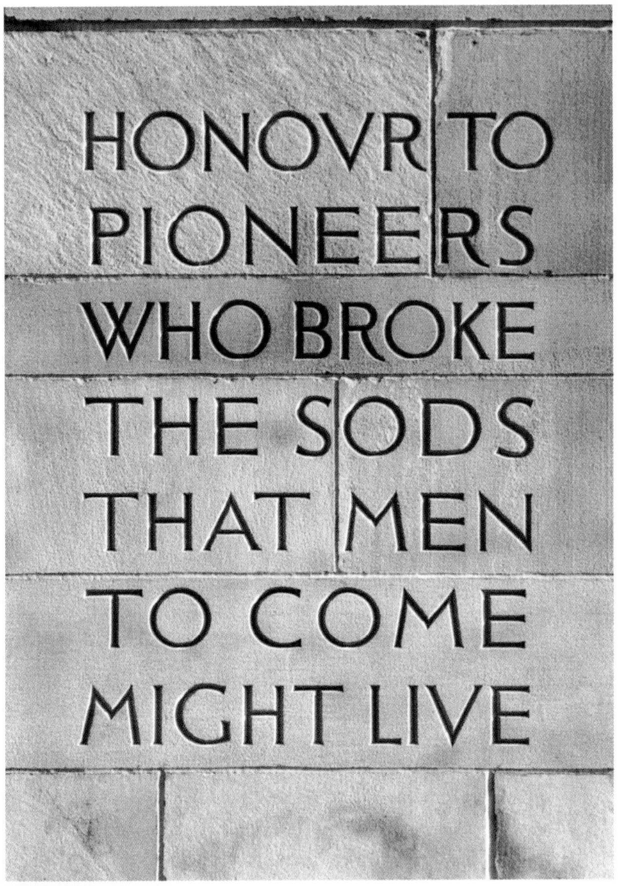

Alexander's deep interest in Native American mythology is evident in all of his writings. To accompany a panel on the Nebraska State Capitol depicting buffalo (ABOVE), he translates into blank verse a song purportedly deriving from the Calumet (the so-called Peace Pipe) ceremony:

> AS ONWARD WE WEND
> THINKING OF OUR CHILDREN
> MANY TRAILS OF BUFFALO WE BEHOLD
> MANY TRAILS OF LIFE

His love of declamatory prose comes through clearly in all of his compositions, whether intended for the walls of public buildings, such as this for the Nebraska Capitol (LEFT), or for scholarly publications. (Photos courtesy Nebraska State Historical Society.)

PETER KIEWIT SONS

Builder

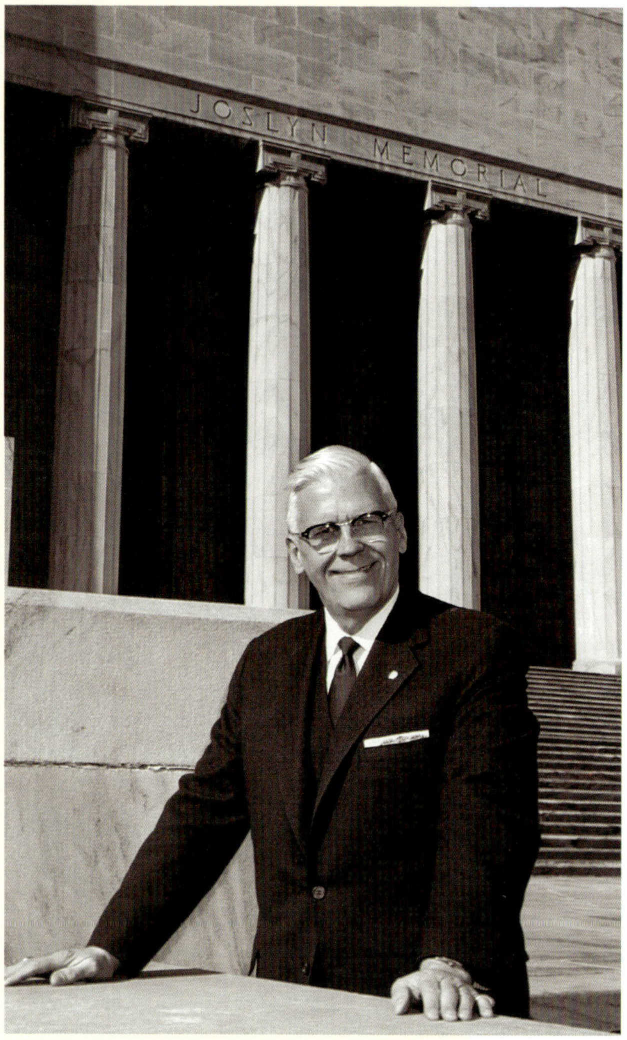

Peter Kiewit, 1960. Along with the State Capitol tower and the Union Pacific terminal, the Joslyn Memorial was a major project early in the career of a man who was to transform a local construction firm into a company with an international presence.

The company was established as Kiewit Brothers in 1884 by Andrew and Peter Kiewit, themselves first-generation Americans, the sons of a Dutch immigrant bricklayer. The family came to Omaha from Keokuk, Iowa, in the late 1870s at the urging of Peter who, like George Joslyn and others, realized the opportunities represented in a city located at the beginning of the recently settled West. When the brothers dissolved their partnership in about 1890, Peter carried on the business alone. In 1912 Peter Kiewit and Sons was formed when he was joined by his sons Ralph and George. Two years later, afflicted by phlebitis, Peter Kiewit died prematurely at age 52. Ralph and George later changed the company's name to Peter Kiewit Sons.

Their younger brother, Peter, was thirteen at the time and worked for the company whenever possible, carrying out a wide range of unskilled tasks wherever needed – from water boy and timekeeper to boss of unskilled labor. By the time he graduated from Central High School in 1918, Peter already had experience as labor foreman at the Omaha Savings and Loan Bank on the corner of 15th and Dodge Streets. In addition to school and construction work, he enrolled in the World War I counterpart of ROTC but, in his eagerness to get to the job site after school, wore brown work boots with his uniform and was repeatedly charged with demerits for not wearing regulation black shoes. Peter entered Dartmouth University but left after his first year, in spring of 1919. "An early," he said, "if not the first, college dropout." He wanted to return to the business he most cared about and became a full-time employee of the company just in time for the Roaring Twenties.

In those boom times, the company won a series of prestigious regional contracts, including the Omaha Livestock Exchange (1924), the State Capitol tower (1927), the Joslyn Memorial (1928), and the Union Station (1930). At the same time, Peter Kiewit Sons underwent further internal reorganization, characterized by Peter increasingly taking center stage. In 1924 George sold out to Ralph and moved to San Diego, where he set up a tile-making business; Peter moved into management. He was renowned for his attention to detail. At the Joslyn Memorial, for example, Peter calculated that a larger brick would simplify construction and, in the face of Alan McDonald's skepticism, prevailed upon Yankee Hill Brick Company in Lincoln to make the necessary molds. He also initiated the use of brass rather than galvanized steel clips to attach the marble exterior to the brick core, a successful innovation repeated at Union Station, another of Kiewit's significant Omaha projects.

Peter Kiewit was renowned for his attention to detail, developing a cost-tracking system that enabled the company to focus on problem areas before it was too late and analyze each project to find significant savings without jeopardizing quality.

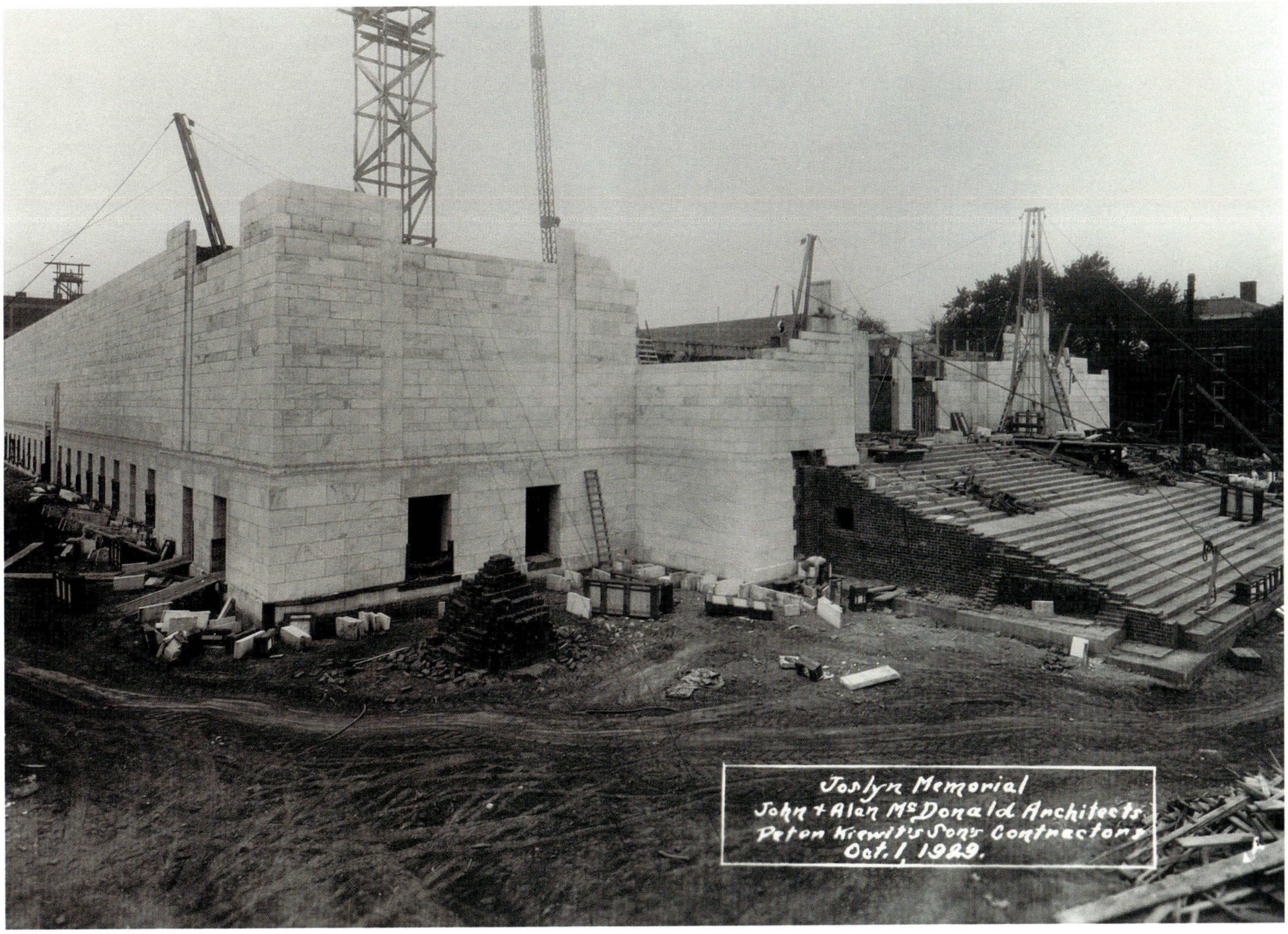

The Joslyn Memorial from the southeast. Unfinished stairs lead up to a ragged entrance facade. Taken one year after groundbreaking, completion is still two years away.

When, in 1931, Ralph Kiewit also moved to California, the company was reorganized one more time. Despite a serious illness in the preceding year, Peter took over the helm of Peter Kiewit Sons, guiding the company through the lean and difficult years of the Great Depression to become a "colossus," in *Forbes* magazine's words, of the construction industry. In 1960, thirty years after his characteristically creative role in the construction of the museum, Peter Kiewit joined Joslyn's Board of Trustees, serving until 1974. He died in 1979.

the DECORATIVE SCHEME

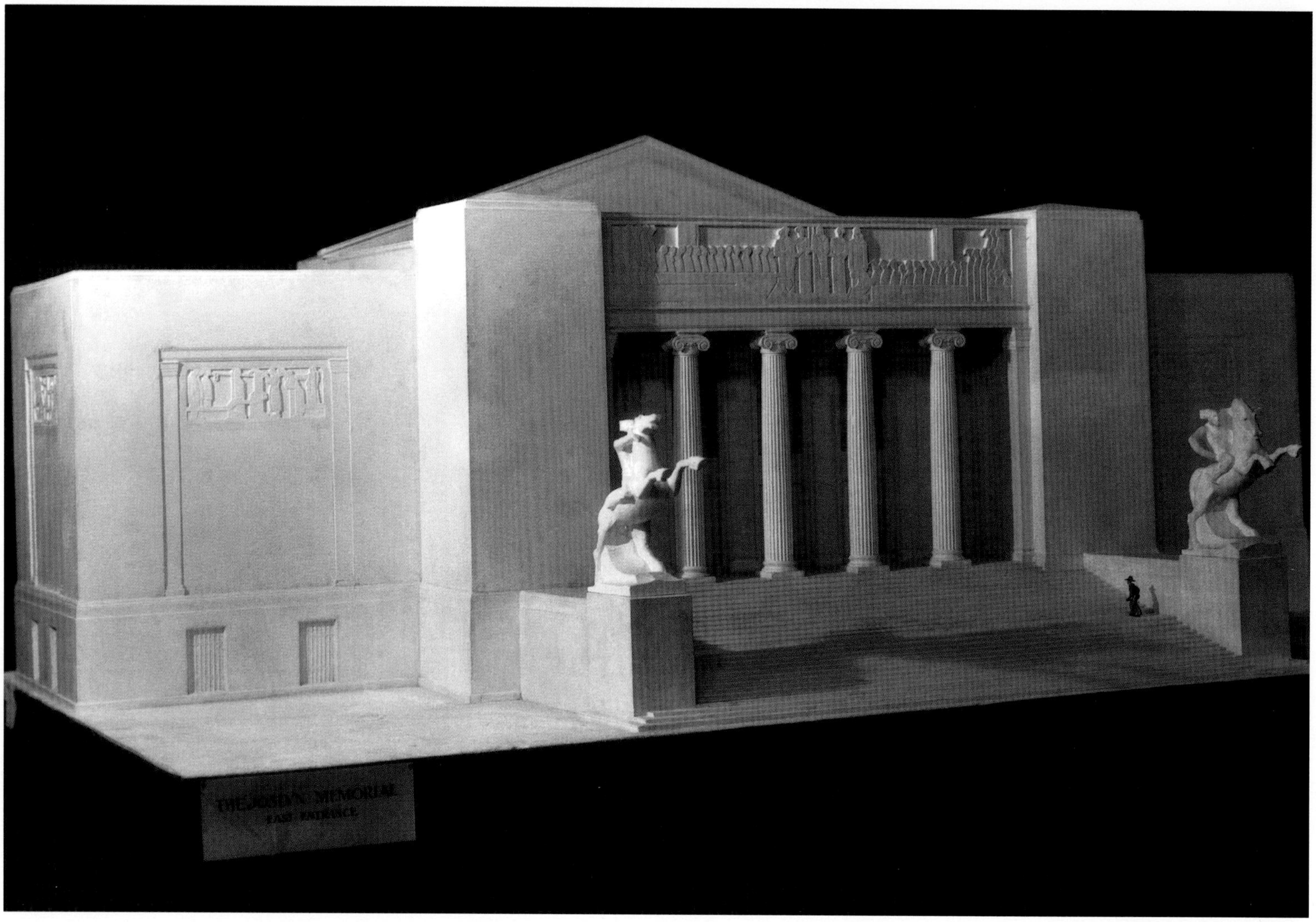

Describing his original proposal, Brcin declared, "I have named the sculptural embellishments 'Episodes of Western Legends and Hero Tales in the Making' . . . a mighty symphonic tone poem, the introductory movement being that of 'Tribute,' a large composition in relief, 53 feet long and 9 feet high placed conspicuously above the columniation of the east portico." The enormous equestrian monuments on each side of the main steps were to represent the Sioux warrior and the Pony Express rider.

On May 22, 1928, Alan McDonald wrote to C. L. Farnsworth, Secretary of the Society of Liberal Arts, outlining, in considerable detail, the work that the McDonalds and Mrs. Joslyn proposed to commission from John David Brcin:

> *8 corner panels 14'6" x 5'6".*
> *1 panel over east entrance 51'6" x 9'.*
> *2 equestrian statues, 18' high or less, cast in bronze and erected.*
> *1 or 2 figure compositions, 3/4 life size or smaller, for court fountain, cast in bronze and delivered to the building.*
>
> *In addition to the above items Mr. Brcin agrees to prepare studies and furnish plaster models delivered to the General Bronze Corporation in New York for the following items:*
>
> *6 different panel inserts for the 6 east entrance bronze doors.*
> *1 memorial tablet of George A. Joslyn with suitable inscription.*
>
> *Mr. Brcin also to prepare studies and furnish plaster models delivered to the Georgia Marble Company for the following items:*
>
> *Column and pilaster capitals for the east entrance.*
> *5' of lettered inscription for cornice treatment south and north elevation.*
> *6 rosettes, 4 different designs, for three grade entrances.*

It is clear from this extensive list that, following the example set by Lee Lawrie's work at the State Capitol, the McDonalds envisioned a single artist providing a uniform scheme for their building. They established a total fee to Brcin of $146,000, of which $108,000 was to cover production "costs for armatures, casting in plaster and bronze, crating, transportation, marble carving, erection of bronze items, approval photographs, traveling expenses, assisting labor and live models . . . leaving Mr. Brcin $38,000 as net fee." This letter Farnsworth passed on to Charles F. Harding, Mrs. Joslyn's representative in Chicago, who responded with a letter on June 3 that is as revealing as it is brief. Keeping salutations to a minimum, Harding wrote:

> *I notice that you advise me that Mrs. Joslyn is in favor of . . . Mr. Brcin. I don't suppose that anyone would desire to go against Mrs. Joslyn's wishes in the matter, and therefore I do not see why your program is not entirely adequate. I myself should be very glad if we could have Lorado Taft, or some other artist of first class reputation, do this work. I would really like to see some stroke of genius in the building. I presume, however, it would simply be an annoyance for me to mention the matter, so I shall let it go. However, I want the contract submitted to Judge Redick before it is signed up; then you and Mrs. Joslyn, who are the ones that will sign this contract, will expect the same to be ratified at the next meeting of the trustees. Yours respectfully.*

Clearly, legal counsel in Chicago felt that some degree of railroading was being perpetrated; but the architects, having covered the bases, got their way and Brcin signed the contract the following month.

In an interview with the *Chicago Daily News* published September 25, 1929, the elated sculptor outlined his approach to the commission. "Folklore," he said, "besides being the real foundation for great art, is the greatest of all arts. . . . Since this building is to be dedicated to . . . the fine arts, I have been prompted to select as my subject matter . . . those incidents of western life upon which most likely will be developed a goodly share of the future legends and folklore of America. . . . I have named the sculptural embellishments 'Episodes of Western Legends and Hero Tales in the Making.' The theme will be developed in the form of a mighty symphonic tone poem, the introductory movement being that of 'Tribute,' a large composition in relief, 53 feet long and 9 feet high placed conspicuously above the columniation of the east portico."

In terms that would have found approval with the most homespun American Regionalist painter, Brcin exclaimed, "If American air is good enough for our lungs and American bread good enough for our food, I do not see why our souls must depend on the Olympian gods of the Greeks of old, or the smoky atmosphere of the artificial bohemian life of Paris for inspiration.

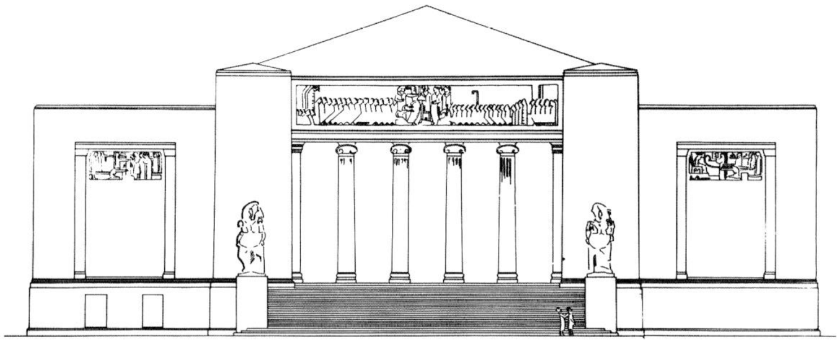

The east facade in classical guise. Brcin's early panels occupy the full width of the spaces between the columns. The giant frieze, depicting a huge congregation assembled in tribute to the arts, was ultimately eliminated. Alexander objected: "It amounts to an assertion of the pre-eminence of the arts (of 'art for art's sake') which is certainly not true of the American consciousness."

Brcin goes on to explain that the main theme – humanity's debt to the arts – will be augmented by "eight shorter movements" – the panels – "picturing to the mind those scenes of western life that fire our imagination with romance and noble sentiment. They are 'Buffalo Hunt,' 'Peace Pipe Ceremony,' 'Early Fur Trading,' 'Lewis and Clark Expedition, the Trail Blazers,' 'Purchase of Louisiana,' 'Cowpunchers,' 'Esteban Martin, First Printer on the American Continent,' and 'Distribution of the News.'" Having mentioned that the last two panels specifically pay tribute to "the man in whose honor the building is erected," Brcin concludes, "The final and dramatic touch will be expressed by two equestrian statues, eighteen feet in height – thirty feet with pedestals [Alan McDonald's "18' or less"!] flanking the steps leading to the main entrance and entitled 'Pony Express' and 'The Mounted Indian,' two subjects as poetic as may be found in any land."

The artist's euphoria is easy to understand, but even as he was preparing his preliminary designs in Chicago, back in Omaha the rules were changing. Constructing a coherent historical program for a building is not a simple task, and the McDonalds had decided to consult Hartley Burr Alexander. On November 4, 1929, the Board of the Society of Liberal Arts hired him to write inscriptions and to be an "advisor on sculptural subjects and treatments thereof." When the McDonalds sent Alexander photostats of Brcin's designs accompanied by their comments, the scholar was quick to respond with his own ideas. He had words of praise for aspects of Brcin's program and retained many of its features, but Alexander's more sophisticated appreciation of cultural crosscurrents in American history allowed him to suggest topics that were more tightly woven yet still capable of personal inflection.

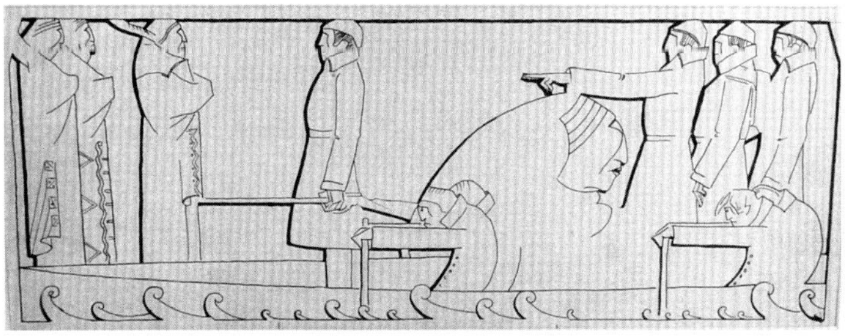

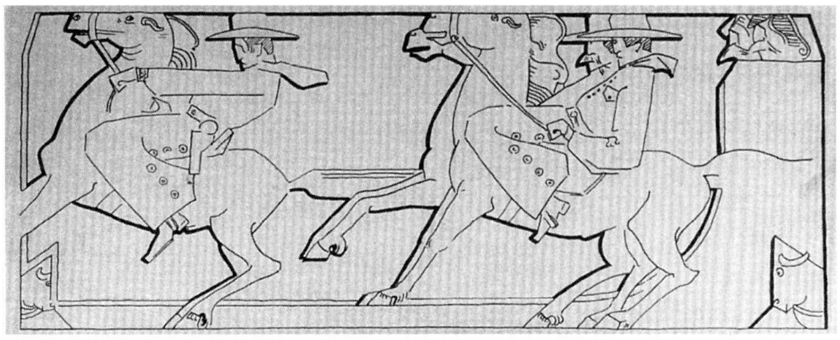

In a letter of December 1, 1929, Alexander offered two schemes, the first of which effectively turned Brcin's proposal on its head. Six panels, *Pioneer Press, Distribution of News, Signal Fire, Sign Language, Indian Picture Writing,* and *Pony Express*, referred to George Joslyn's career. Two other panels, *Advancement of Learning* and *Communication of Beauty*, were meant to symbolize cultural advancement. Alexander's second plan was more historically based and retained, with some re-titling, six of Brcin's original topics: *Pioneer Press, Distribution of News, Indian Council, Buffalo Hunt, Fur Traders,* and *Cowboys.* He suggested completing the second scheme with panels depicting *Homesteaders* and *Civic Builders.* Alexander preferred the first scheme.

Relief in the modernized style. Proposals for the panels depicting Lewis and Clark and cowboys show Brcin's great simplification of sculptural form to parallel the streamlining of architectural details.

The architects were delighted with the suggestions; not so the sculptor. Alexander had not limited himself to discussing the panels relating to American history. He had criticized the main frieze – Brcin's "introductory movement" – and disapproved of the rearing equestrian statues, feeling, with some justification, that presenting the exposed underside of a horse was not the noblest way to greet a visitor; Brcin's "final and dramatic touch," he thought, was superfluous. Finally, the Anglo-Saxon philosopher-poet suggested that some of the Serb sculptor's renderings of both European and Native American figures were altogether too "Slavic," characterized by heavy brows, broad faces, and flowing beards. Offended, Brcin protested to Alan McDonald, "My work has been exhibited all over the country, architects and sculptors praising it for the very reason about which Dr. Alexander is complaining."

But, over the next few weeks, it was Brcin's relationship with the architects rather than that with the professor that rapidly deteriorated. By February of 1930, Alan McDonald and Brcin had exchanged letters charging each other with breach of contract. The dispute was only settled when Alexander had a personal meeting with Brcin and managed, somehow, to convince the aggrieved artist to accept a number of changes. Alexander had already written to McDonald that he found it more difficult working with Brcin than with Lee Lawrie, but balanced this implied rebuke with the observation that he had found his collaborator on the State Capitol almost too eager to take his suggestions. Ever diplomatic, Alexander managed to bring McDonald back into the collaboration by suggesting a procedure based on that employed successfully for the State Capitol. He and Brcin would exchange ideas and sketches until they had mutually agreed upon a design; only then would it be submitted to the architects. After they had approved the concept, Brcin would execute a clay model which, in turn, had to be approved. From the clay model, he would create a final plaster cast that would be sent to Omaha and used as a template for the stone carvers, Edward and Gino Ratti, to cut the panel into the Georgia Pink marble of the exterior facades.

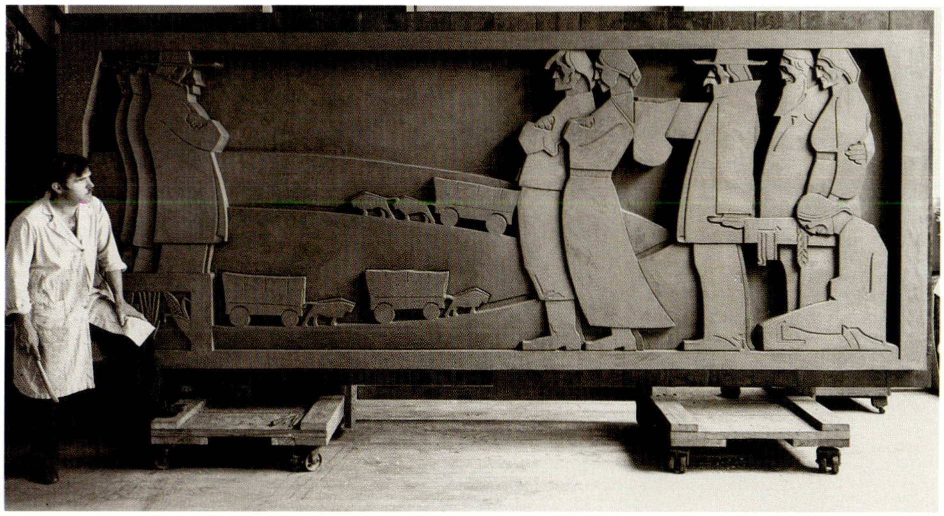

Brcin poses in front of the completed plaster model for the *Homesteaders* panel.

On this basis work progressed, but the damage to the collaborative effort was never fully repaired, and ensuing letters both ways were never entirely free of misunderstandings or reproaches. Alan McDonald and Alexander tended to unite against Brcin, who increasingly took on the role of a "difficult foreigner." In the end, the ambitious young artist saw his "mighty symphonic tone poem" reduced to something like a counterpoint to the imposing music of the architecture.

The final scheme, as approved and executed, combines elements of both contributors but is, overall, closer to the spirit of Alexander than that of Brcin. The sculptor had protested that Alexander's *Communication of Beauty* was impossible to translate into stone, and the solution was to drop such abstract notions altogether. Also abandoned were the specific and, to Brcin, colorful heroes of frontier history: the Indian hunter, Lewis and Clark, the fur trader, and the cowpuncher. Instead, reflecting Alexander's view of cultural development in America, the eight panels were divided equally between the Native American and the European contributions. They were: *The First Printer* (or, subsequently, *The Pioneer Press*), *Distribution of News* (or, subsequently, *Dissemination of Intelligence*), *Civic Builders, The Homesteaders, Indian Prayer for Life, Indian Signal Fire, Indian Sign Language,* and *Indian Picture Writing.*

The location of the eight reliefs had been decided in the original Beaux-Arts design, but the relative position of each topic was matter for further discussion. There was never any doubt that the two panels most closely associated with George Joslyn's life, *The Pioneer Press* and *Dissemination of Intelligence,* should appear on the main, east facade, flanking his name and close to the bronze doors that, it had been decided, would be dedicated to his particular virtues. Not only was this the most important aspect of the building, it faced downtown Omaha, the hub of Joslyn's empire. The south facade, running alongside Dodge Street, also required special consideration, as did the relationship between adjacent panels on each corner which, from certain vantage points, are viewed as pairs. Finally, as well as relating thematically, these corner elements had to complement each other compositionally. So, for example, it was decided to place *Civic Builders* on the east end of the south facade next to *Pioneer Press,* where the pair combine to augment the overall portrait of George Joslyn as well as work together formally.

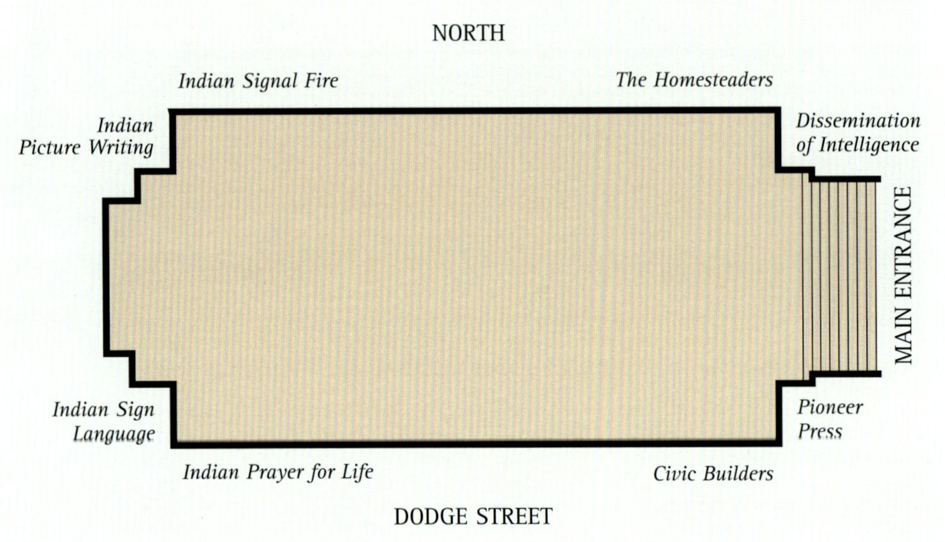

In this arrangement, the theme of each panel bears a distinct relationship to its neighbors. The main and, today, somewhat unsettling caesura occurs between the east and west ends, with the former referring to the white settlement of the area and the latter to the native culture it was effectively to replace.

RIGHT: In this undated photograph, the main elevations are essentially complete. The main stairway, however, has only progressed down to the first landing; the ground has yet to be cut away to accommodate the wider flight of stairs reaching to street level.

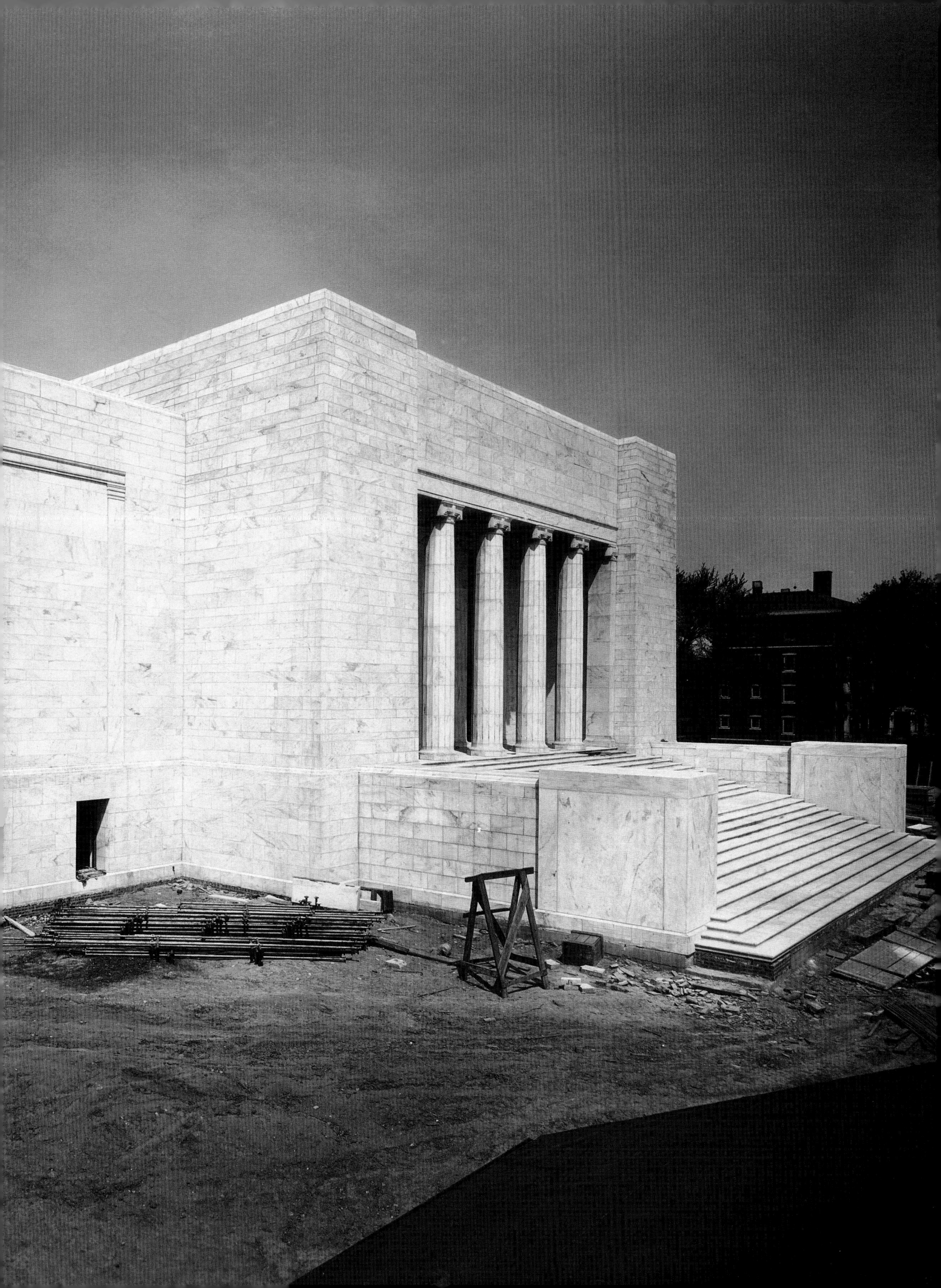

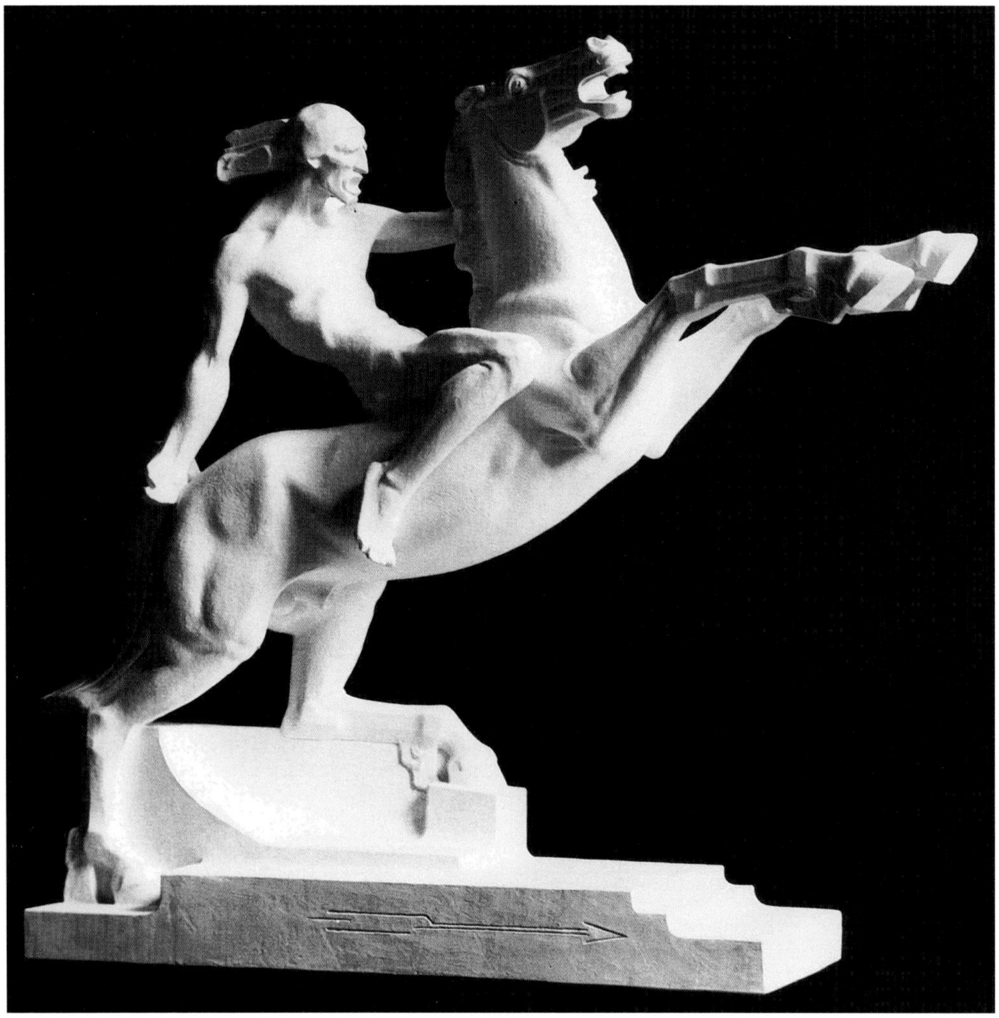

Brcin's original scheme called for a rearing horse on each side of the east steps: one mounted by a Native American, the other by a Pony Express rider. His collaborators, Alexander and McDonald, did not share his enthusiasm for what they felt to be the horses' unseemly and intimidating poses. The sculptures were never executed and this 3½-foot-high plaster prototype is the sole sculptural relic of Brcin's dramatic proposal.

THE EXTERIOR

THE EQUESTRIAN MONUMENTS

Brcin's initial scheme called for a sculptural frieze along the full length of the front entablature and two horsemen – a Sioux warrior and a Pony Express rider – one on each side of the main steps. Early renderings clearly show aspects of this scheme, but neither component survived the early stages of the collaboration. Alan McDonald was quick to tell Alexander that the equestrian statues appealed to no one apart from the artist. Accordingly, Alexander wrote to Brcin objecting that they "will rise like threats above the entrant to the building, and will give first and most vividly a belly-view of the unusual form, with virtually no sense of its intended significance." Brcin responded that he wanted these forms "to rise like threats" and "strike with awe every entrant to the building." Brcin attempted to dismiss what he called the "belly criticism" with the assertion that the sculptures were meant to be seen from a distance. The disagreement straggled on through the length of the commission, with McDonald and Alexander variously suggesting carved reliefs of Pegasus (shades of Lee Lawrie's *Buffalo* on the State Capitol steps), reclining Indian figures, and classical urns. In the end, nothing was done.

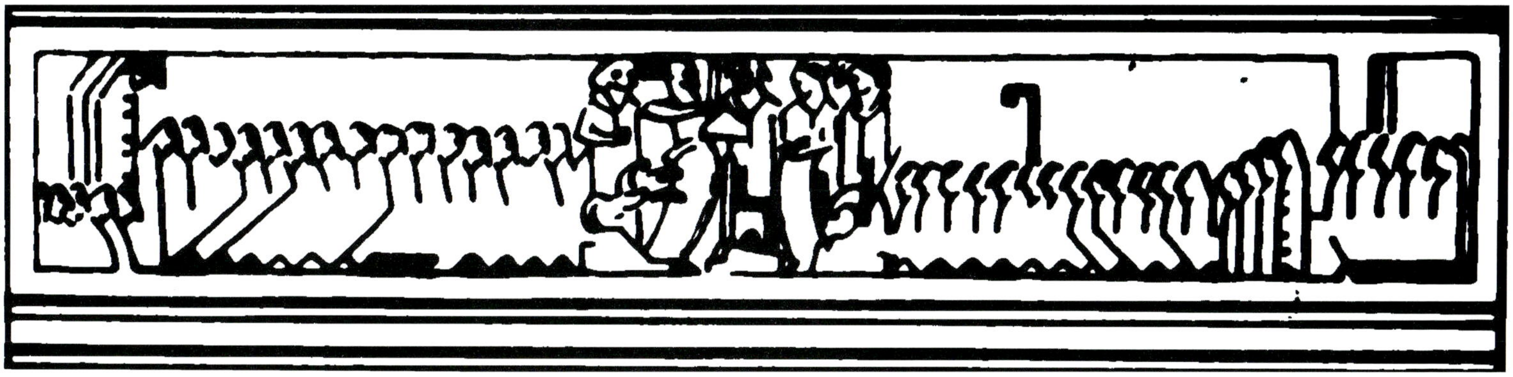

THE FRIEZE

Brcin's great frieze also fell victim to Alexander's sense of propriety and, to a lesser extent, the McDonalds' concern to be modern. For his *Tribute to the Arts,* Brcin depicted five figures personifying the arts – sculpture, music, architecture, literature, and painting – surrounded by rows of people with bowed heads. From the beginning, Alexander disliked it. In keeping with his criticism of Brcin's tendency in the early panel designs to depict gloomy or servile people, Alexander said he found the bowed heads expressive of depression rather than adulation. More importantly, he felt the whole idea of "tribute to the arts" unsettling. "What it amounts to is an assertion of the pre-eminence of the arts (of 'art for art's sake') which is certainly not true of the American consciousness." Given Brcin's status as an immigrant and his public insistence on his "detailed Americanization," it is not hard to sense how disquieting such criticism must have been to the young artist in the middle of a commission that could make or break his reputation. When Alan McDonald, concerned that the frieze might be "a bit overwhelming," weighed in with supporting opinion from leading architects in favor of a simple inscription, there was little room for Brcin to maneuver and the idea was dropped completely.

THE MARBLE

For the first sixteen years, guided tours of the Joslyn Memorial focused on the extraordinary variety and geographical diversity of the materials in the building. To some extent, "streamlining" the exterior further increased emphasis on the large expanses of stone unrelieved by decoration, and the choice of Georgia Pink (Etowah Fleuri) marble for the exterior was a bold one. Usually preferred for smaller interior spaces, this extremely variegated stone provides the Joslyn building with an outer skin full of visual incident. Colors range from pink and white to shades of gray and green; flaws that, in other circumstances, would cause many blocks to be rejected, here simply add to the delicate texture. The marble's finish was hand-hammered, which initially gave it an appearance quite different from today. In a newspaper article, somewhat cheekily titled "Widow Joslyn's Mystery Memorial," one writer referred to it as "a great box-like building . . . its plain white exterior ornamented only with a series of modernistic panels." Within a few years, its sparkling surface had been softened by the effects of weather and industrial pollution. The writer of a 1936 guide meant for internal use refers to its "pink marble glory" and the "variations in weather that produce an ever changing effect on the exterior. Rain, particularly, brings deep rich tones of pink."

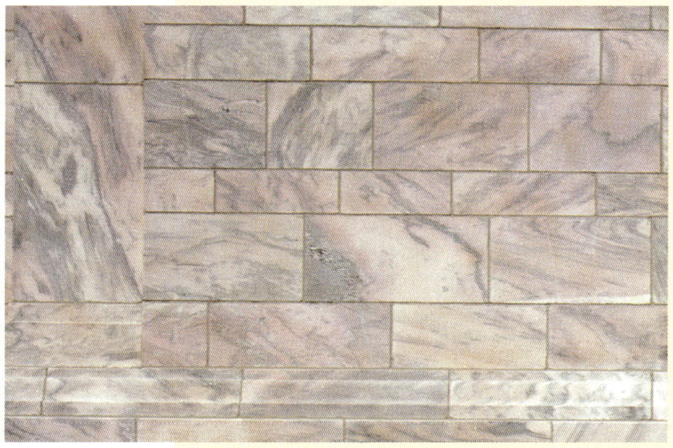

The exterior of the Memorial building consists of a thick veneer of marble blocks laid like masonry over massively thick brick walls, a building technique as old as the monuments of Egypt.

THE PANELS

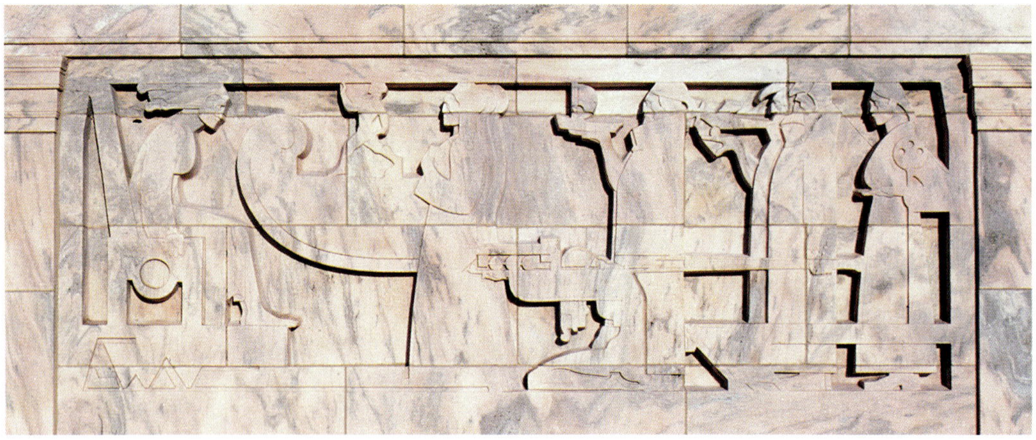

Dissemination of Intelligence (or, Distribution of News)

The first of the panels to be carved, *Dissemination of Intelligence,* is also the most allegorical. The seated figure on the left symbolizes Intelligence; the small figure of a Greek runner stands before her. Other figures variously hold out to Intelligence a boat, a locomotive, and an airplane, all representing travel; two more hold objects symbolizing the telegraph (lightning bolts) and radio (a microphone). George Joslyn's own considerable professional contribution to the spread of intelligence through newspaper journalism was reserved for the other panel on the east facade, a focus that may have influenced Alexander in his final preference of the more general title *Dissemination of Intelligence* over the original and more specific *Distribution of News.*

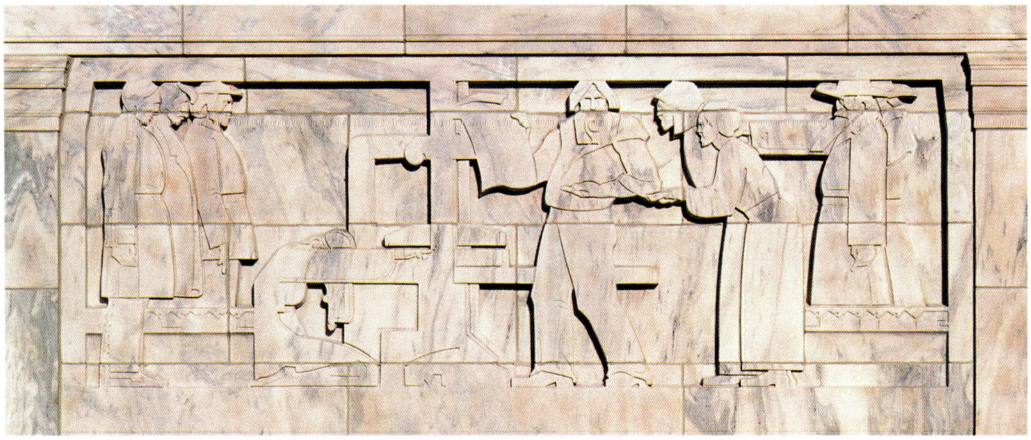

The Pioneer Press (or, The First Printer)

Brcin had originally outlined a composition featuring Gutenberg, but readily accepted Alexander's suggestion that an American treatment would be most appropriate here. The change was one of costume rather than composition, and in final design features a variety of frontier types – city fathers, women, a soldier – looking at a printer holding up a newspaper in front of his press. A somewhat exhausted-looking kneeling figure in the center symbolizes the Genius of the Press. The last change that Brcin made was to convert the figure on the far left from a tunic-clad immigrant (perhaps a reference to his own life) to that of a Native American wearing buckskins.

The Homesteaders

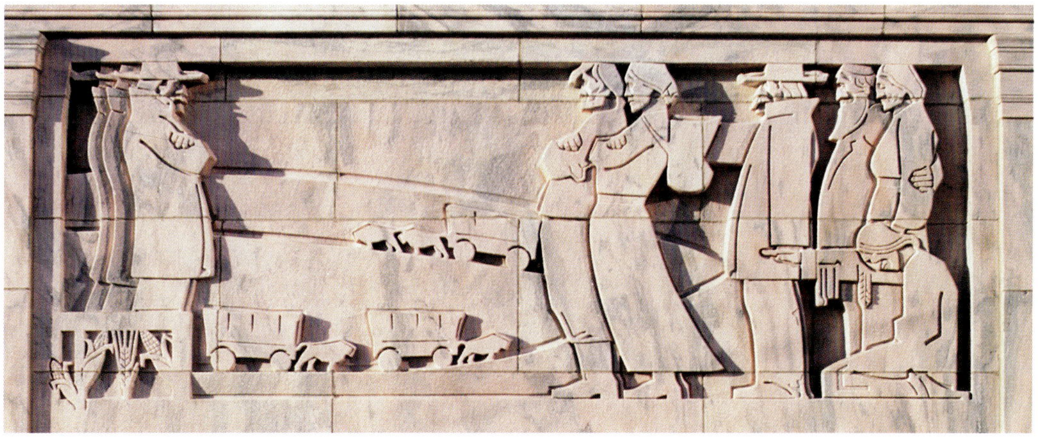

Progress on this panel illustrates the perils inherent in collaboration at long distance and might be called "the non-dissemination of intelligence." Not included in Brcin's original listing, *The Homesteaders* was suggested by Alexander as a companion piece for *Civic Builders* and a replacement for *Lewis and Clark* or *Louisiana Purchase.* Authorized to start work on *Homesteaders*, Brcin worked out a design which Alexander found acceptable. Unfortunately, by this time Alexander had begun to have second thoughts about his own scheme and wrote to Alan McDonald suggesting that the *Pony Express* (the subject of one of Brcin's two rejected equestrian pieces!) would go well with *Dissemination of Intelligence.* McDonald conveyed this to Brcin, who replied that *Homesteaders* was more than half completed. Though irritated that Brcin was essentially forcing them to stay with their own idea, McDonald asked Alexander to accept the panel on the grounds that it would expedite carving on-site. Alexander concurred.

The Homesteaders depicts a stern group of established farmers, planted corn at their feet, staring at a group of equally determined-looking settlers. The kneeling Native American, Alexander said, "expresses surrender of the old way of life." Between the groups, prairie schooners travel a road winding into the distance. Alexander felt that a sun would enliven the middle section, but Brcin demurred and McDonald wrote in agreement that "after seeing the *Dissemination* panel actually carved on the walls we do not feel that the space . . . will be objectionable. The scale of this building is so great . . . that these rather blank spaces on the panels do not seem nearly so blank on the wall."

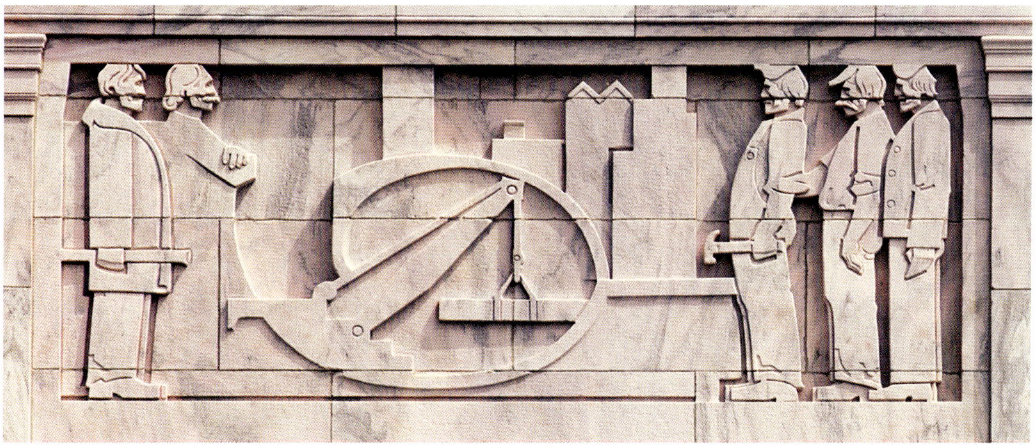

Civic Builders

Complementing *The Homesteaders*, its counterpart on the north wall, *Civic Builders*, completes the story of George Joslyn embodied in the panels on the east facade. *Civic Builders* describes the stage of progress after *The Homesteaders* and shows two groups of purposeful men: planners and entrepreneurs on one side, artisans and craftsmen on the other. Between them rises a cityscape. Because of the significance of this panel – it described the very act of civic building represented by the erection of the Joslyn Memorial itself – Alexander was especially anxious about its composition and made a number of suggestions concerning the way the city was represented. In the end Alexander declared the panel to be satisfactory rather than exciting, commenting, "My objection being only that it lacks lift."

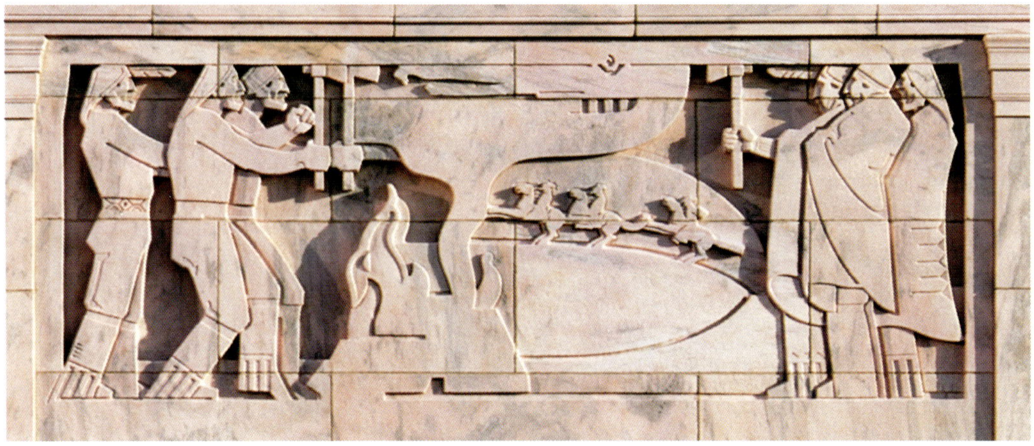

Indian Signal Fire

Peace Pipe was another of Brcin's original proposals, and his initial attempts to transfer the design, more-or-less wholesale, over to Alexander's *Indian Signal Fire* led to a lengthy exposition by the folk-lore academic to the folk art-admiring artist. "There is no 'peace pipe ceremony' in the strict sense – the ritual smoking of a pipe opens all councils." Further, the thunderbird that Brcin had depicted in the smoke was at cross-purposes with the peace pipe ritual. "The Thunderbird would be fine in the smoke as it is a frequent war emblem. I should have told you all these things, but somehow it did not occur to me that they would not be familiar." As usual, Brcin had taken an essentially narrative approach. In his mind the scene captured the moment that "the Indians . . . are pictured at . . . their first sight of the fire. Most of them are in a meditative mood. . . . They do not hold fighting implements because they just got the signal." But, bowing to Alexander's superior knowledge and incorporating detailed information about costume, Brcin swiftly evolved a design depicting a war dance ceremony with three horsemen (the reason for the signal fire and the war preparations) in the distance. The final composition of *Indian Signal Fire* neatly matched that of *Homesteaders* at the other end of the north wall.

Indian Prayer for Life

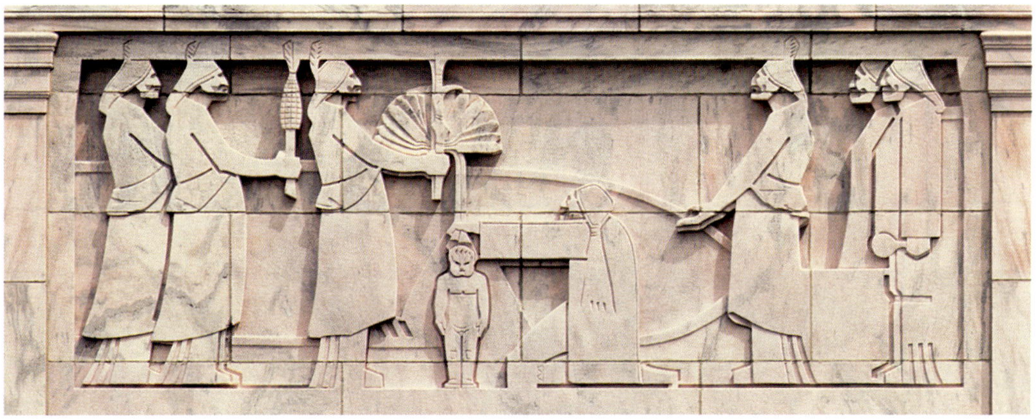

Of all the panels, *Indian Prayer for Life* stems entirely from Alexander's special knowledge of Native American culture, and none of Brcin's initial designs could be used as a starting point. The scene, he insisted, should show the "beautiful Hako Blessing the Child ritual, which was the Indian's prayer for the future of the race." Alexander, convinced that the panel was a necessary complement to the forward-looking spirit of *Civic Builders,* overcame Alan McDonald's reservations about its relevance. Once again, Brcin's initial attempt to interpret Alexander's ideas met with detailed criticism. The long-suffering artist learned that his composition was "decidedly the least 'Indian' of any in this series. This is mainly due to the attitudes of the figures. . . . Except in a Christian church I have never seen Indians kneel in devotion . . . . It would be wrong, too, to put eagle-plume headdresses . . . [it] is a war symbol, and would never be worn . . . near the child who is a symbol of life, not death . . . . I am wondering if you may not care to attempt another composition for the same subject." Brcin patiently incorporated all of Alexander's suggestions into the next design, and the final relief depicts a child at the center of a ceremony. Surrounded by "acolytes" with the "Kurahus in profile, uplifting the winged stems, . . . the old man . . . just lifting the blanket from the boy."

Indian Picture Writing

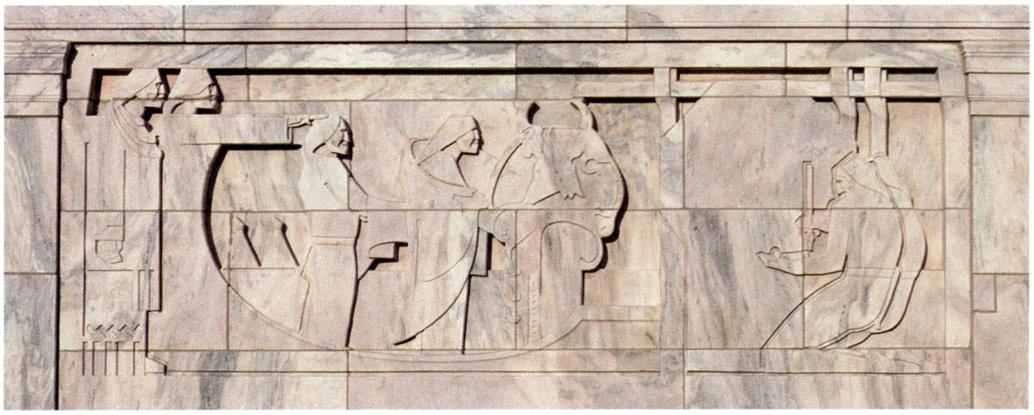

Alexander outlined to Brcin his image of the design as "a painted tipi, with before it a woman working with a beading frame and a man painting a dressed skin [buffalo hide stretched on a frame]. . . . Spectators or children could be added, at option. . . . A second possibility could be a 'record keeper,' with a pile of painted skins before him . . . chanting the tribal history to seated auditors." Brcin took the first option and depicted a group of figures on the left who "may be anything and everything" watching a man kneeling before a stretched skin to write. Alexander was adamant that an unprepared hide be included to associate the act of writing with that of sign language. Reworking a buffalo skin motif from his design for the discarded fur traders panel, Brcin placed it in the center of the composition and pronounced it "as fine as any I have done so far."

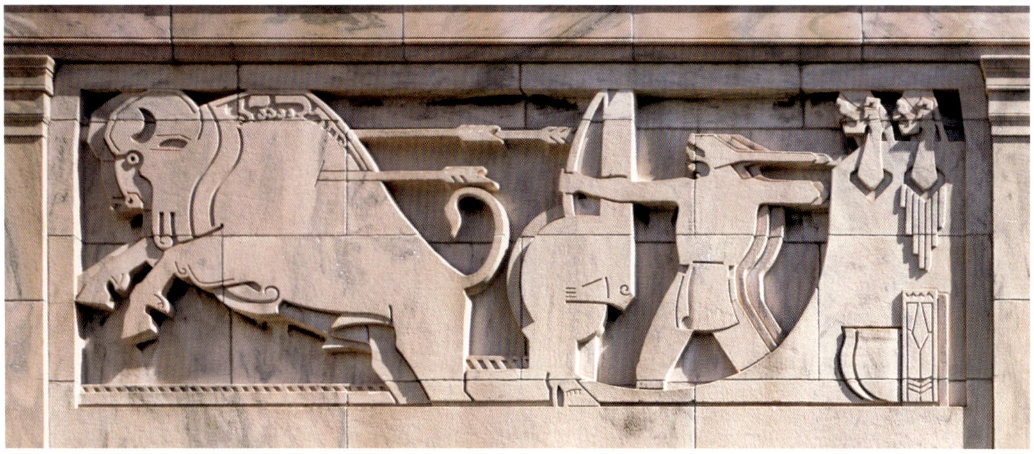

Indian Sign Language

Brcin's original scheme included a panel titled *Buffalo Hunt,* the design of which Alexander applauded as "the high point in the panel design . . . quite corking." So enthusiastic was he that, when the subject was eliminated at his own suggestion, he went along with Brcin's request that he try to rework the design for *Indian Sign Language.* It was a stretch, but Alexander eventually came up with the expedient of having the figures on the right crook their hands at the sides of their heads – the sign for buffalo. Alexander also suggested that the silhouettes of both buffalo and archer be repeated, thereby suggesting a herd of animals and a phalanx of hunters. Finally, cautioning Brcin that the bowls he had included in the original sketch were not characteristic of Plains Indians, he suggested that the artist visit the Field Museum to study so that appropriate vessels be depicted.

THE INSCRIPTIONS AND THE MEDALLIONS

The main, east facade, where Brcin had envisioned an enormous, elaborate relief elucidating humanity's debt to the arts, was, in the end, dedicated to George Joslyn. A simple inscription – *Joslyn Memorial* – runs across the entablature, and in the portico are two of Alexander's inscriptions.

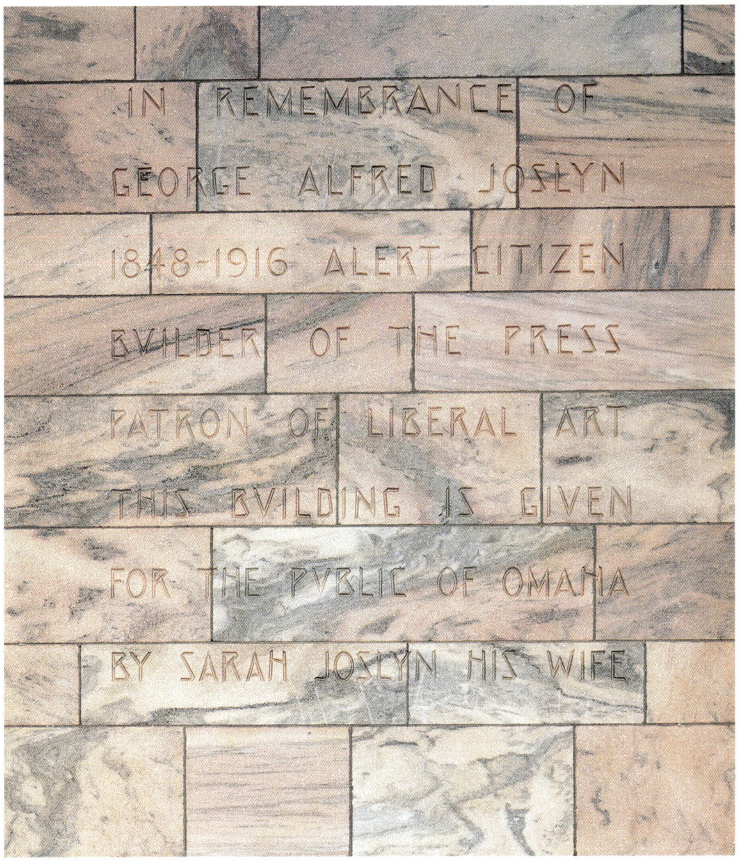

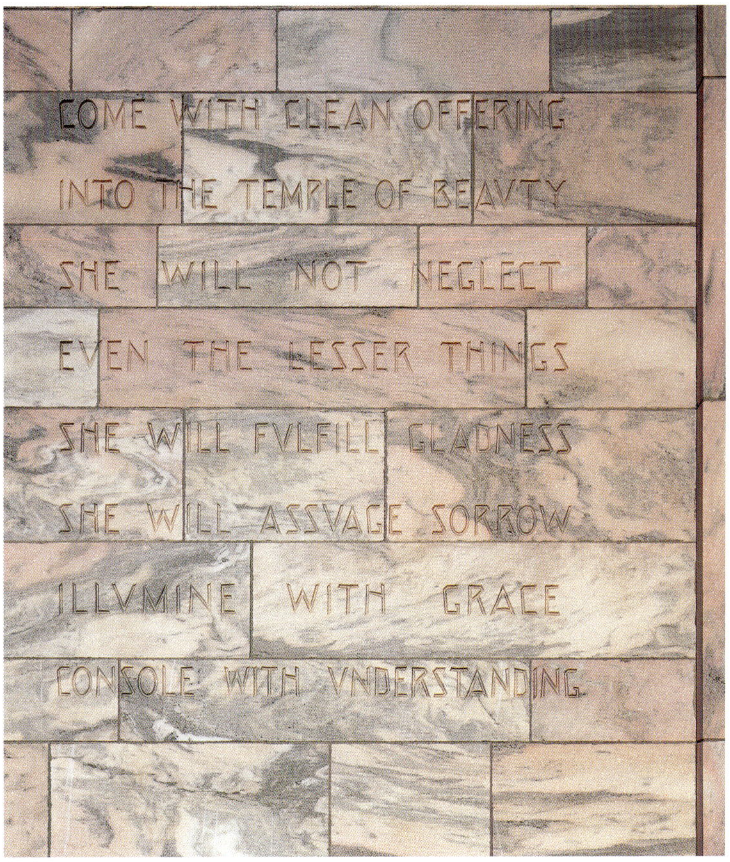

IN REMEMBRANCE OF

GEORGE ALFRED JOSLYN

1848-1916 ALERT CITIZEN

BUILDER OF THE PRESS

PATRON OF LIBERAL ART

THIS BUILDING IS GIVEN

FOR THE PUBLIC OF OMAHA

BY SARAH JOSLYN HIS WIFE

COME WITH CLEAN OFFERING

INTO THE TEMPLE OF BEAUTY

SHE WILL NOT NEGLECT

EVEN THE LESSER THINGS

SHE WILL FULFILL GLADNESS

SHE WILL ASSUAGE SORROW

ILLUMINE WITH GRACE

CONSOLE WITH UNDERSTANDING

Above each of the subsidiary entrances on the south, north, and west facades, the collaborators decided to place a pair of rosettes, or medallions, on each side of an inscription commemorating the contributions of the historical inhabitants of the region: Native American man and woman, Spanish conquistador and priest, prospector and farmer. The medallions appear to have been the first sculptural elements designed by Brcin and, unlike any other aspect of the collaboration, seem to have occasioned little, if any, discussion between artist, architect, and rhetorician.

IN THE MORNING OF TIME THEY CAME

THEIR DRUMS WERE BEATING

THEIR HEARTS WERE HIGH

THE LAND SUMMONED THEM AND THEY LOVED IT

THEY ENTERED THE LAND TO DISCOVER IT

IRON WAS IN THEIR HANDS

THEY ENTERED THE LAND TO

REDEEM IT LOVE WAS IN THEIR HEARTS

THE HOUSE OF HIS PROTECTION THE LAND GAVE

TO HIM THAT SOUGHT HER OUT

AND UNTO HIM THAT DELVED

GAVE RETURN OF HER FRUITS

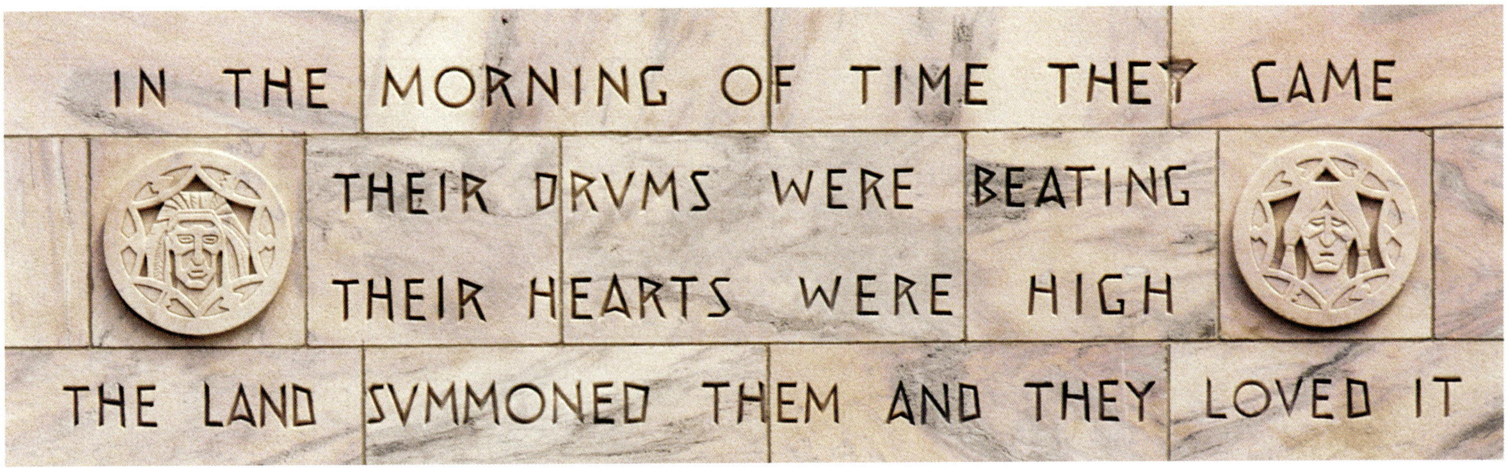
IN THE MORNING OF TIME THEY CAME
THEIR DRVMS WERE BEATING
THEIR HEARTS WERE HIGH
THE LAND SVMMONED THEM AND THEY LOVED IT

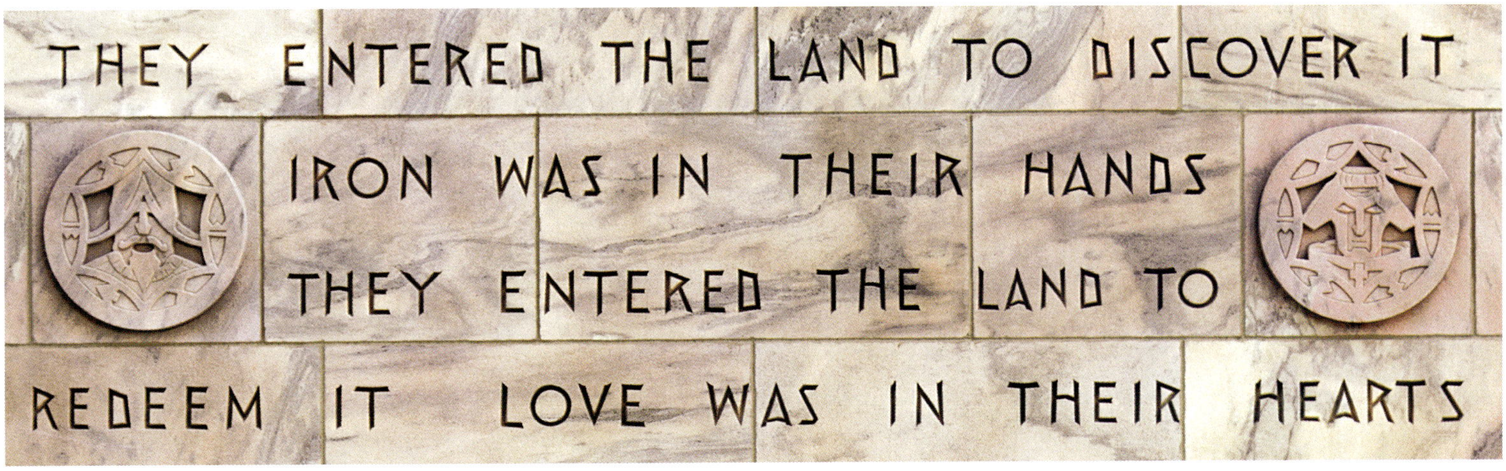
THEY ENTERED THE LAND TO DISCOVER IT
IRON WAS IN THEIR HANDS
THEY ENTERED THE LAND TO
REDEEM IT LOVE WAS IN THEIR HEARTS

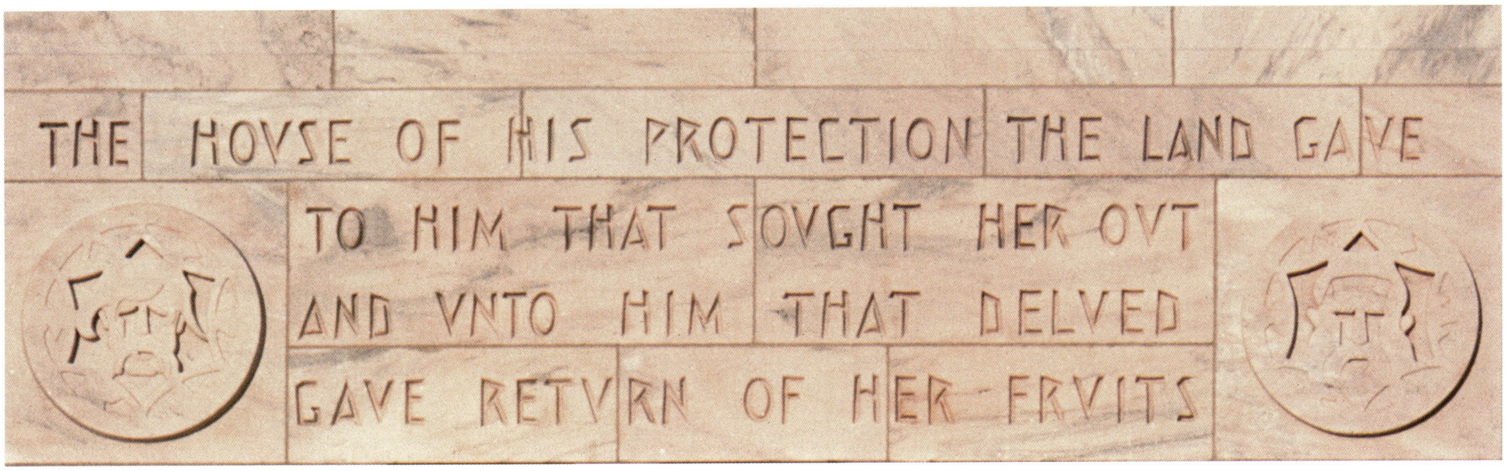
THE HOVSE OF HIS PROTECTION THE LAND GAVE
TO HIM THAT SOVGHT HER OVT
AND VNTO HIM THAT DELVED
GAVE RETVRN OF HER FRVITS

THE EAST DOORS

As part of the scheme worked out by Alexander, Brcin, and McDonald, the six bronze doors guarding the main entrance were to represent six virtues particular to George Joslyn, thereby completing the public values outlined in the nearby relief panels. From the beginning, the stylistic treatment of the doors was a matter of sharp debate.

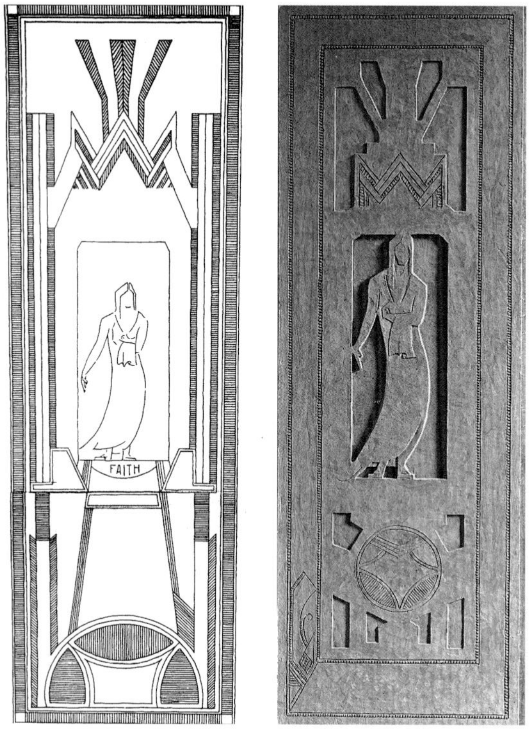

As before, the concern lay in how to express a particular American modernism within an essentially historical and cultural building. Alan McDonald described the interior as an attempt to "combine the spirit of the modern with the culture of the past. Therefore, there must be a transition between Brcin's sculptural modernism and our architectural modernism of the interior." Although siding with McDonald in general terms, Alexander added, "I think you are mistaken in divorcing the doors from the panel treatment too emphatically. The panels create a style and the building is rather more in keeping if this style is maintained with some unity."

Alan McDonald rejected Brcin's first model on the grounds that the figures were too small and much of the detailing was superfluous and – in criticism that must have been especially galling for the ambitious sculptor – unfavorably compared it with a design prepared by Herschel Elarth, their architectural draftsman, which was sent to Brcin as an example of what was required. In particular, McDonald felt that Brcin had lost the "beautiful character of the head as shown on Elarth's drawing, and has replaced it with one of his own characteristic faces, of which," he added gratuitously, "we will have plenty by the time the eight panels are complete."

Brcin's original drawings for the east doors (ABOVE AND BELOW) show relatively small figures intended to be set in deep relief with elaborate geometric designs. Alan McDonald rejected this approach and had his assistant, Herschel Elarth, send the sculptor a drawing of the kind of design he wanted. Because of this collaborative approach, the more delicate linear patterns of the finished doors mediate between the bold forms of Brcin's external wall reliefs and the decorative scheme of the interior.

Following this short and unequal tug-of-war, Brcin once again acquiesced to the architect's vision, and he worked with Elarth to complete the designs. In the final versions, the linear delicacy of the faces and detailing is clearly related to the young architect's design work elsewhere in the Memorial but retains Brcin's strong diagonals as well, limiting the modeling to two planes, a solution in harmony with both the bold "modernism" of the relief panels and the more decorative interiors.

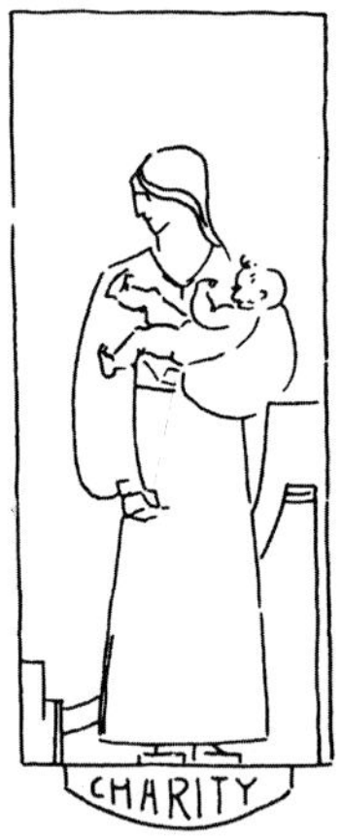

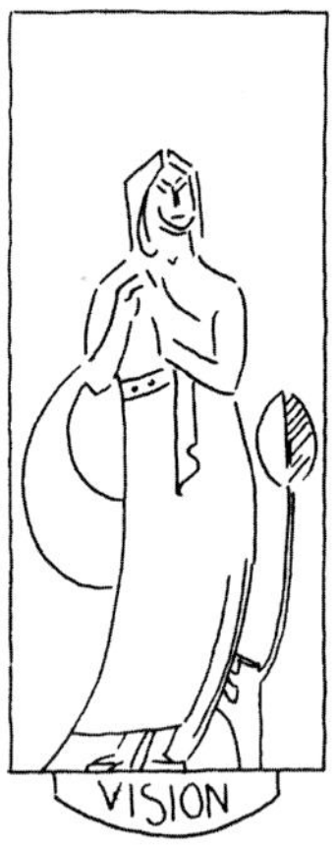

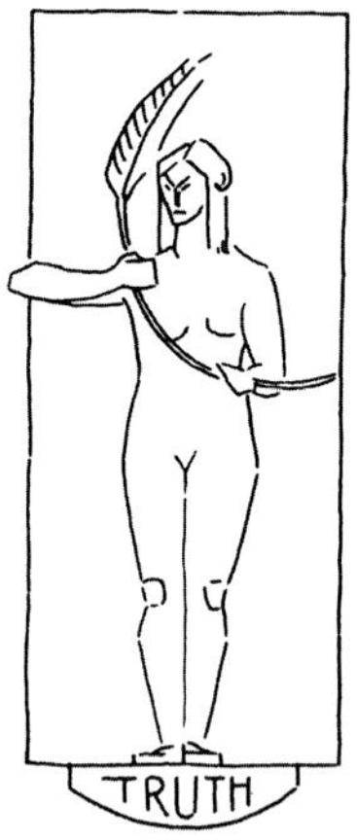

The subject matter of the six panels of the east doors was chosen to express George Joslyn's personal virtues and to pair the three traditional values of Faith, Hope, and Charity with individual qualities that lay behind his worldly success: Courage, Vision, and Industry.

South Pair

LEFT: *Labor (Industry)* holds a scythe, building, machine, and tools; signifies determination and hard work.

RIGHT: *Caritas (Charity/Love)* holds in one hand the sun, in the other hills with ripening grain and trees; signifies the beauty and bounty of the natural order.

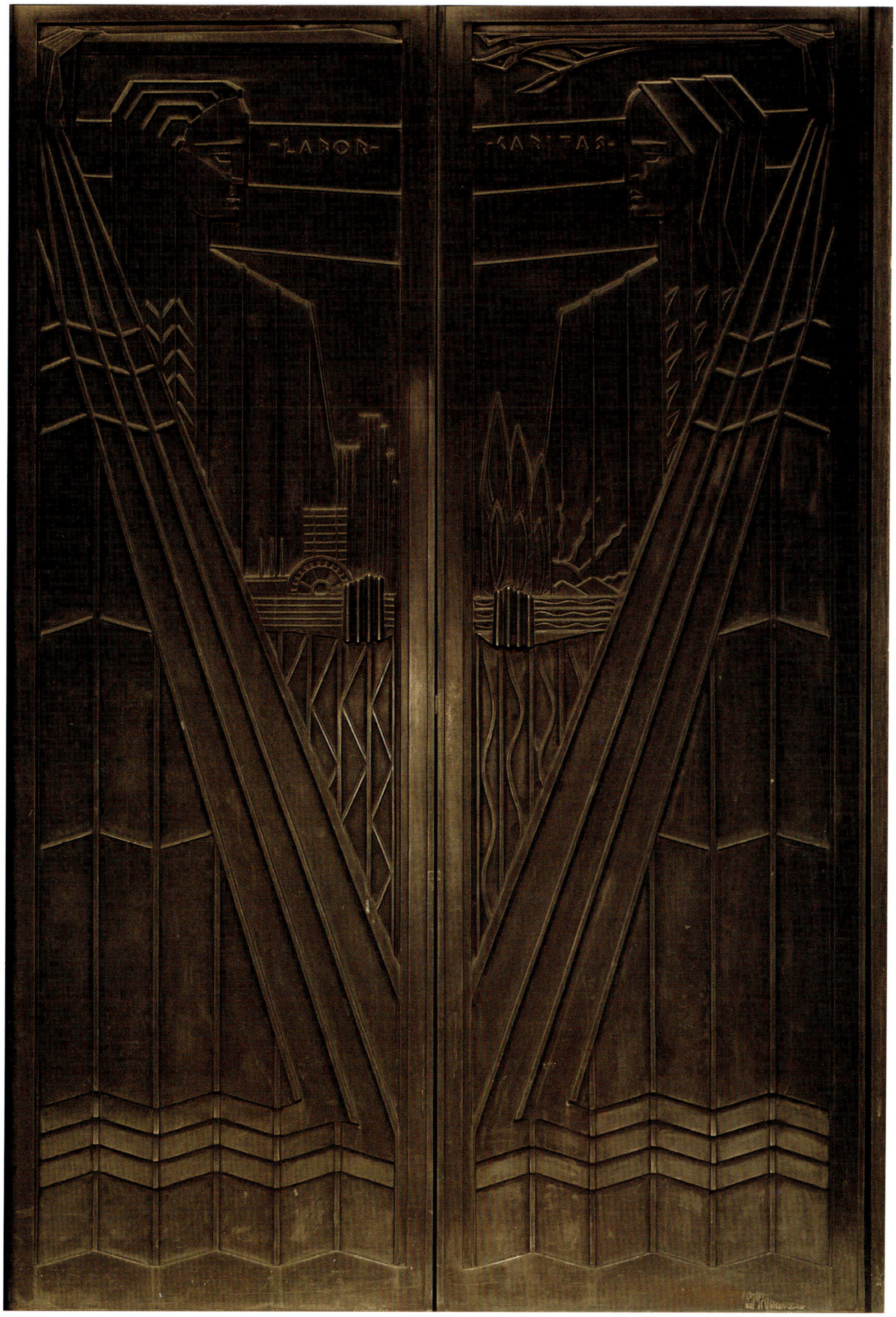

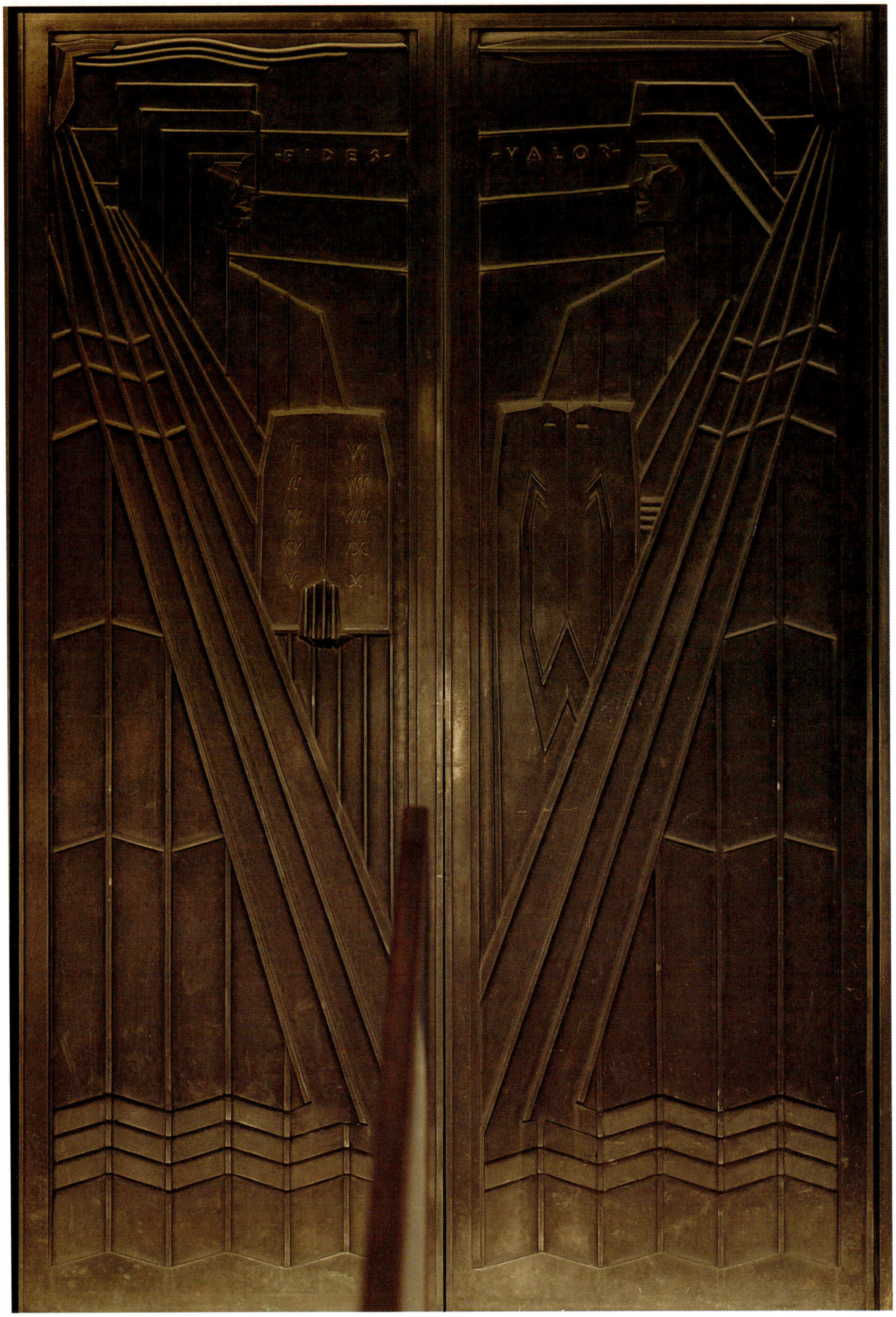

Center Pair

LEFT: *Fides (Faith)* holds the numbers of divine law, representing the Ten Commandments; signifies obedience to God.

RIGHT: *Valor (Courage)* holds a shield and lifts a sword aloft; signifies fortitude.

North Pair

LEFT: *Visio (Vision/Foresight)* holds a lamp; signifies clear vision into the future.

RIGHT: *Spes (Hope)* holds in one hand a crystal ball, in the other a flaming torch; both signifying faith in the future. The fountain alongside the figure signifies hope for future life.

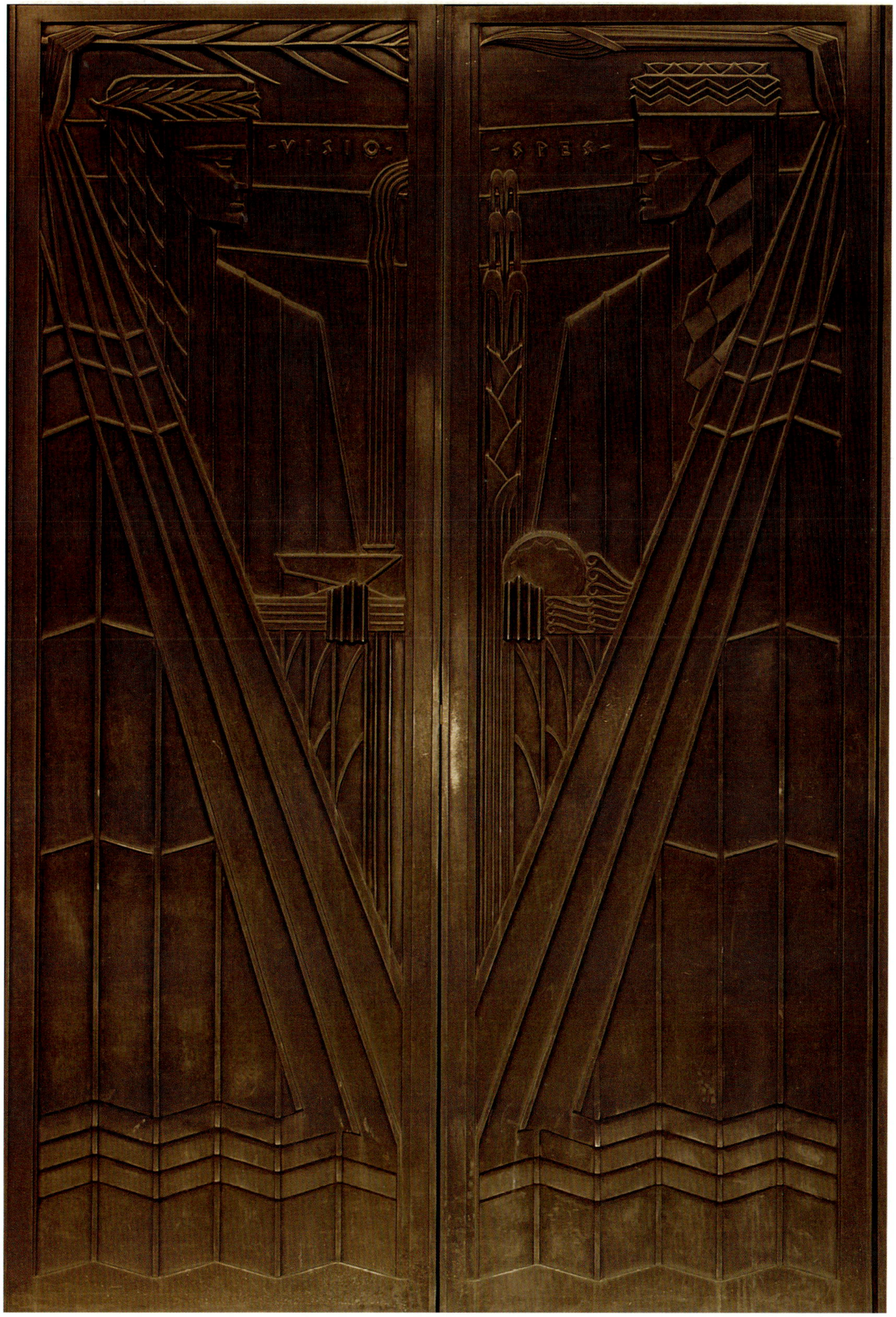

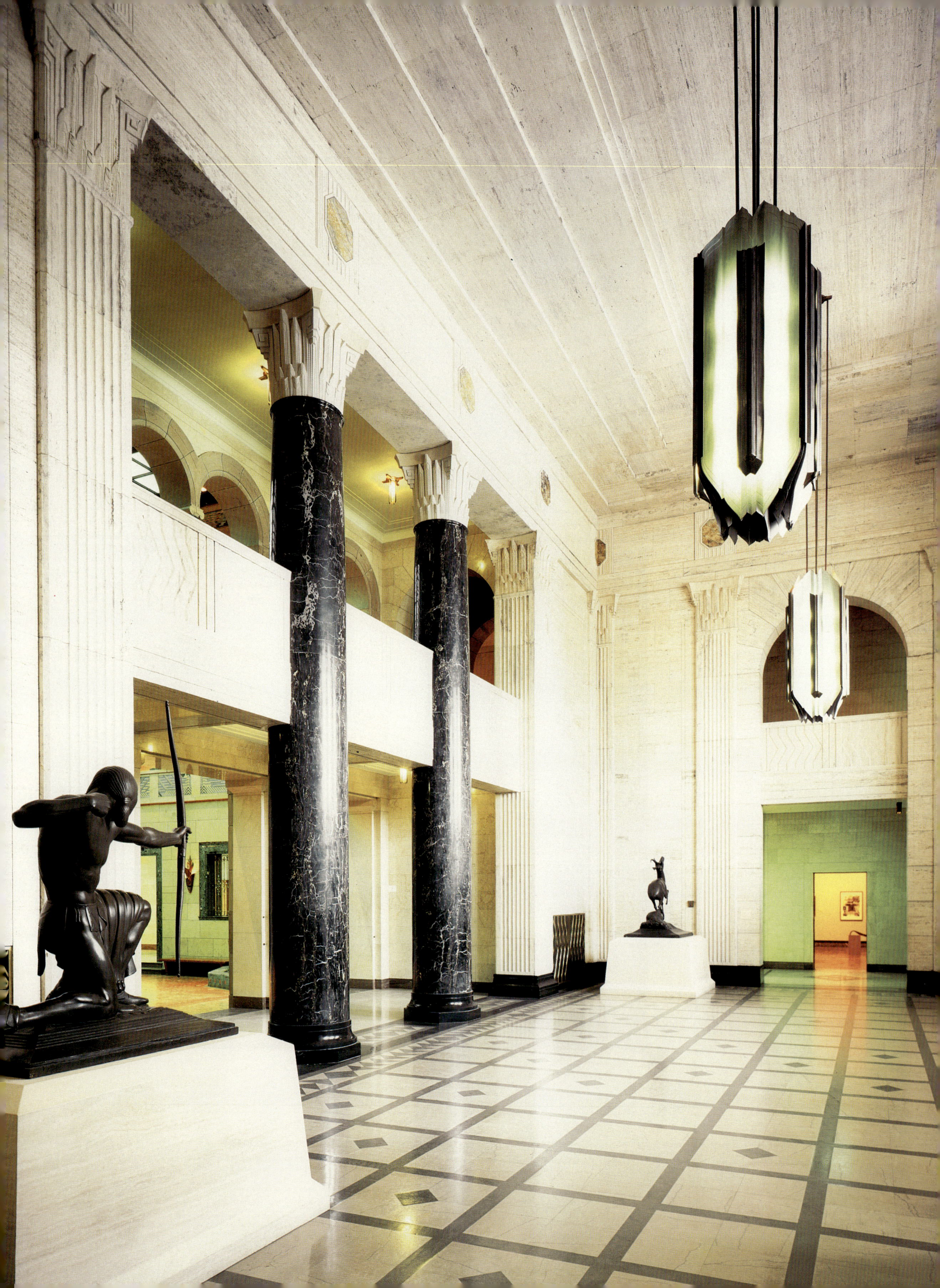

THE INTERIOR

The architects' original notion of the visitor moving from a boldly modernistic exterior to a "quiet" interior is hardly sustained in the finished product. The overall effect is one of considerable opulence. Ceiling heights and room proportions change dramatically from space to space, as do the colors and textures of the wall, ceiling, and floor surfaces. There is some evidence – and this may be one factor behind her oft-cited complaints that she could not afford new clothes because of the cost of the Memorial – that the architects repeatedly coaxed Mrs. Joslyn into upgrading the quality of the surfaces. Initially, they were delighted that the streamlining of the exterior resulted in $50,000 savings; the money saved was soon consumed by the interior. Originally, all floor surfaces outside the main lobby and floral court areas were specified as rubber tile, and, although this humble material was present in the finished building (concert hall and the four large galleries), it was almost completely replaced by marble, tile, and terrazzo throughout public and private areas on both levels.

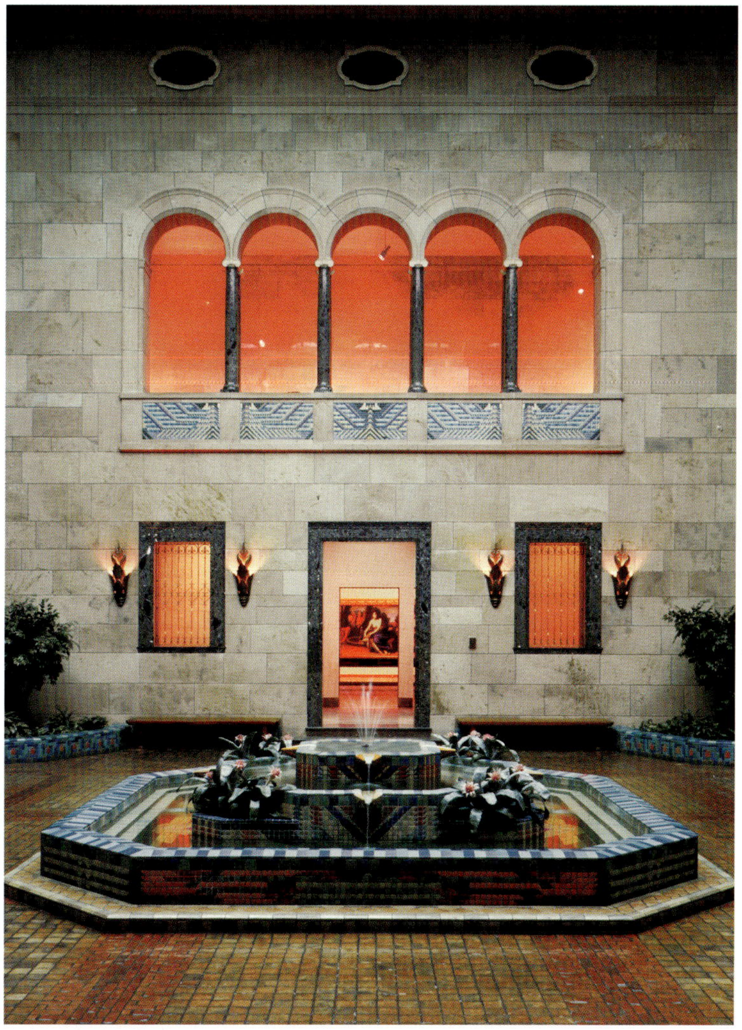

LOBBY

Walls, ceiling, and pilasters of the lobby (OPPOSITE) are Roman Travertine; the column capitals, panels, and column bases are of French and Belgian marble; the floor is of Badger Pink Tennessee marble and Vermont Green slate. The distinctive columns of black-and-gold marble are from the Italian island of Palmaria. (The same material is used in the reception room fireplace in the Joslyns' home, Lynhurst.) The walls of the antechamber leading to the floral court are clad in Botticino marble from Italy, the bases are Dark Cedar and the floors Badger Pink marbles, both from Tennessee.

FLORAL COURT

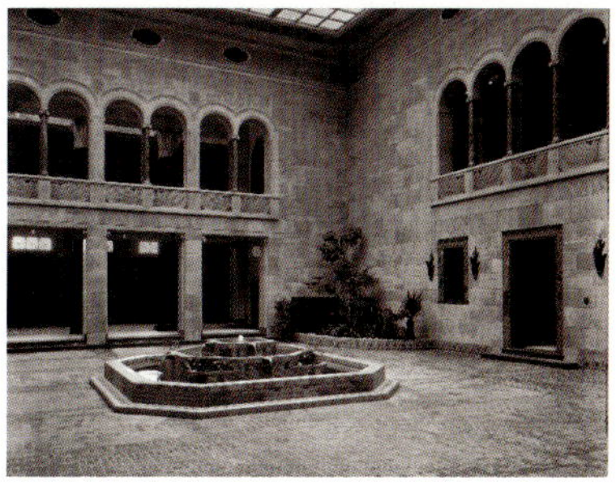

floral court, 1931

This bright, top-lit fountain court was intended as a contemplative space and clearly derives its inspiration from floral courts the architects would have seen on their research trip "back east," such as those at the Isabella Stewart Gardner Museum in Boston and the Frick Collection in New York. Walls are Aquia, or George Washington, stone from Virginia; columns and door trim, Vert Antico marble from Greece; column capitals are Hauteville marble from France; steps are Dark Cedar marble; the floor is Moravian tile from Pennsylvania; the decorative panels on the fountain and walls are of faience tile made in Ohio. Originally illuminated during the day by natural light, the skylight was covered over in 1980 and artificial lighting installed.

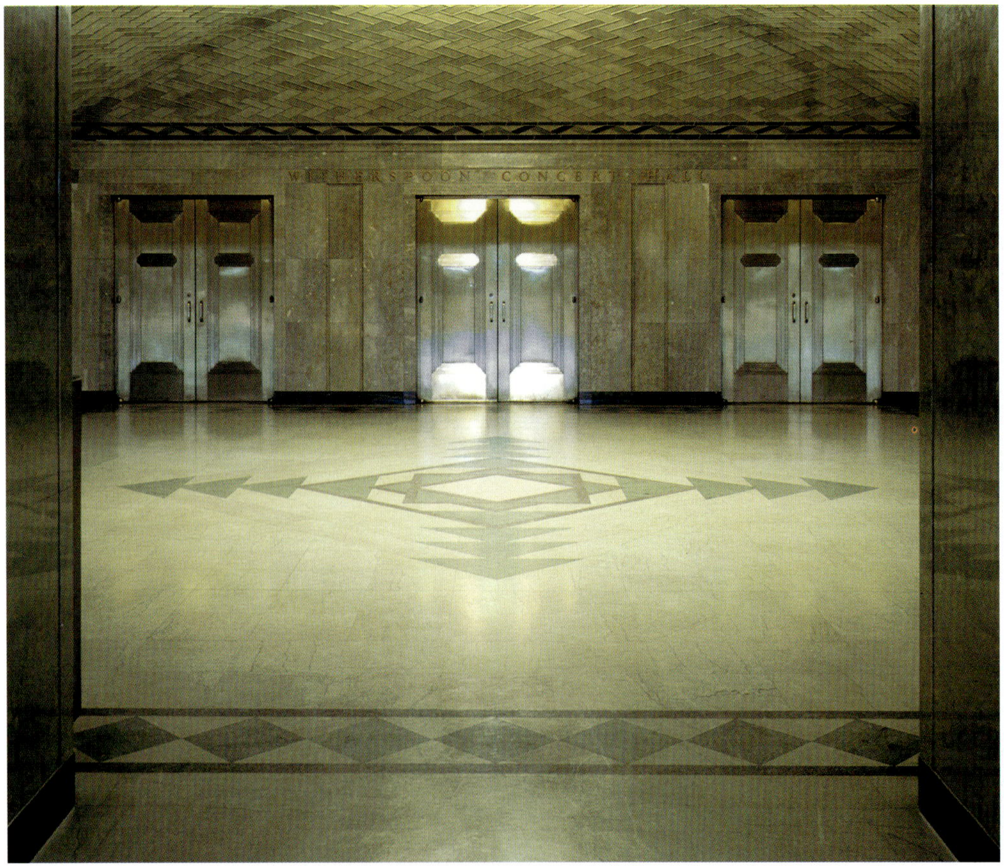

FOYER

Beyond the floral court is the foyer to the concert hall. Here wall panels are St. Genevieve Rose marble with St. Genevieve Golden Vein, both from Missouri; the floor is Badger Pink marble and Vermont Green slate. The ceiling is, in the words of the 1936 guide, "low, arched, self-supporting" and "fashioned of Guastavino Akoustolith, a very expensive, sound absorbing tile made by a secret process."

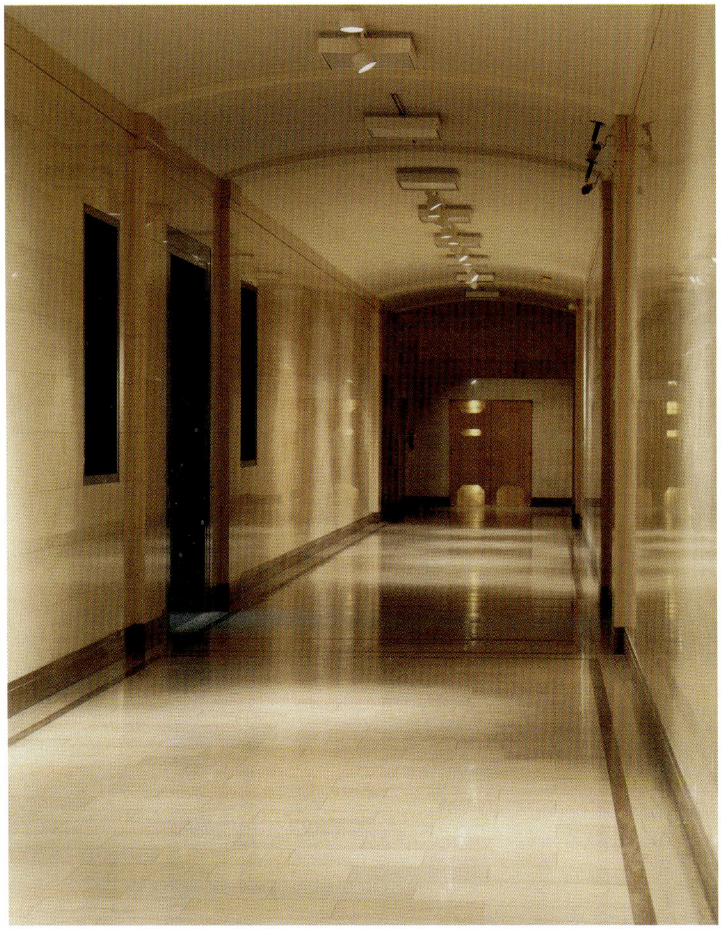

SIDE CORRIDORS

Separating the floral court from the art galleries are two corridors. Echoing the treatment of the transitional space between the lobby and the court, the walls are Botticino marble from Italy and the floors Badger Pink Tennessee marble.

CONCERT HALL

Situated at the very heart of the Memorial, the concert hall embodied George Joslyn's love of music. Seating 1,178, it originally housed the organ he had bought as a gift for his wife and installed in their music room at Lynhurst. The inaugural event at the Joslyn Memorial, when it opened on Thanksgiving weekend in 1931, was a concert by the nationally acclaimed organist Christian Palmer. The ten doors piercing the north and south walls below the balconies were intended to be opened to permit music to waft into the galleries (RIGHT). The concept that gallery visitors would be treated to the sound of organ music did not long survive Mrs. Joslyn's death. Citing cost of maintenance, the organ was dismantled in the late 1940s; one of Eugene Kingman's first acts when he became director

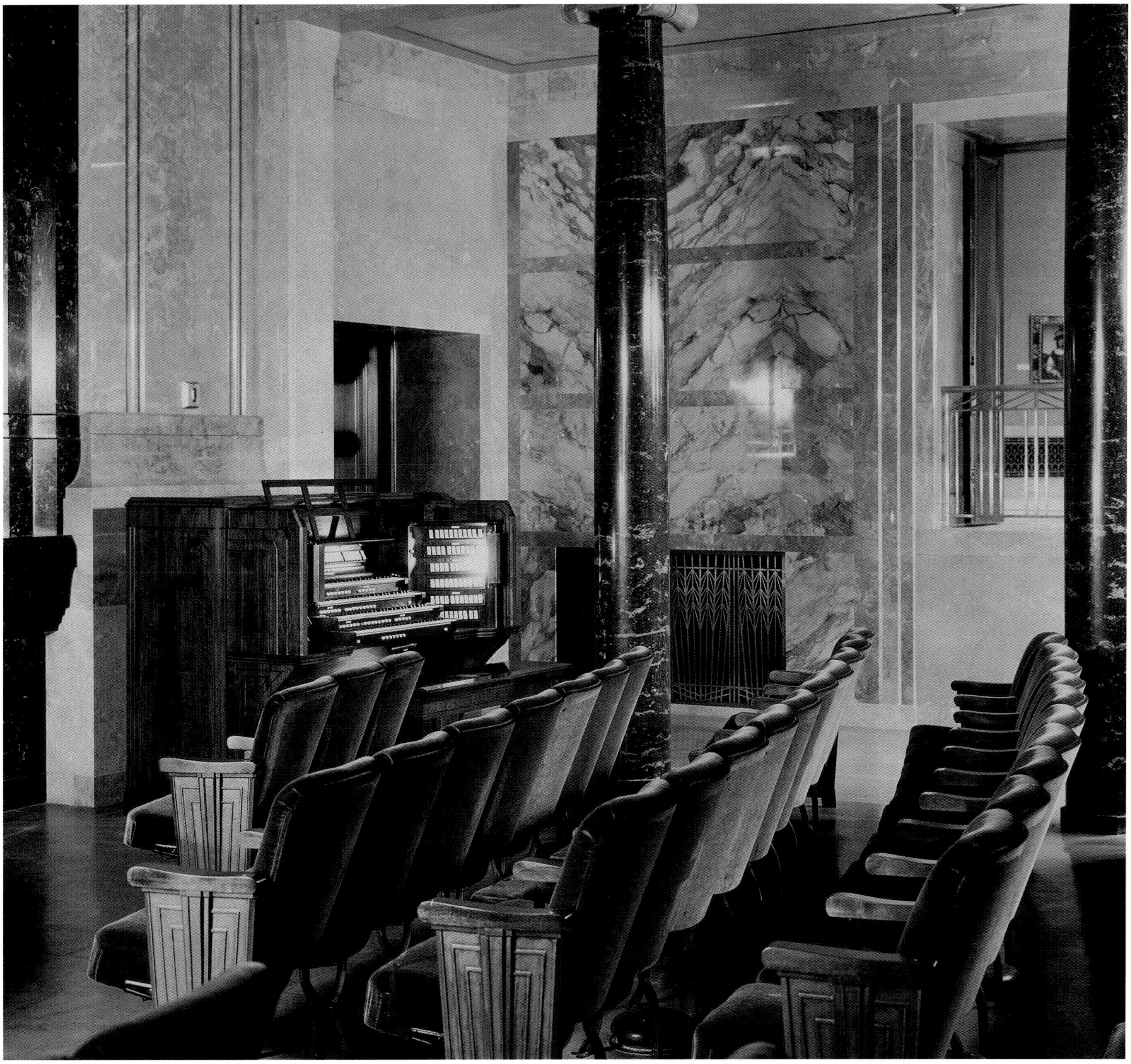

in 1947 was to have the doorways closed and walled over on the gallery sides to provide continuous hanging space for art.

The concert hall wall panels and trim continue the use of the St. Genevieve marbles encountered in the foyer; column shafts and the proscenium arch are Westfield Green marble from Massachusetts, and the column bases Belgian Black marble. The column capitals are paired, stage to entry doors, in marbles from France, Morocco, Italy, Germany, and Spain. Upper walls and the ceiling were covered with the same Akoustolith tile as the foyer ceiling.

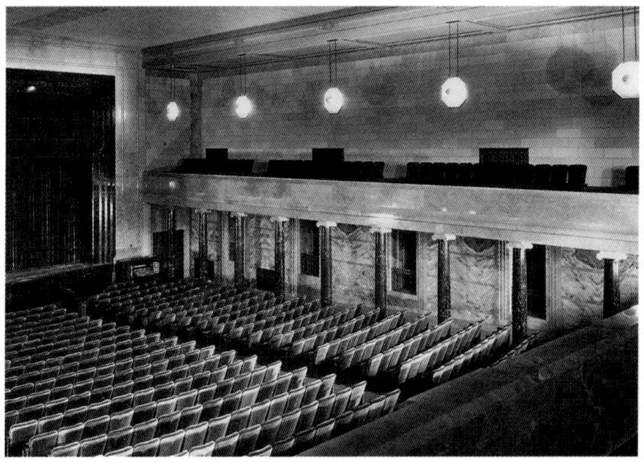

TOP AND ABOVE: concert hall, 1931

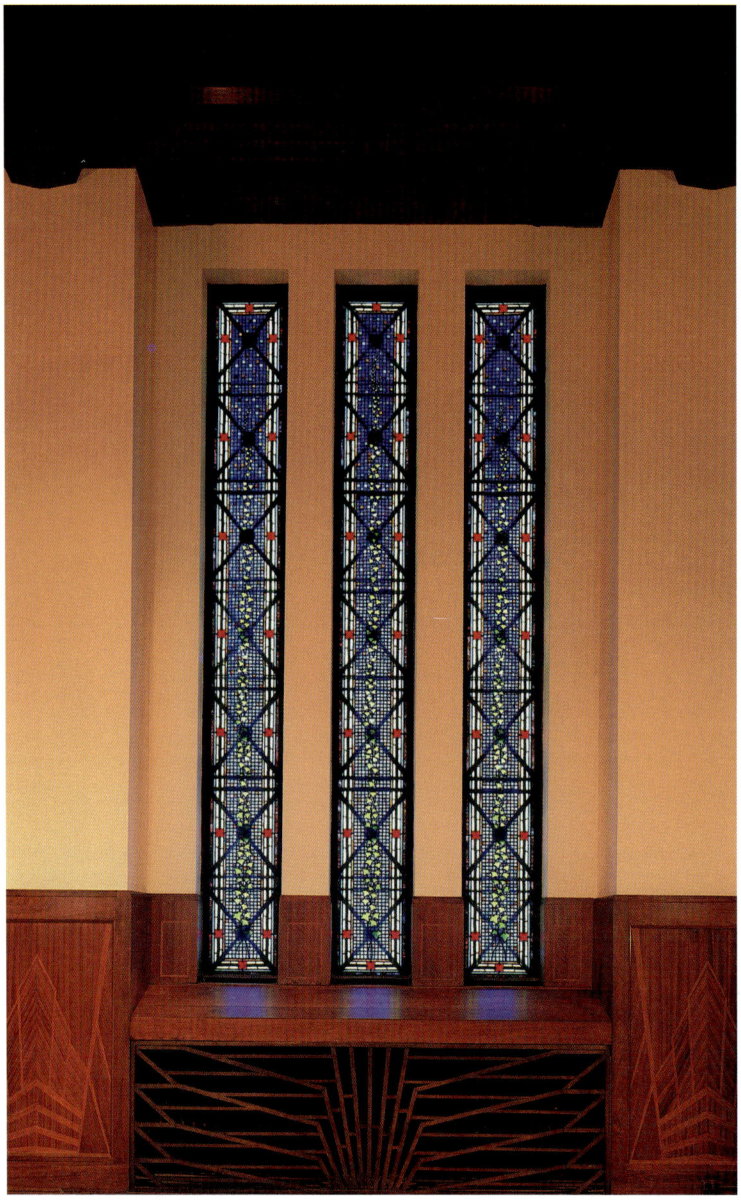

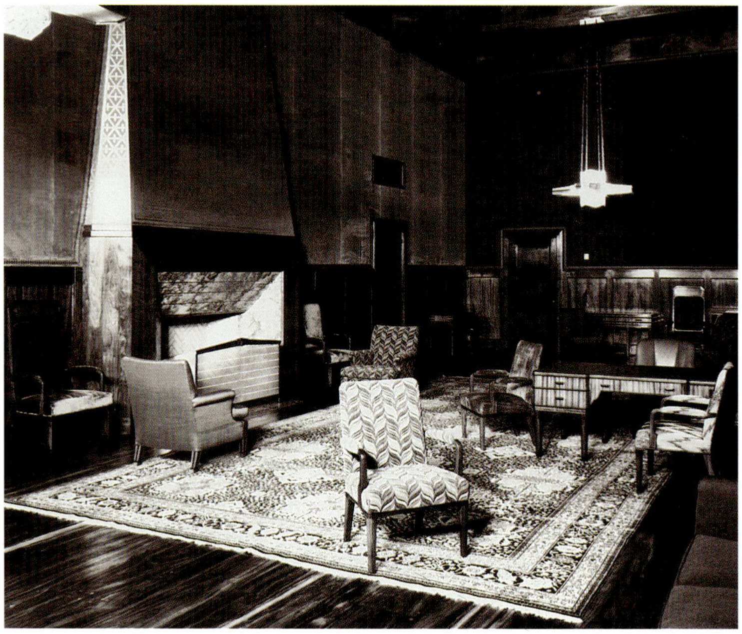

lounge, 1931

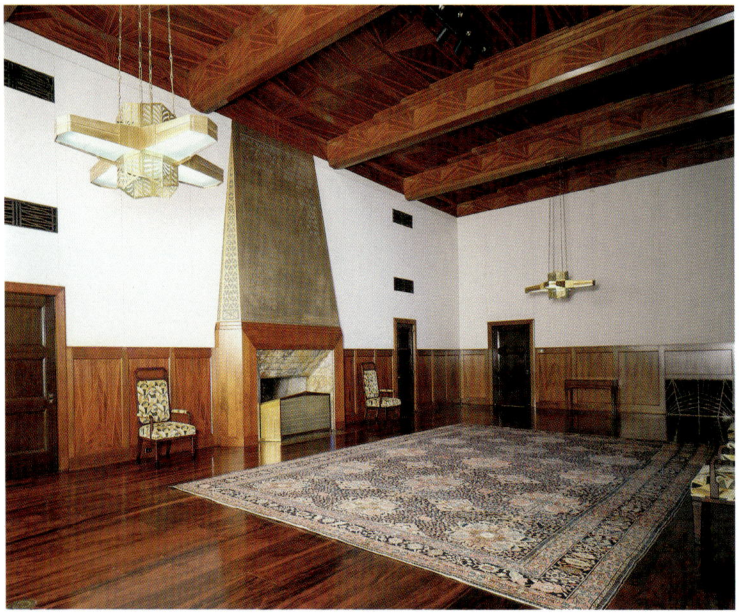

LOUNGE/RECEPTION ROOM

Designed to be a "luxurious setting for the reception of distinguished musicians, lecturers and dramatic artists" (the 1936 guide again), this westernmost room has served a number of functions over the years, most notably, until her death in 1940, as Mrs. Joslyn's place of retreat. Walnut inlaid with peroba wood was used to create the thunderbird design in the ceiling and the flame of life in the wainscoting; the floor is teak. Originally, the walls were covered with silk velvet. That this room was intended to be more intimate is indicated by two personal references. The fireplace is made of the same Benou Jaune marble as that in the Joslyns' home; the clinging ivy motif of the stained glass windows refers to everlasting devotion. The overall effect is highly imposing; too much so, perhaps. According to her granddaughters, Mrs. Joslyn once made a comment to the effect that the architects got the room wrong: "They made it too big," a comment that also reinforces the notion she did not take a very active role in the evolution of the plans, regular visits to the architects' offices notwithstanding.

THE GALLERIES

Running *en suite* along the north and south of the building, the galleries, like the floral court, incorporated natural light through the ceiling. An early handbook describes them as having "a jute cloth wall covering in soft tones . . . wainscoting of various marbles, and floors of tile, rubber tile and slate." The galleries were converted to artificial lighting and the wainscoting and walls recovered with linen in 1971.

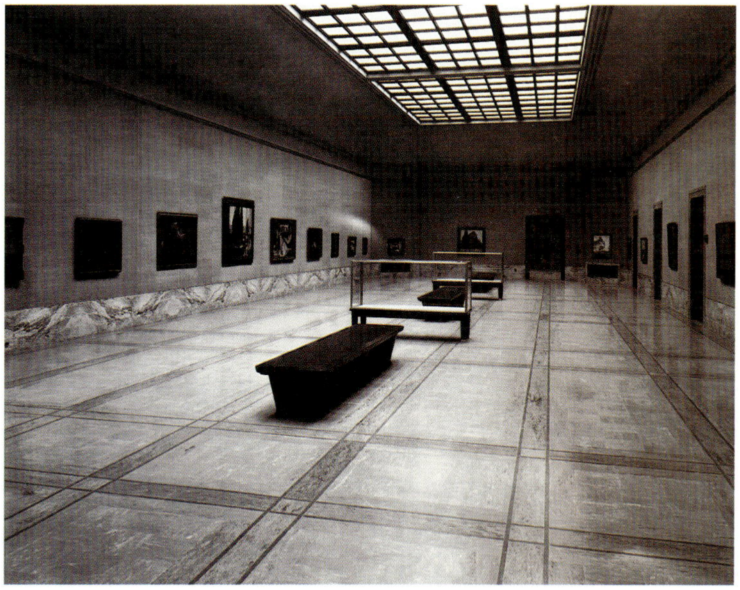

galleries, 1931

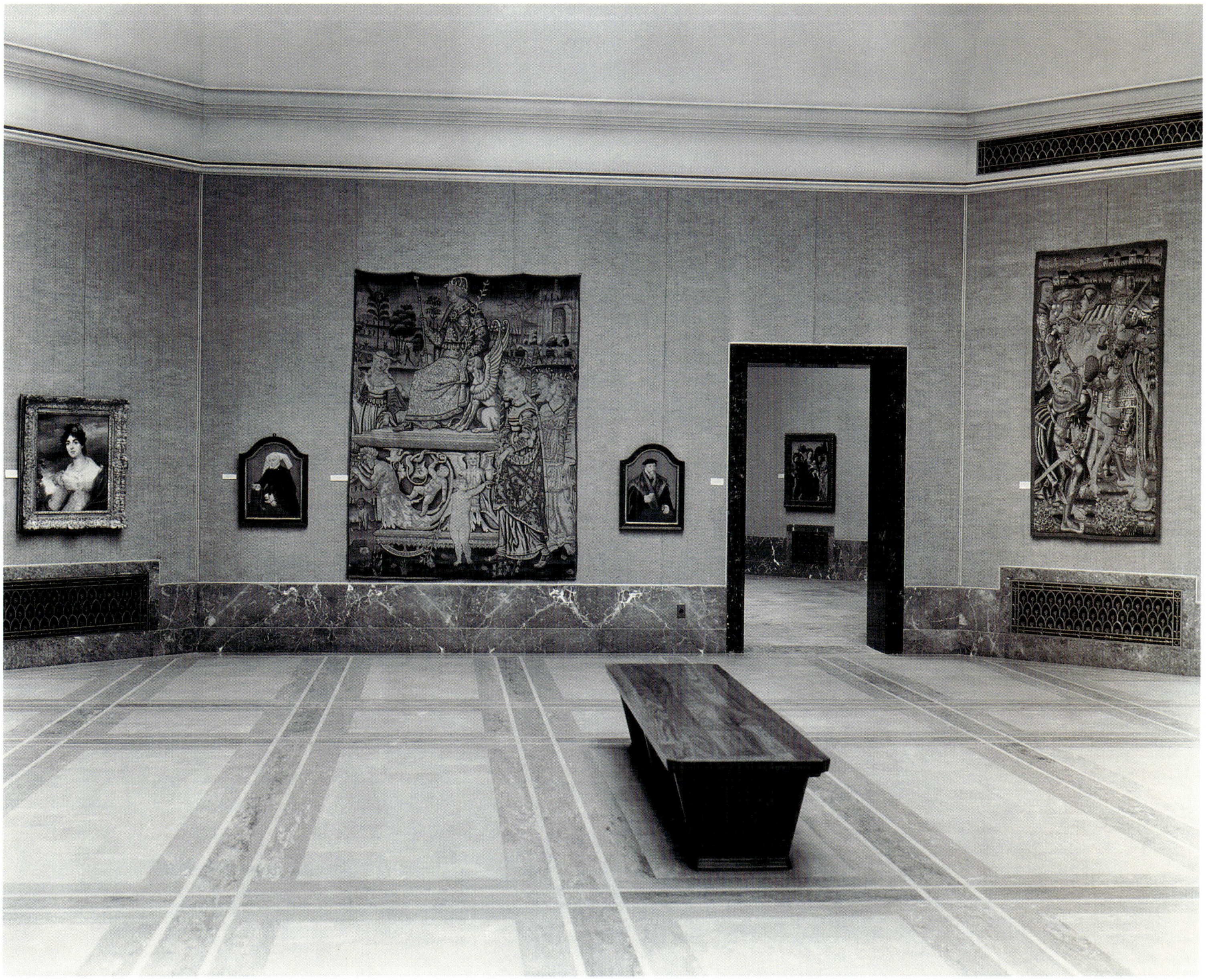

THE METALWORK

Doors and Grills

Perhaps nowhere is the overlapping nature of the Joslyn Memorial building's stylistic evolution as apparent as in the metalwork. It would seem (the records are incomplete) that Hershel Elarth carried out work for the thunderbird grillwork. The doors along each side of the concert hall are in the redesigned geometric style, as are the railings in front of them, and relate to the thunderbird grillwork throughout the main level. The three secondary Museum entrance doors and the entry doors to the concert hall, as well as

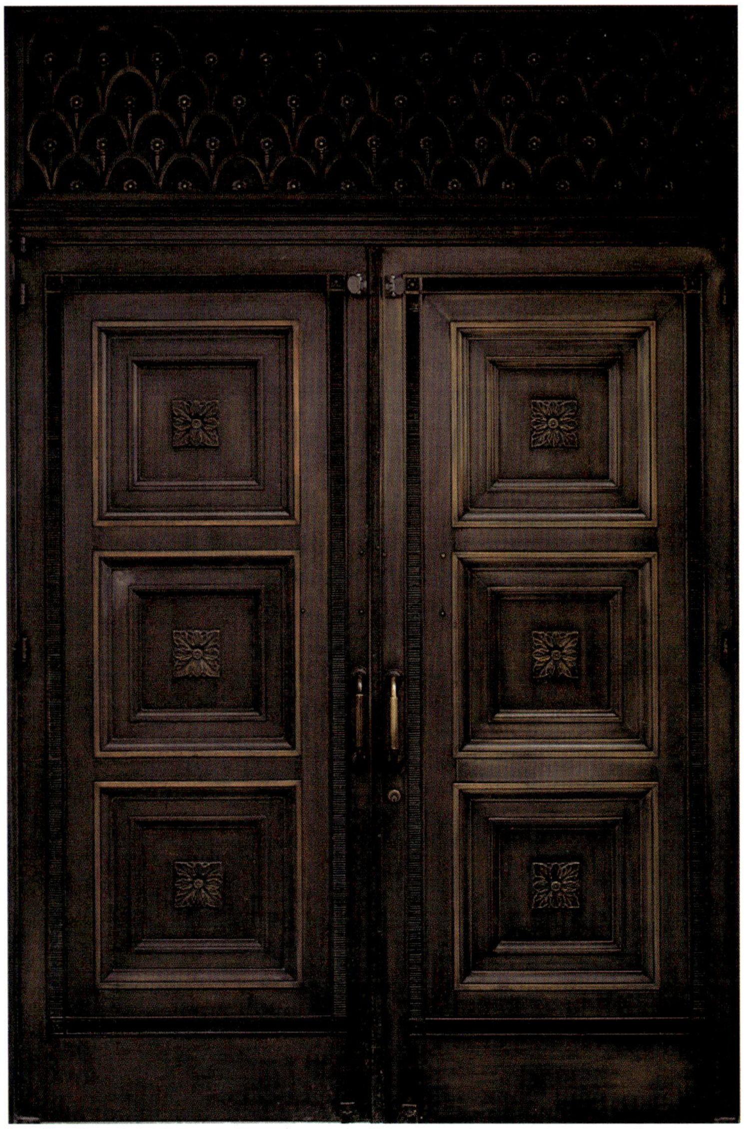

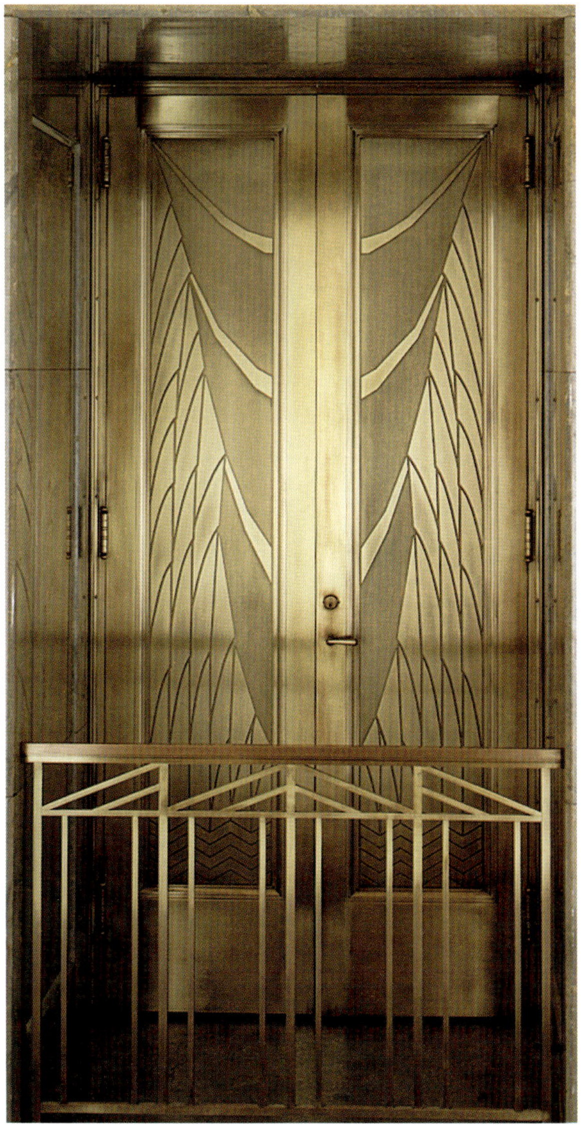

Much, if not all, of the metalwork had already been ordered in the original classical language when the McDonalds decided on their Moderne redesign. They were apparently able to modify the order and to persuade Mrs. Joslyn to pay for new metalwork, but much of the Beaux-Arts design remains scattered throughout the building. The dense and delicate classical detailing of the original design is most apparent in the north (ABOVE LEFT), west, and south entrances, as well as in the doors leading from the concert hall foyer to the hall itself. Elarth's doors for the apertures between the concert hall and the galleries (ABOVE RIGHT) use graceful, curving forms that act as a foil to the strong verticals and diagonals of the railings.

the grills in the floral court, the grills on the lower level, and those on the outside of the windows, all are in the original Beaux-Arts style. Although this gives a fairly clear indication of the relationship between construction and redesign, it seems there was some degree of reworking even after certain components had been cast. In a letter of October 29, 1929, John McDonald wrote to Elarth:

> *Your sketches in connection with front entrance bronze doors and grilles arrived and are very interesting. We . . . have forwarded same to General Bronze Corporation in order to see if we can possibly afford these doors.*
>
> *Word comes of General Bronze that the ten railings in the auditorium are cast and nearing completion. This eliminates the possibility of changing the design of these at present. Yours cordially.*

Apparently they were able to talk Mrs. Joslyn into paying for redesigned railings.

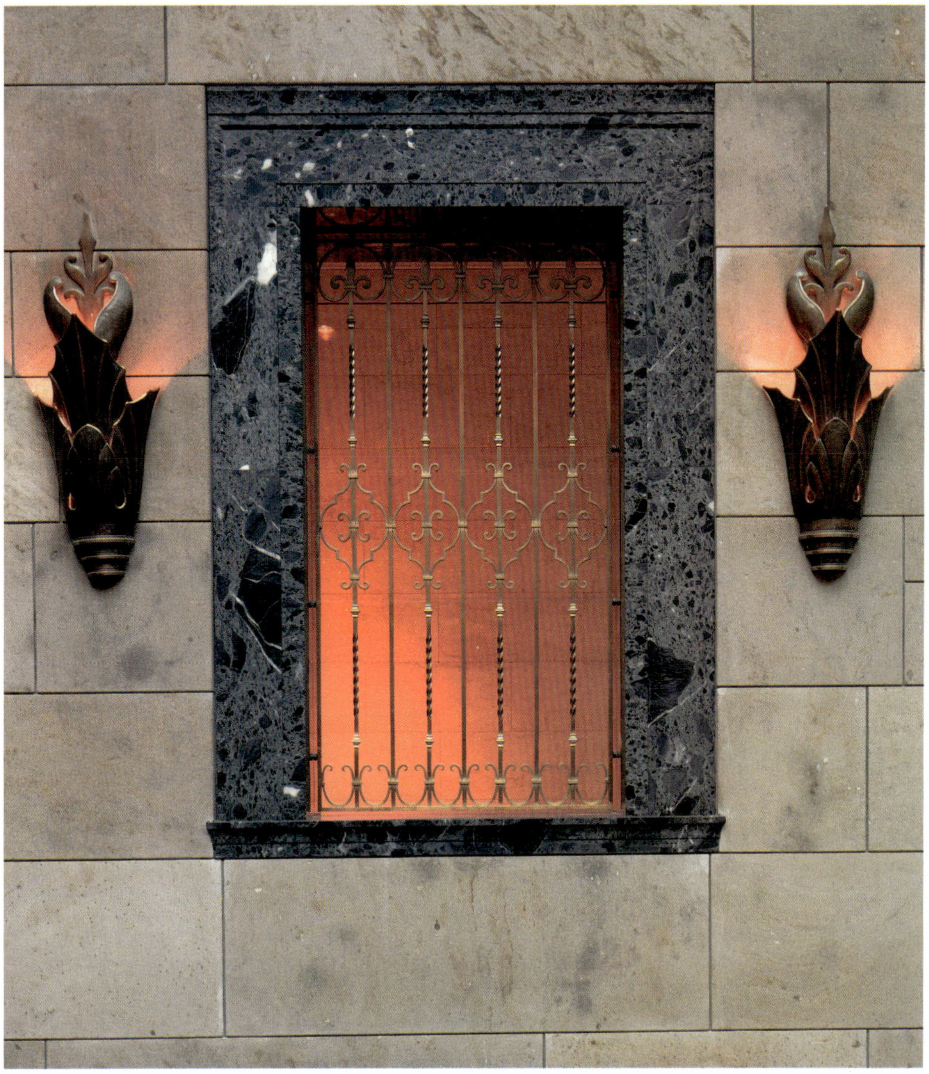

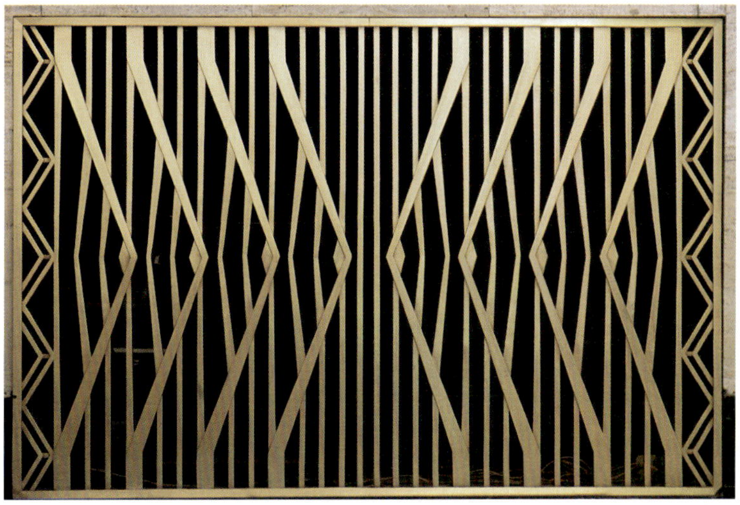

The lobby grill (RIGHT) dramatically introduces the thunderbird motif to the visitor and, with its bold verticals and diagonals, offers a considerable contrast to the classicizing window grills in the floral court (ABOVE). These forms from the original designs blend well with the florid tile patterns and flamelike sconces in the Moderne refit.

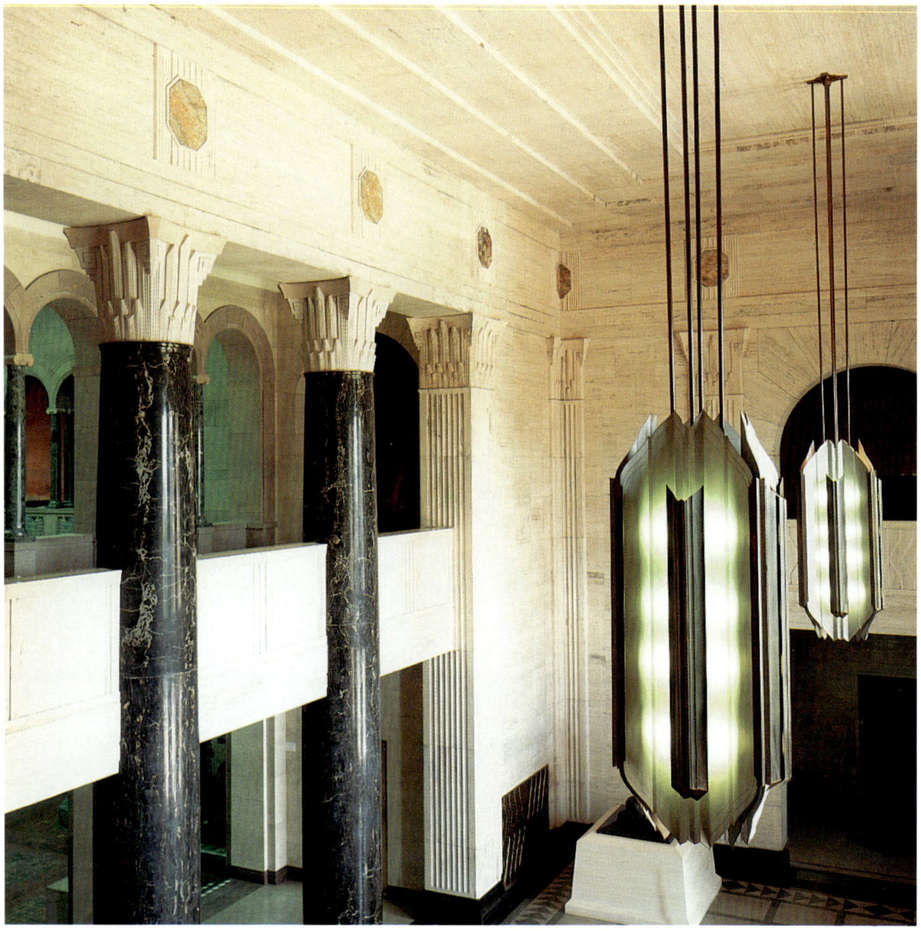

LIGHTING FIXTURES

In the words of the original guidebook, "The lighting fixtures carry out the simple lines and details of the architecture and in every instance use electricity in a fluid and modern manner." In correspondence over fifty years later, Elarth wrote that the "wall sconces and ceiling hung lighting fixtures elsewhere in the interior" were designed by specialists in New York. Walter Kantack, who executed the commission, was a leading lighting designer of the period. *Kaleidoscope,* the quarterly house journal of Kantack and Company Inc. of New York City, featured Joslyn's lights on its cover as illustrations to an article on metal alloys in a 1932 issue.

Lobby

Made of aluminum and bronze, to harmonize with the main doors, the lobby chandeliers (ABOVE) use concealed fluorescent tubes to reflect light from the strongly vertical facets. These fittings are closely related to those in the lobby of Ralph Walker's Barclay-Vesey Building (1922-26) in New York, an early classic of American Moderne architecture.

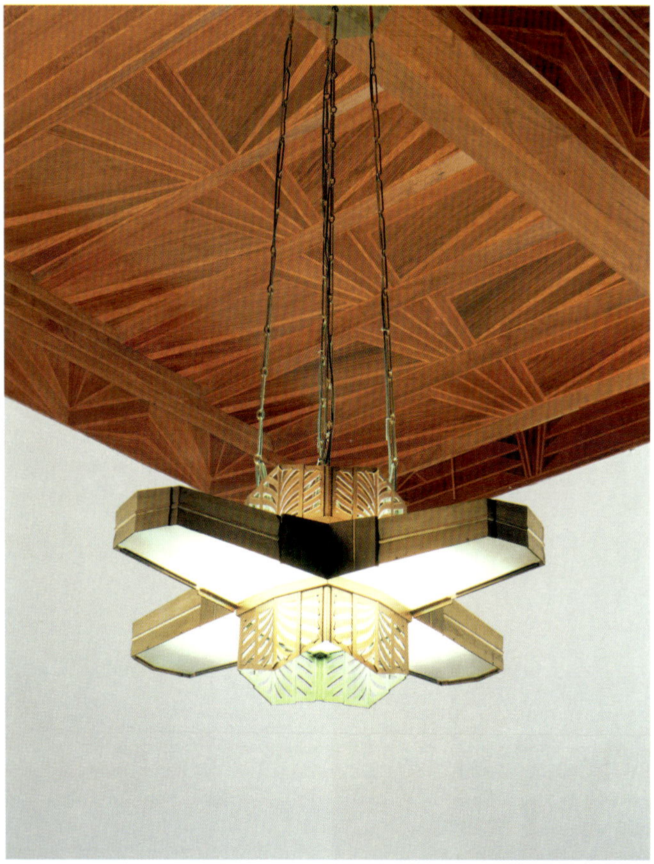

Lounge/Reception Room

The two large bronze lighting fixtures that dominate this room (LEFT) contain elements of Art Nouveau design, a feature not uncommon in American Art Deco interior decoration of the 1920s.

Foyer

Set directly onto the curved Akoustolith ceiling, the foyer light (RIGHT) combines a geometric glass fitting with unconcealed fluorescent tubing.

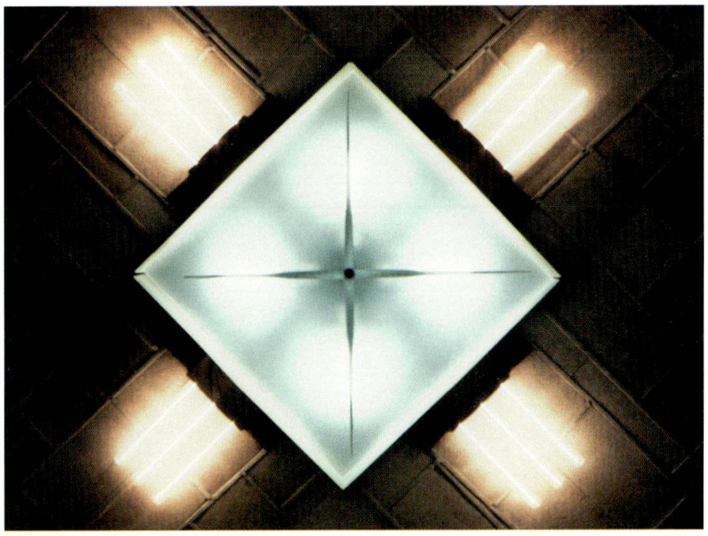

Floral Court

In keeping with the floral nature of this grand space, these subsidiary lighting fixtures (BELOW RIGHT) combine leaf and flame forms with the thunderbird wing motif.

Concert Hall

The most striking feature of the lights in the concert hall (BELOW) is the large octagonal aluminum reflectors that create a subdued, indirect glow. With their unadorned metal surfaces and hublike centers, these fittings are the boldest and most "machine age" of the building's Moderne decorations.

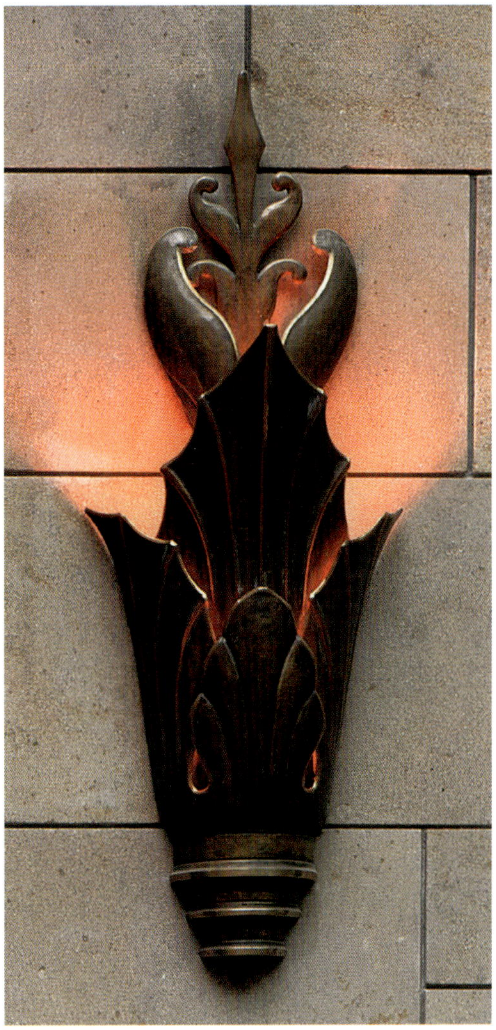

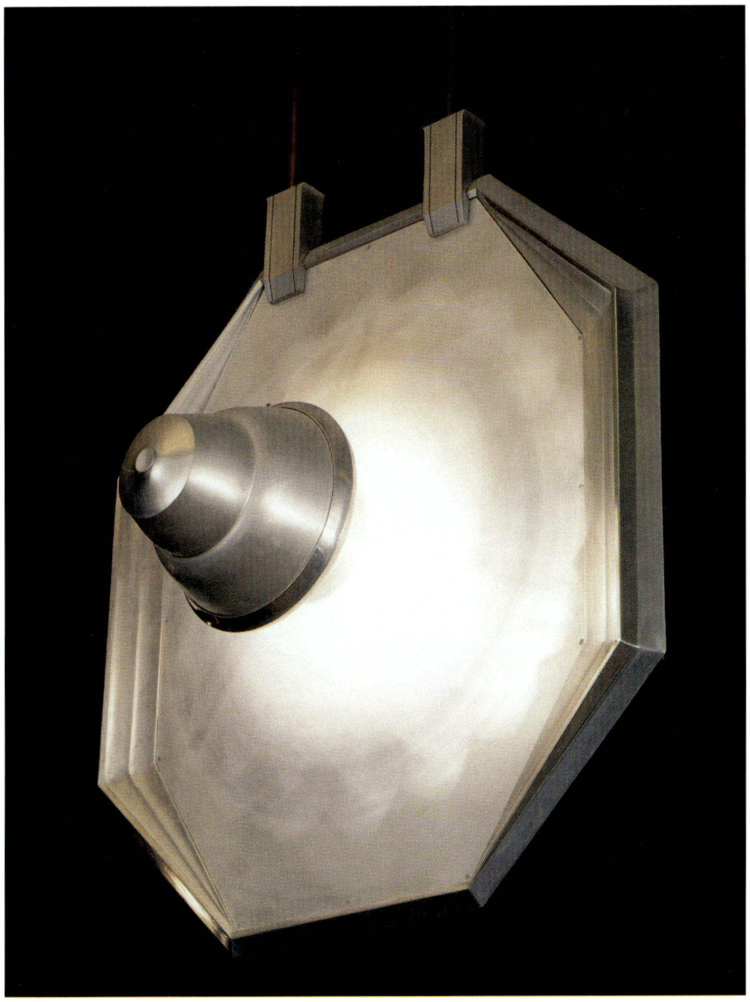

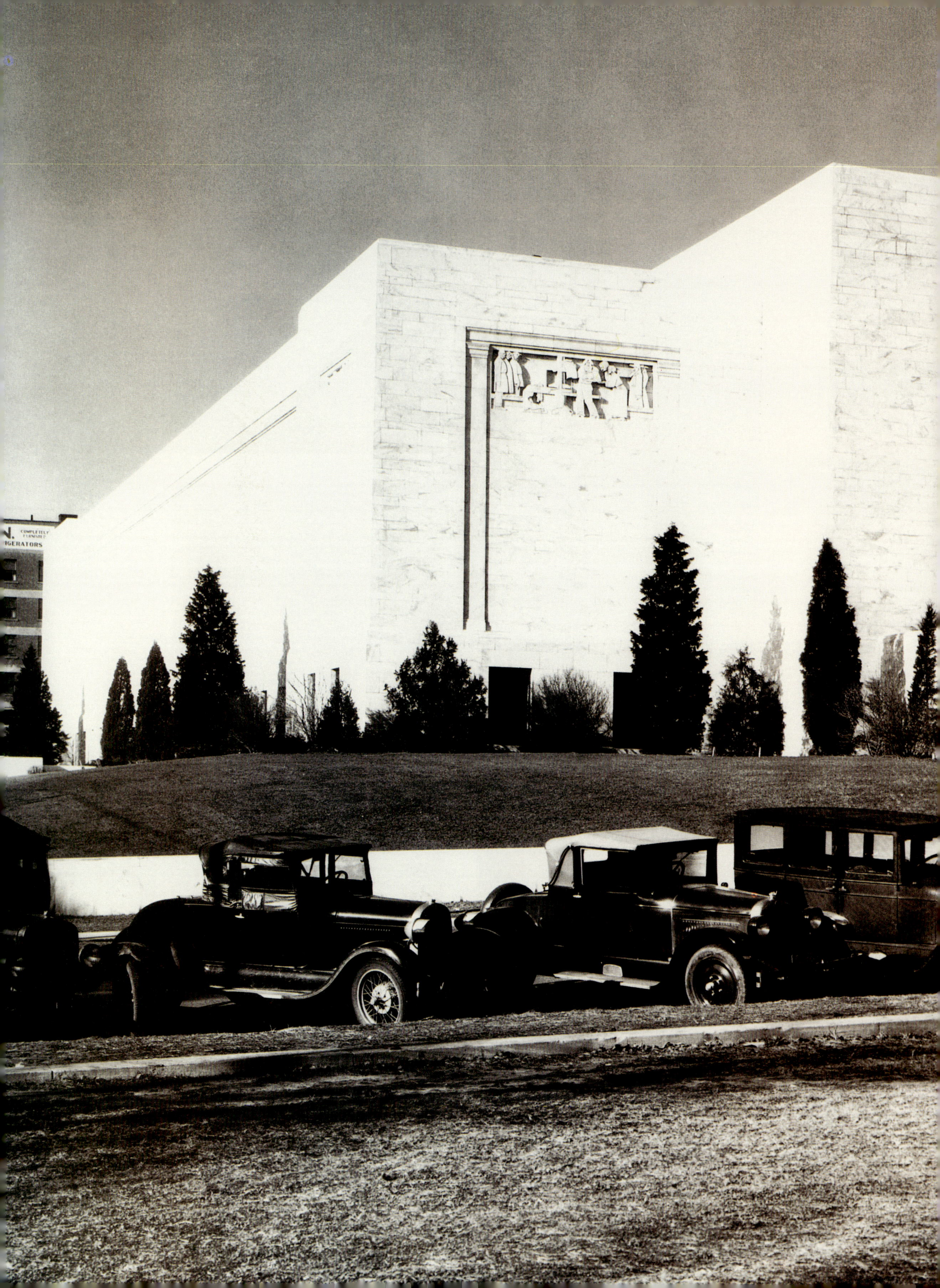

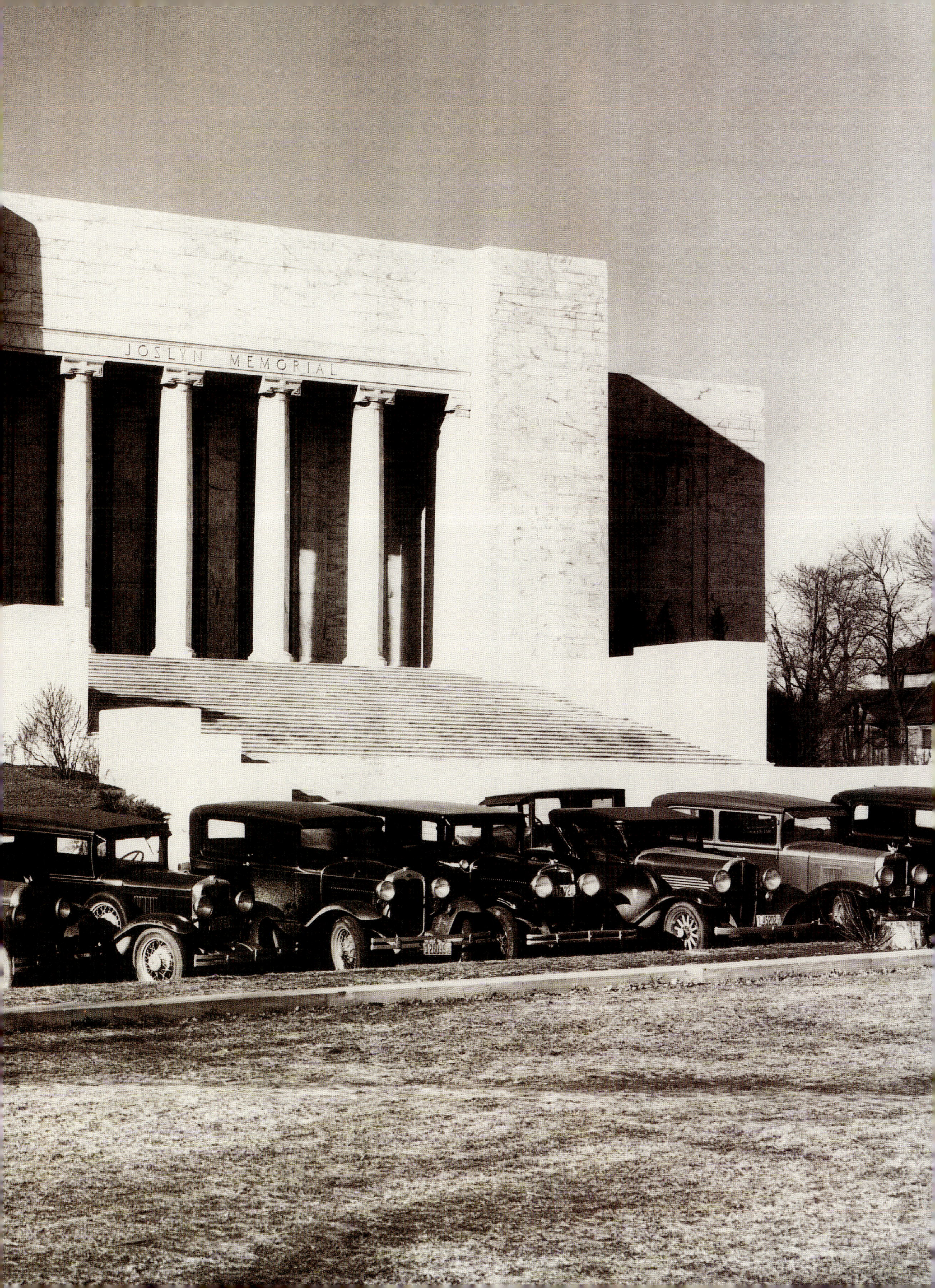
JOSLYN MEMORIAL

The opening of the Joslyn Memorial on November 29, 1931 – Thanksgiving weekend – gave Omaha a sensational cultural building that was greeted with pleasure and astonishment. If the newspaper reports can be believed, 25,000 people attended the inauguration, an event that was characterized by a complete lack of ceremony. There were no speeches, and Mrs. Joslyn attended incognito, so to speak. When asked how the building was to be used, she replied with New England economy, "That's up to them."

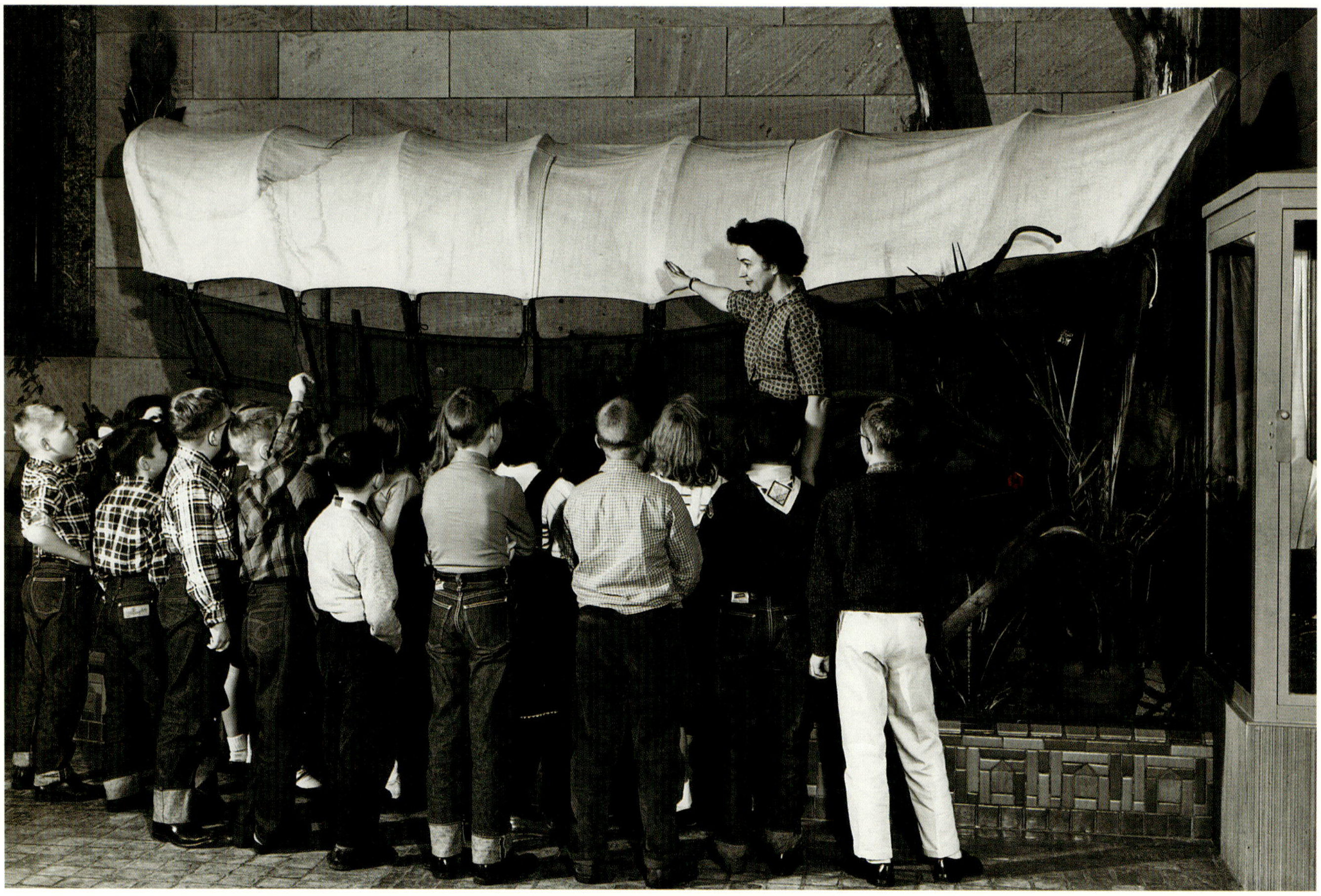

ABOVE: Children view an original Conestoga wagon nestled in a floral court planter and part of ambitious long-term historical displays.
BELOW: An early presentation of material from the collection of Western American art.

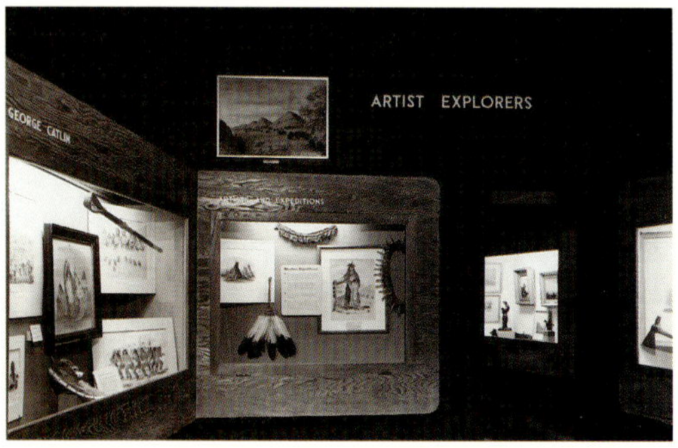

For many years the Joslyn Memorial remained the focus of much cultural activity. As had been anticipated, some of the best collections in the region were turned over to its care, and Dr. Paul Grummann, the first director, was able to use the ample funds of his benefactor to make fine acquisitions, a program continued after her death, thanks to the handsome endowment – a little over two million dollars – she left in her will. In 1947 Grummann retired and was succeeded by the curator, Eugene Kingman. A painter of considerable skill and a pioneer of Western American art history, Kingman had a clear vision of the Joslyn as the Smithsonian of Omaha: a full-blown center for the arts and sciences, embracing all aspects of human intellectual endeavor. To this end he converted the marble halls and storerooms of the lower level into information-packed installations on regional history and culture, complete with plains panorama (painted by himself), photos and photomurals, period rooms, and art and artifacts describing the development of the Omaha area from prehistoric Native inhabitants through the pioneer days (a log

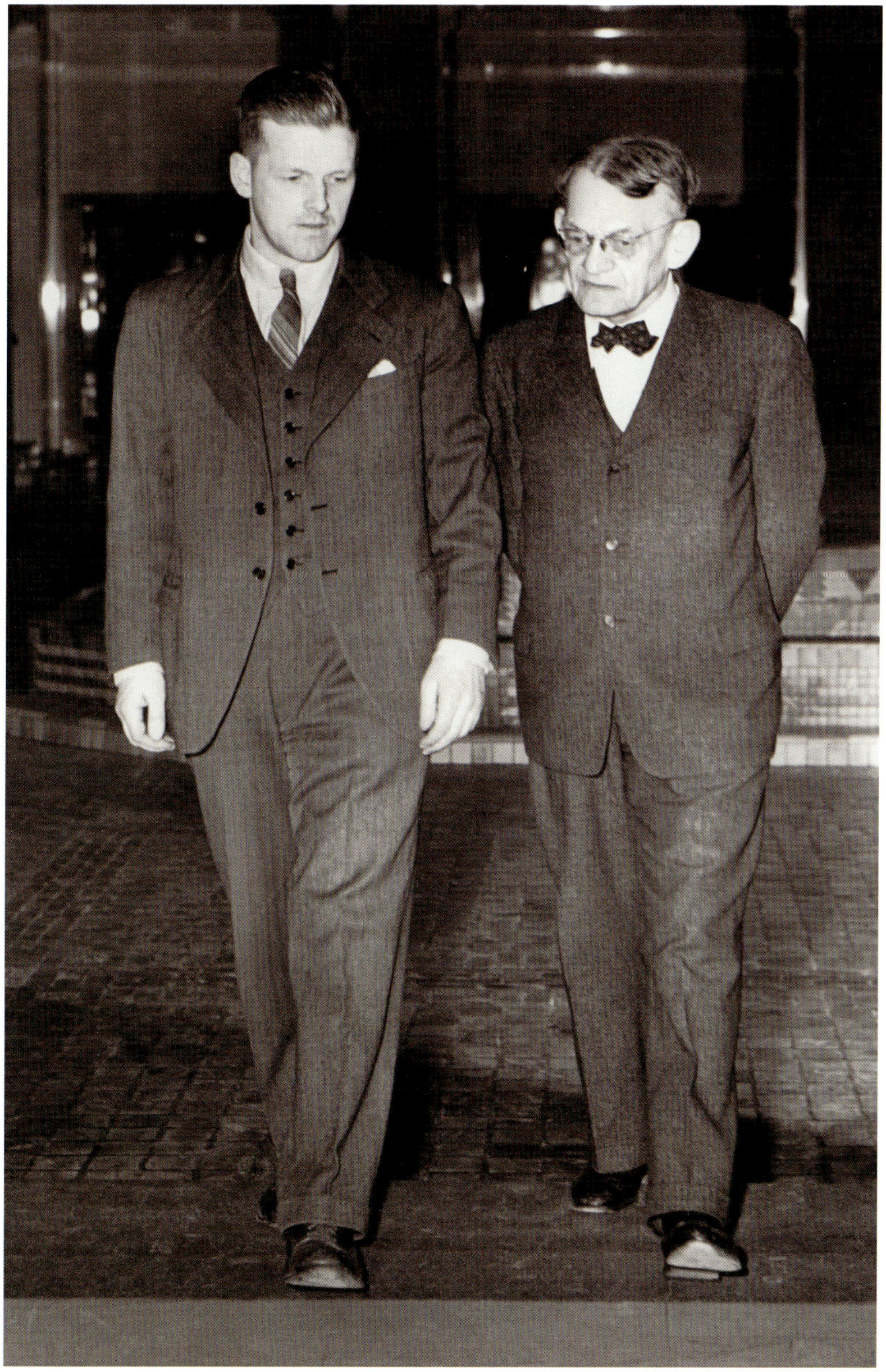

Curator Eugene Kingman, on the left, walks across the floral court with Paul Grummann, Joslyn's first Director. On Grummann's retirement in 1947, Kingman became director and immediately embarked upon a range of innovative projects.

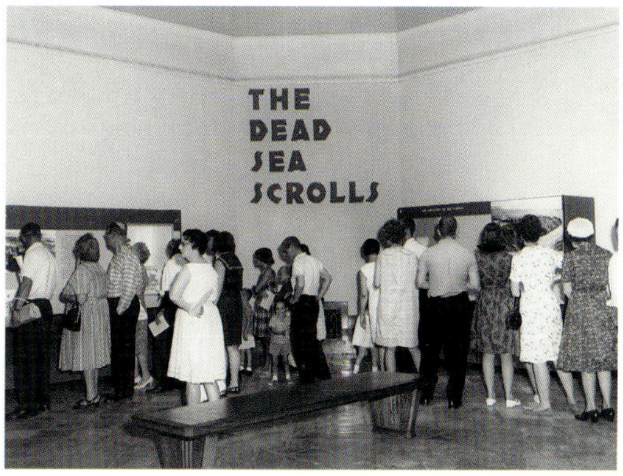

Kingman's wide-ranging interests and connections led to the presentation in Joslyn's galleries of ambitious special exhibitions, such as *Scrolls from the Wilderness of the Dead Sea* in 1965.

cabin) to contemporary suburbia (ranch-style houses and melamine tableware). Opened in 1954, the initial installation, "Life on the Prairie," was recognized with a major history award, bringing Kingman national attention and the invitation to advise the Smithsonian itself on such matters. He expanded the exhibition program to include such historically based exhibitions as *Scrolls from the Wilderness of the Dead Sea* and, long before the era of the blockbuster, *Tutankhamun's Treasures*.

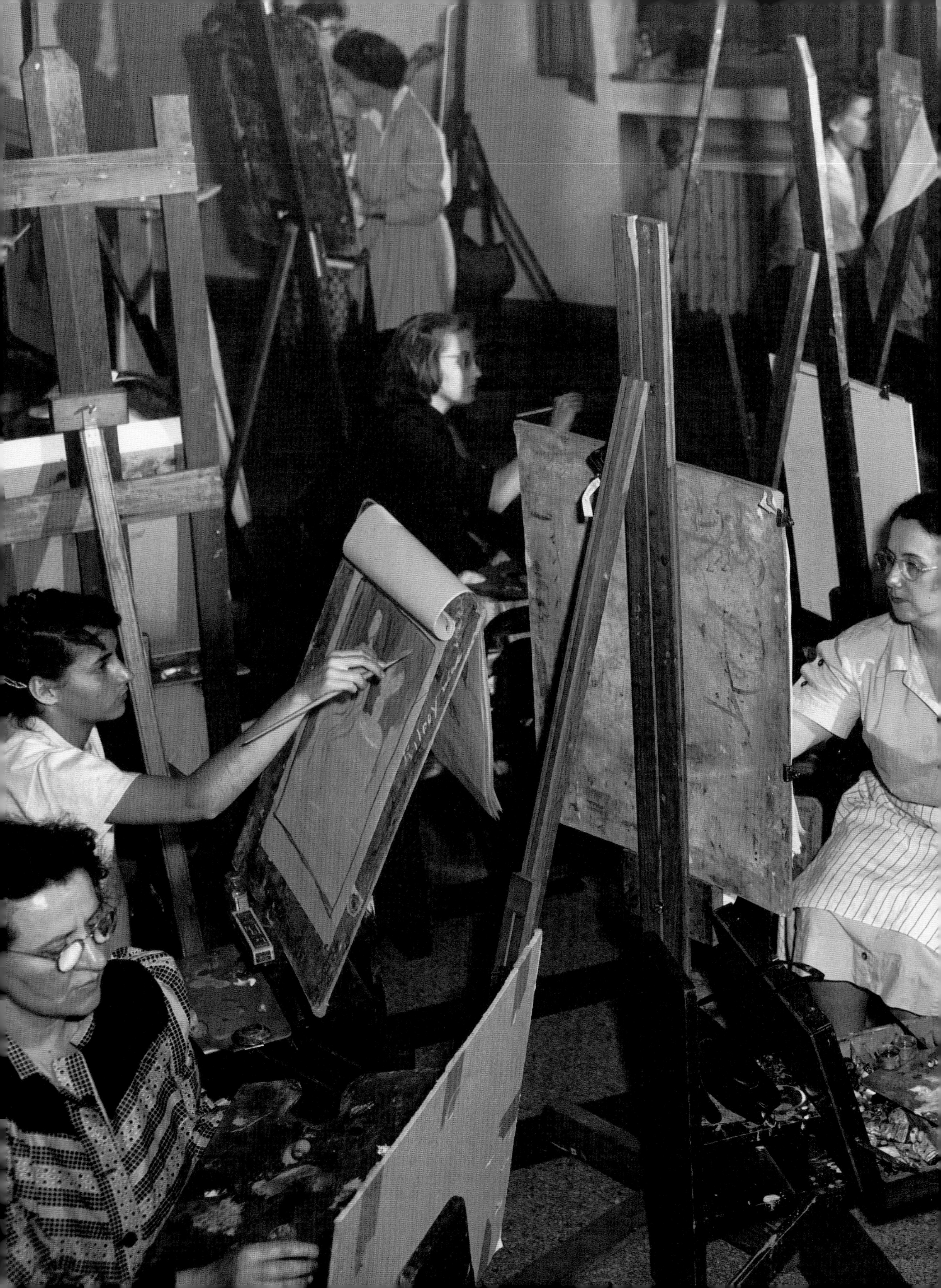

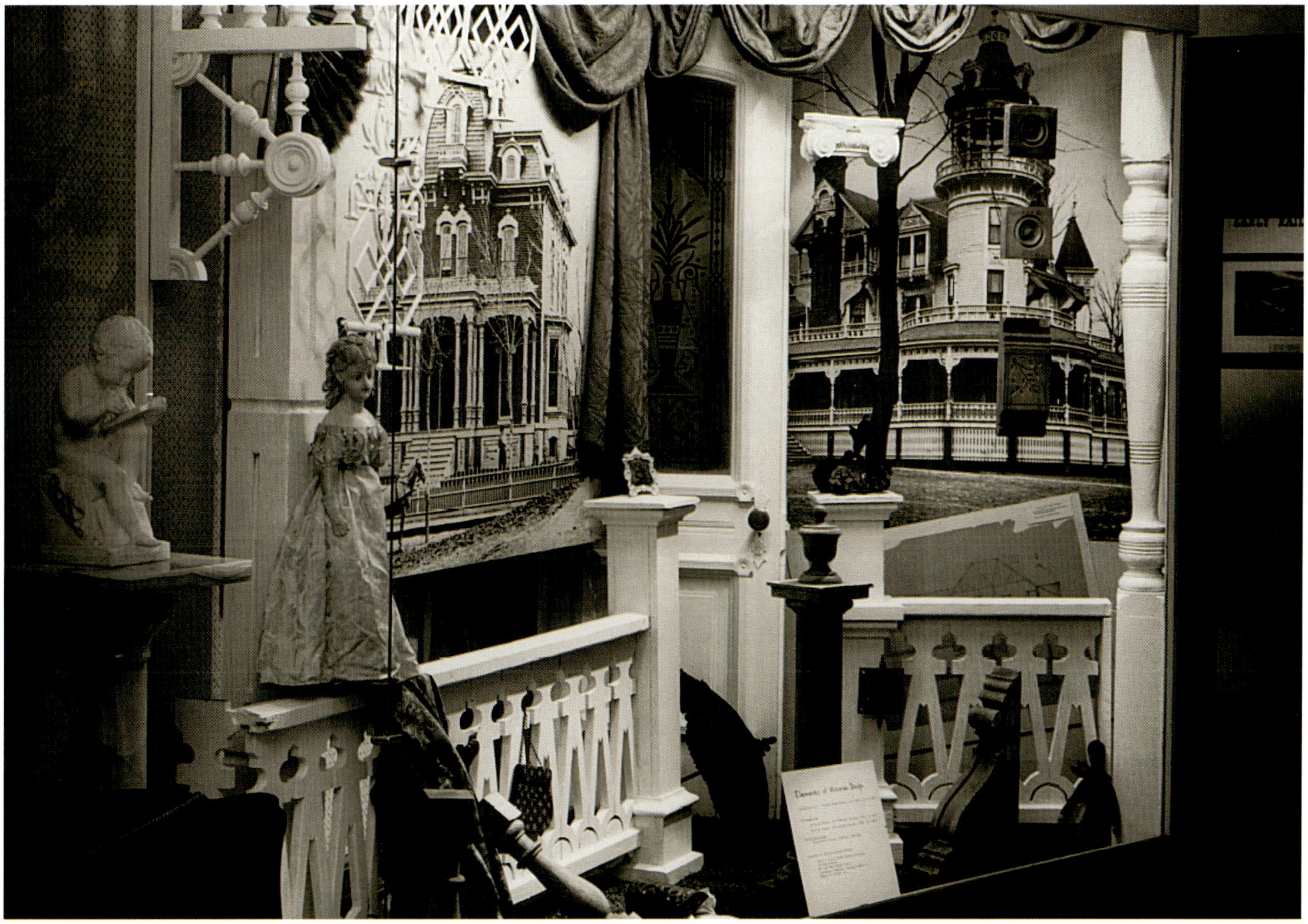

LEFT: A crowded painting class in Joslyn's classroom, originally situated in the southeast corner of the lower level.
ABOVE AND BELOW: Ingeniously inserted in what had been lower level storage areas, Kingman established a sequence of period rooms, including a pioneer's log cabin and a view of Omaha from a turn-of-the-century parlor.

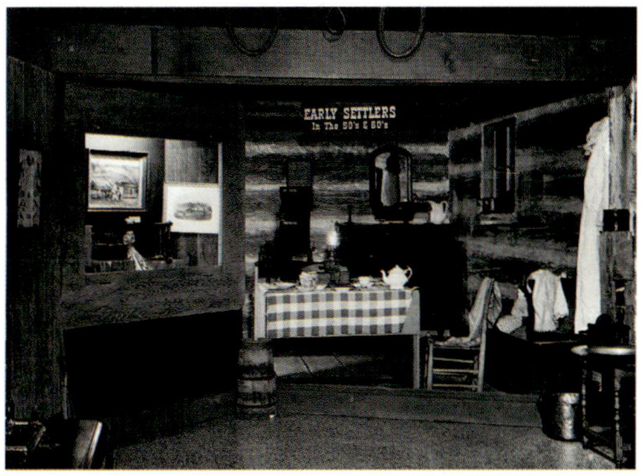

In the 1960s Kingman initiated an expansion scheme: an ambitious master plan calling for a complex of buildings added to the Memorial that included a science museum and planetarium. Nothing came of it, and in 1969 he left to take up the position of director of the Museum of Texas Tech University at Lubbock where, in 1975, he died. Although frustrated in his grand ambitions, Kingman's vision saved much of Omaha's material culture that would otherwise have been lost. He personally salvaged interiors of old mansions that were being demolished without regard to their historical worth, and stood in the archway of the main entrance of the old post office building, defying the wrecking ball, until guaranteed its safety.

Most importantly, though fully realizing that Joslyn was highly unlikely to exhibit them, he accepted into the Museum's care almost anything that was offered. It was a far-sighted policy. The Smithsonian is often referred to metaphorically as "the Nation's Attic"; Kingman literally made the Joslyn Memorial building "Omaha's Attic." Many thousands of objects that were stored there for decades have, in recent years, been transferred to a number of regional history museums, where they now are used for display and research.

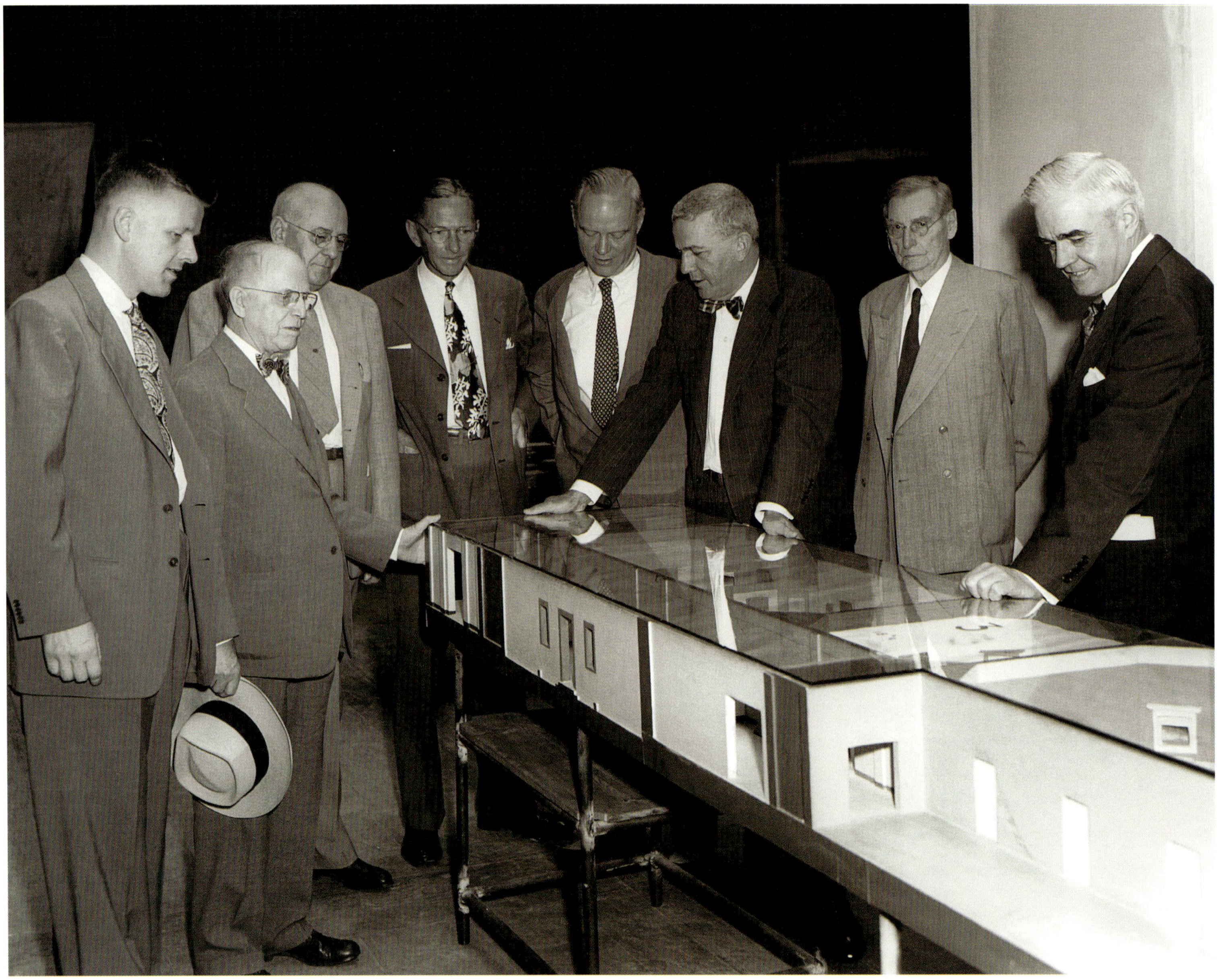

ABOVE: Director Kingman reviews with Trustees plans to remodel the exhibition spaces, including blocking the side doors in the concert hall to create more hanging space in the adjacent galleries. Left to right: Eugene Kingman, William Watson, Frank T. B. Martin, W. A. Cassidy, Casper Y. Offutt, Roy Page, John McDonald, and W. Dale Clark, 1948.

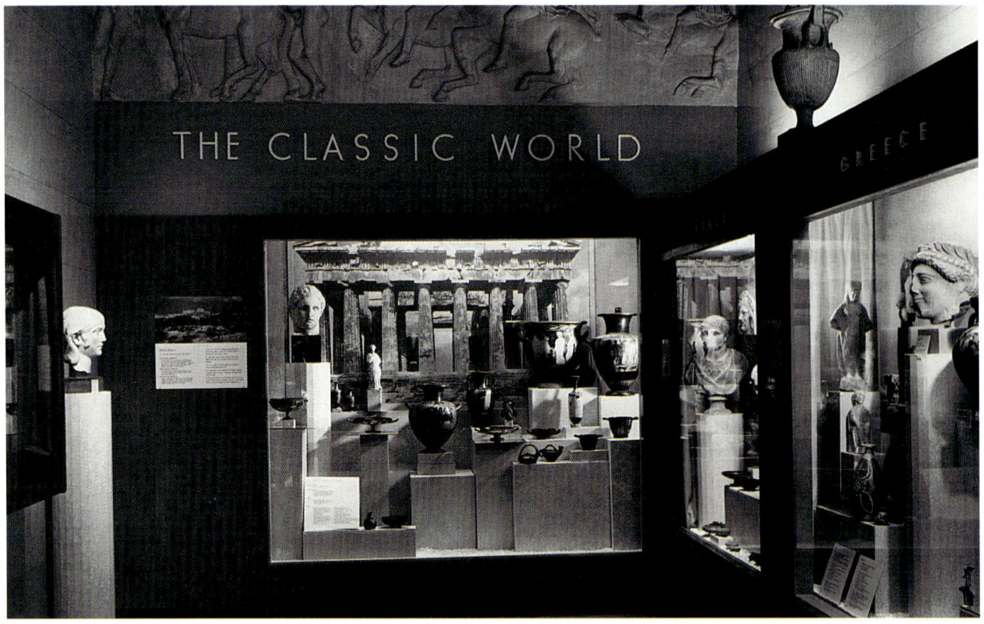

RIGHT: Kingman and his staff embedded art and artifacts within displays that discussed broader cultural conditions, resulting in a "contextual" approach well in advance of its time.

Following Eugene Kingman's departure in 1969, the Joslyn Liberal Arts Society (renamed in 1962) quickly returned to emphasizing art over history and, during an inflationary period that saw the power of its original endowment drastically curtailed, the institution's best efforts went toward maintaining its position as the region's most significant general-purpose art museum.

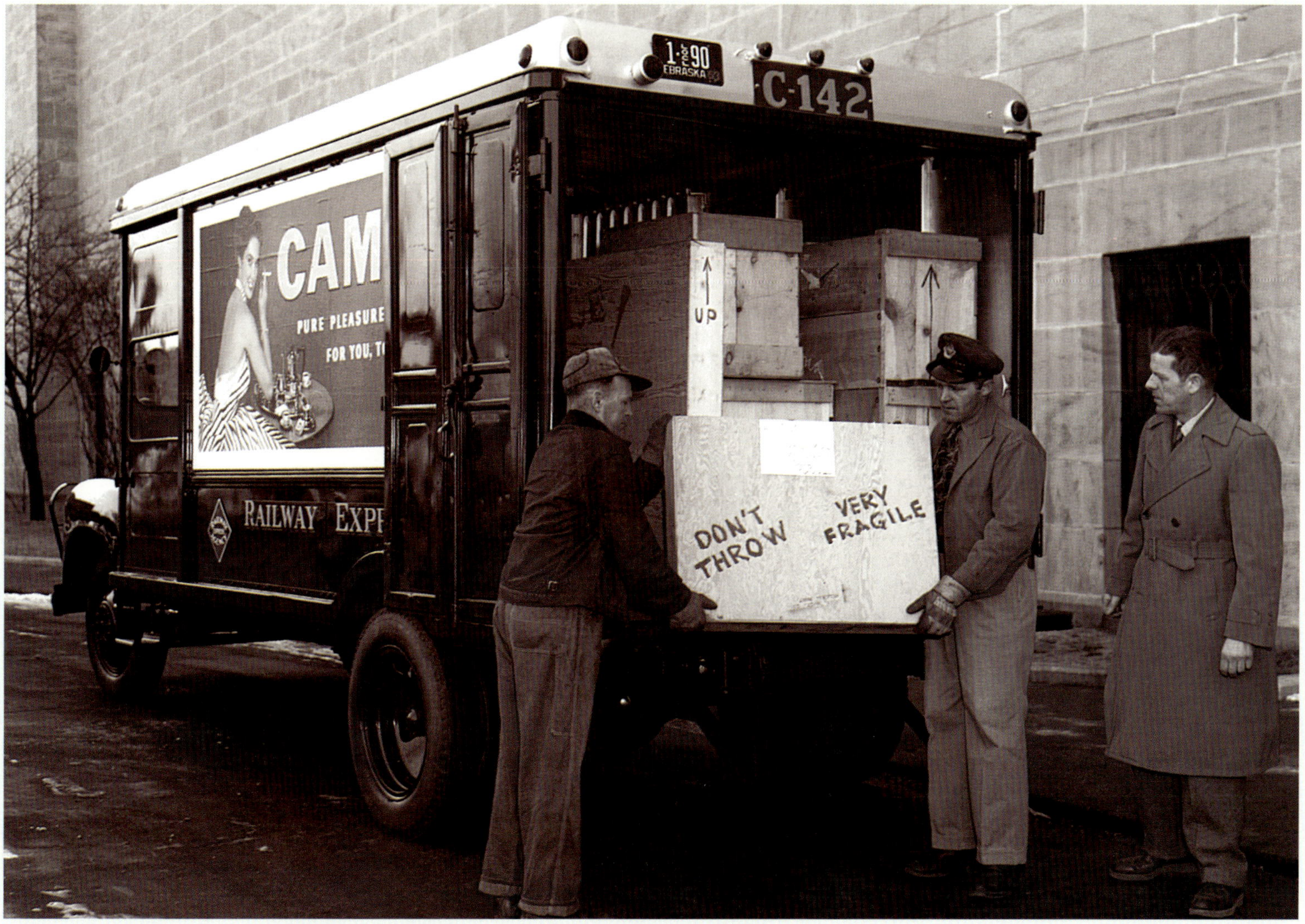

Eugene Kingman oversees the delivery of art at the north door of the Memorial building, the original "loading dock." Shipments were then taken into the rooms on the lower level immediately to the right.

A second expansion plan in the mid 1970s was abandoned for lack of funds but, a decade later, with generous and enthusiastic support from Northern Natural Gas Company (subsequently InterNorth, and now Enron Corp.), the newly established Center for Western Studies produced a series of publications and exhibitions that drew national attention to the Western American collections owned by the company but housed in purpose-built facilities in the Museum.

At the same time, however, Joslyn's attraction as a concert and performance hall had greatly diminished, its increasingly antiquated facilities no longer adequate for the leading professional music organizations of the city. Furthermore, other institutions took up the mantle of local history and, despite some refurbishing for the Bicentennial

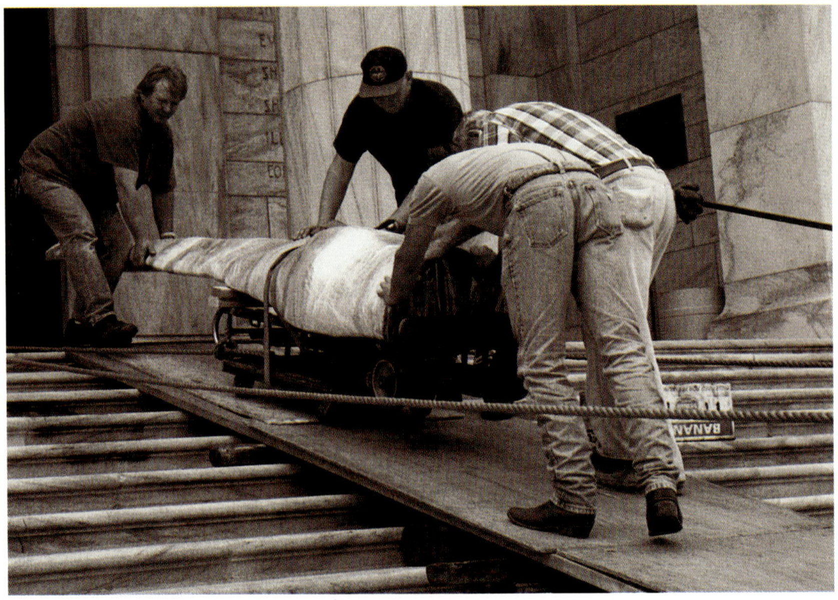

Subsequent remodeling of the lower level in the 1940s, 50s, and 60s moved the loading dock to the northwest corner of the Memorial building. As this was a single door, shipments of any size still had to be brought up ramps through the main doors; an unsightly activity that, ironically, echoed ancient Egyptian building techniques and the Memorial building's architecture.

celebrations, after thirty years a heavy layer of intellectual, if not actual, dust had settled over the award-winning historical installations carved out of the lower level corridors by Eugene Kingman.

Where possible, aspects of the building were modernized. In 1970, with funds provided by Mr. and Mrs. D. J. Witherspoon, the building was provided with environmental conditions now generally considered necessary for the loan and display of art. In 1983, 22nd Street was closed and a land exchange arranged with the Omaha Public School authorities to enable an extensive sculpture garden to be laid out immediately to the east of the Memorial. As part of the same project – all carried out by the Omaha-based architectural firm Leo A. Daly, Inc. – the lobby at the north door was extensively remodeled to permit easier handicapped access to the three main floors of the building. In 1984 funds were provided by Robert H. and Mildred T. Storz to restore the floral court (also referred to as a fountain court) to something close to its original condition. By this time, however, the very facility that had once seemed almost too spacious (there are stories of children roller-skating in the lower level in its early days) now seemed crowded and inflexible, ill-suited to the requirements of contemporary art museum programming. All aspects of the Museum's operations – from food service to shop, education department to library – were in desperate need of additional space.

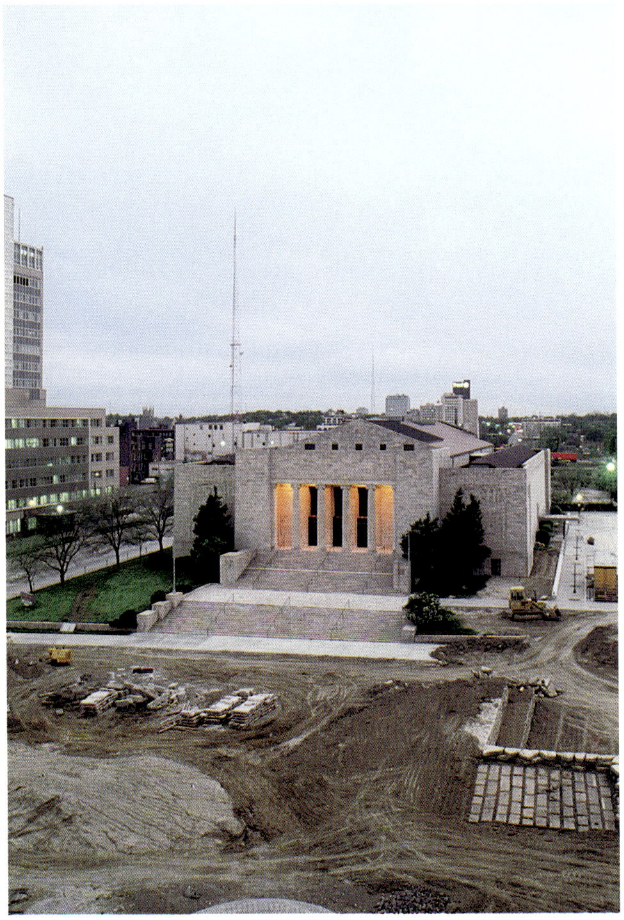

A land exchange with Central High School in 1983 permitted a major alteration of the grounds surrounding the Museum. This allowed for the addition of a sculpture garden to the east, an expanded parking lot, and an improved, handicapped-accessible entrance to the north. The property gained by Central to the northeast of the Memorial was turned into a football training field and track.

Most obvious from the regular visitor's point of view, parts of the permanent collection were frequently consigned to storage to accommodate large special exhibitions. Objects had to be stored in spaces throughout the building, including, more often than not, one of the main galleries.

In 1987 the perceived need to re-examine the institution's mission reached a critical point and, at the request of the Joslyn Liberal Arts Society Board of Trustees, a new governing structure was established. Under the chairmanship of Walter Scott, Jr., the new Board of Governors and the Museum staff embarked upon a thorough analysis of the shortcomings and potential of the institution, the end result of which was the adoption of Joslyn Art Museum as the legal name, a revised and focused mission statement, and the identification of the need for approximately 50,000 square feet of additional facilities for art exhibition and storage as well as for public-service functions.

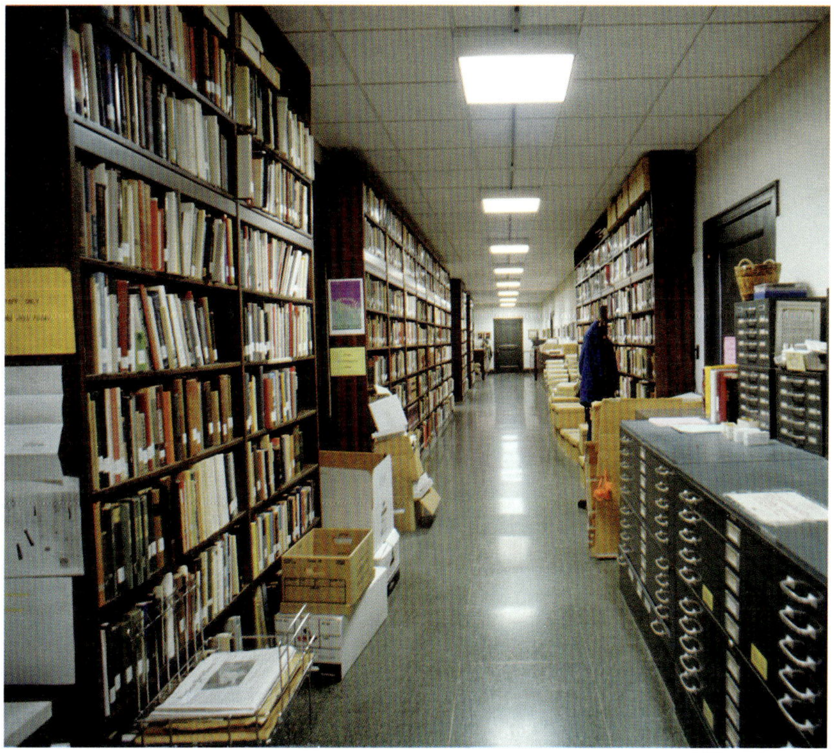

By the 1980s the library had long since outgrown its original southeast corner reading room, and its shelves had spread into staff corridors, an example of the "crowding" problem in all areas of the Museum.

At the same time, the needs of the more recently established local history museum, Western Heritage Museum, had also been examined and, in June 1989, a special committee representing both institutions determined to proceed with a $60 million development campaign – an unprecedented scale for Omaha museums – to secure their future and identity. Of this amount, $45.5 million was designated for specific aspects of Joslyn Art Museum: approximately $16 million for renovation and new construction, $17 million for art purchase and endowment, the remaining $12.5 million for operating and program endowment. A complete review of all objects in the Museum's collections – from baby buggies to bas-reliefs – was undertaken, resulting in the transfer of thousands of artifacts to Western Heritage Museum, the Nebraska State Historical Society, and other regional institutions.

Rapid success in fund-raising efforts led by Joslyn Governor Robert B. Daugherty, highlighted by a $20 million matching grant from the Peter Kiewit Foundation as well as several large gifts from Omaha individuals and companies, permitted the Museum to go forward with plans for new facilities.

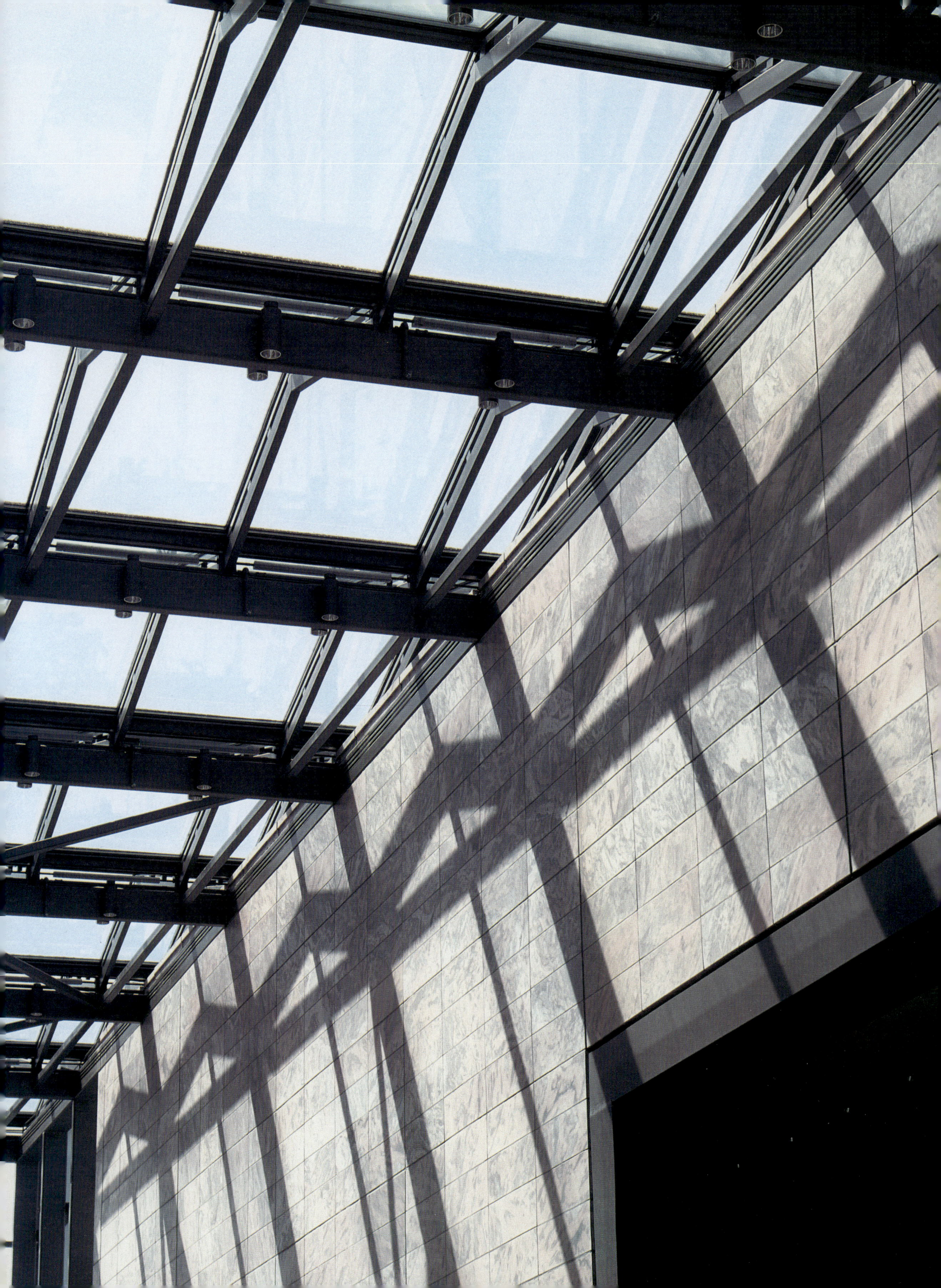

In 1991 the Board of Governors appointed a committee to select a design architect for the Museum's capital expansion. Headed by Michael B. Walsh, the other members of the committee were Sylvia B. Cohn, Margre H. Durham, Willis A. Strauss, and, in an advisory capacity, the Museum's director, Graham W. J. Beal.

It was decided to spread the net as widely as possible in searching for an architect and that a professional advisor be appointed to assist the committee. Bill Lacy of Bill Lacy Design, architect, author, and secretary to the prestigious Pritzker Award Committee, was selected for this task. When Michael Walsh moved to Houston, Willis Strauss took over the chairmanship and Harold W. Andersen joined the committee.

At the end of a five-month proccss, starting with the names of fifty-five firms from across the United States and Europe, as well as one in India, a short list of five architects emerged; all had proven experience both in building new museums and in restoring architecturally significant cultural buildings. They were: Sir Norman Foster and Partners of London; James Ingo Freed of Pei, Cobb, Freed and Partners in New York; Renzo Piano of Genoa; Christian de Portzamparc of Paris; and Antoine Predock of Albuquerque, New Mexico. Piano subsequently withdrew and, after traveling to see examples of the architects' work, the committee convened for two days of interviews with the four finalists in mid June 1992. Impressed by his penetrating analysis of the Joslyn's situation and assured by his recent inventive and sensitive work at the Royal Academy in London, the committee selected Norman Foster.

Best known for his aggressive use of "high-tech" materials, Foster outlined an approach to Joslyn's summary building program that combined visual deference to the original structure with potential solutions for the Museum's several, seemingly conflicting, requirements.

The shadows cast on the south wall of the new building by the steel framework of Sir Norman Foster's atrium roof produce slowly changing patterns that, by a happy coincidence, seem to echo Elarth's thunderbird motif of the Memorial.

SIR NORMAN FOSTER
Design Architect

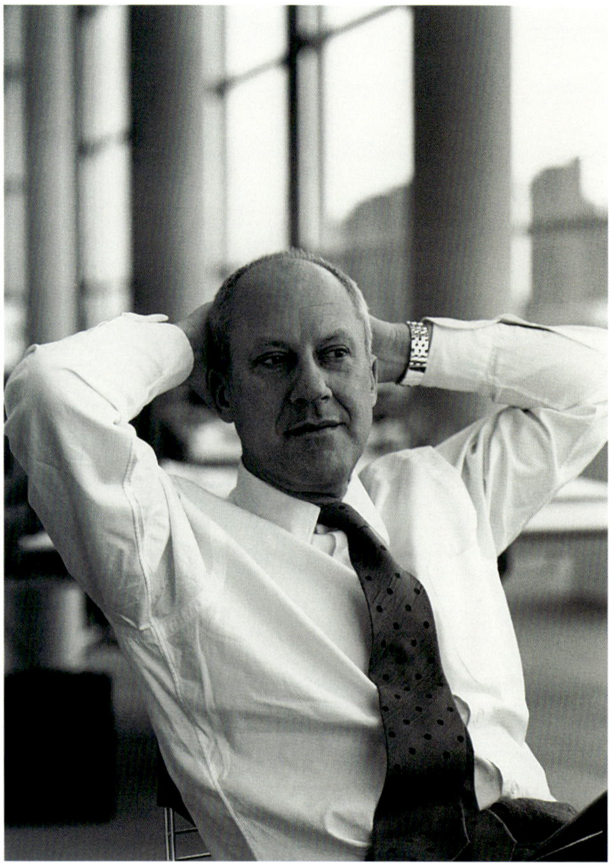

Based in London, Sir Norman Foster (ABOVE) has built one of the world's largest architect practices through consistent and highly innovative use of modern materials. Critical attention to Foster's high-tech approach – exemplified by his 1986 Hong Kong and Shanghai Bank, Hong Kong (BELOW) – has tended to obscure his equal concerns for context and environment.

Born in Manchester, England, in 1935, Sir Norman Foster earned a degree in architecture and town planning from the University of Manchester in 1961, after which he was awarded a Henry Fellowship to study architecture at Yale University. Inspired by such pioneer architectural thinkers as Buckminster Fuller, Foster returned to England transformed by his American experience. In his 1994 American Institute of Architects' Gold Medal Award acceptance speech, Foster simply but potently stated, "In England, I was the odd one out, but when I came here, I felt that I had come home. I felt liberated. It's no exaggeration to say that I discovered myself through America."

Working first in partnership with Richard Rogers, Foster's fascination with the lightness and simplicity of steel construction quickly gave him the reputation as an uncompromising modernist, a description that tended to obscure his concern for environmental context. His success with a series of commercial commissions, notably the 1971-75 Willis Faber & Dumas Head Office in Ipswich, England, (the "youngest" building to receive Britain's Grade I protective listing) was followed by his first cultural commission: the Sainsbury Centre for Visual Arts at the University of East Anglia, Norwich, England. Lean, elegant, and sited like a defiant full stop to the suddenly old-fashioned-looking, "brutalist," 1960s concrete campus, the Centre was also a high modernist manifesto at a time when architectural confidence in twentieth-century Modernism was eroding and many architects were, in the name of Post-Modernism, once again busily ransacking styles of the past to give relevance and credibility to their role as responsible members of the community. (In Foster's own country, the shifting debate among conservationists, environmentalists, and architects took on a particularly British character when Charles, Prince of Wales and heir to the throne, personally intervened to lead the charge against the evils, real and perceived, of much contemporary architecture and called a proposed addition to London's National Gallery "a carbuncle on the much-loved face of the nation"; the scheme was subsequently abandoned.)

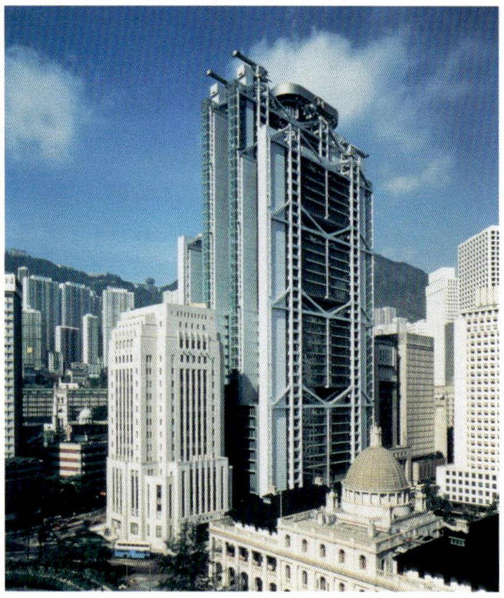

His design of the Hong Kong and Shanghai Bank did nothing to deflect attention from the public perception of Foster as a high priest of high-tech Modernism. This audacious building, designed to express the confidence in the future of a powerful capitalist institution in a place soon to be returned to Chinese communist rule, rethought the skyscraper. For a building type whose blank anonymity had become a fact of life in cities from New York to Tokyo, Foster devised a structure full of incident and variety. Interweaving public and private areas, he created a building permeated with space and light; in place of the inert block, an expressive building speaking of life and continued growth.

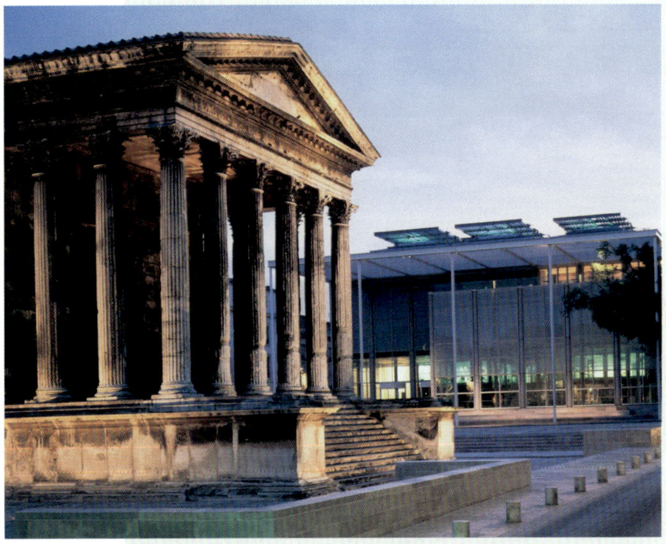

While many observers concentrated on his lavish use of materials usually associated with the aerospace industry, the Bank building also made clear Foster's involvement with environmental issues. Every feature of the structure can be traced back to a concern for its inhabitants as well as a determination that the building wear well. Increased emphasis on a precise context of a given project was further apparent in Foster's design for the Carré d'Art in Nîmes, France, where he successfully situated an unequivocally modern design across the way from the famous Maison Carrée, a remarkably intact Roman temple greatly admired by, among others, Thomas Jefferson.

Foster's *médiathèque* in Nîmes (ABOVE), situated across from the Roman temple, caused its share of controversy, but demonstrated that the old and the new could coexist on their own terms without compromise to either. The old and the new are thoroughly integrated in Foster's Sackler project at London's venerable Royal Academy of Art (BELOW).

Perhaps appropriately, it was a relatively modest project in London that finally allowed Foster to demonstrate his full engagement in issues raised by preservationists and their allies. In 1985 the Royal Academy engaged Foster to refurbish three disheveled fourth-floor galleries. Realizing that the key to the full use of these galleries lay in proper access, Foster inserted an elegant glass-and-metal, free-standing staircase into the fifteen-foot-wide "light well" that separated the eighteenth- and nineteenth-century Academy buildings. Restoration of the facades of these old buildings (not seen in their original state for over 100 years) produced what one critic described as "a result that puts to shame the pastiche of architects who had been working with historic buildings for years." Opened in 1991, and the recipient of fourteen national and international awards, the Royal Academy project was a major factor in the selection of Foster as design architect for Joslyn Art Museum's renovation and extension.

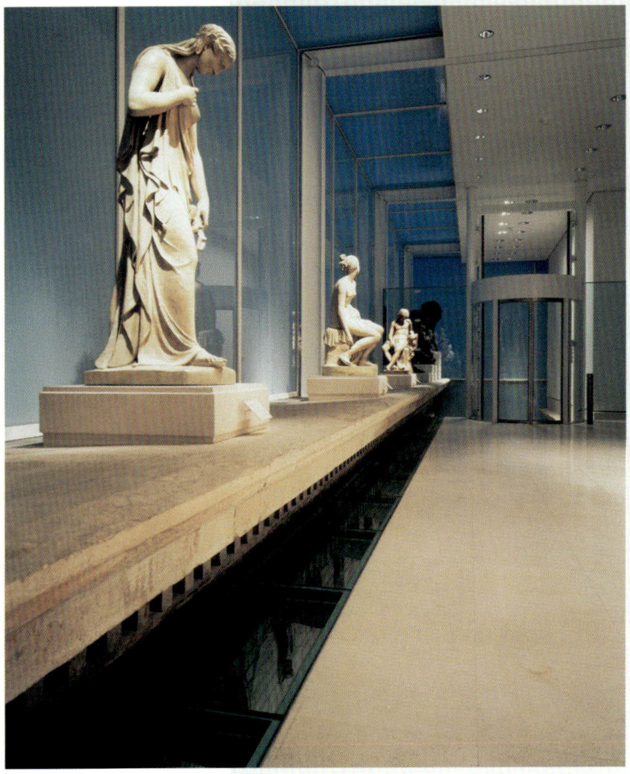

Knighted in 1990, Sir Norman Foster has built an enormous practice, with offices around the world. Ironically, the United States – the country whose technological innovations so inspired him – was slow to embrace his work. Although he had been considered for a number of projects in this country, none had yet been built, and Joslyn Art Museum was Foster's first essay in his spiritual home.

THE TEAM

As is always the case with major cultural commissions, the selection of an out-of-town firm was a controversial one. Sentiments ranged from pride and excitement to dismay that Joslyn seemed to be snubbing regional architectural talent. From the beginning of the proceedings, the committee of Joslyn Governors responsible for selecting the design architect had stressed the requirement for the successful candidate, if not from the Omaha region, to affiliate with a local firm and develop the design on-site. Following interviews with seven Omaha firms, the Museum requested that Sir Norman Foster and Partners work with HDR, Inc. (Henningson, Durham & Richardson).

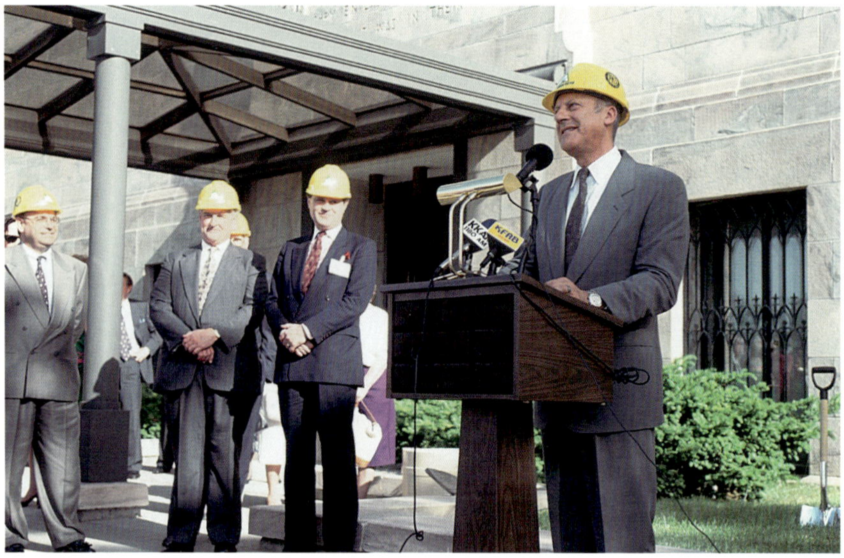

Sir Norman Foster speaks at the June 1993 groundbreaking. Also pictured, left to right, are HDR's CEO, Francis Jelensperger; Walter Scott, Jr., Chairman of Joslyn Art Museum's Board of Governors and President and CEO of Peter Kiewit Sons', Inc.; and Joslyn's Director, Graham W. J. Beal.

To expedite design and construction, "partnering," a relatively novel procedure in the United States, was adopted. Traditionally, architect and client work together to design the building they want. When their plans are in a state of advanced development, they are sent out to bid with construction companies. As often as not, the result is a building well over budget, necessitating a considerable amount of redesign. The partnering process was devised to short-circuit this time-honored and often

Kiewit Construction Company, a division of Peter Kiewit Sons', Inc., provided the initiative for a genuinely successful collaborative effort. In Cascade, Oregon, Kiewit worked with the Army Corps of Engineers to construct a huge lock and dam to allow larger shipping vessels on the Columbia River. The Bonneville Lock and Dam project (RIGHT) was given the 1994 Marvin M. Black Excellence in Partnering Award by the Associated General Contractors.

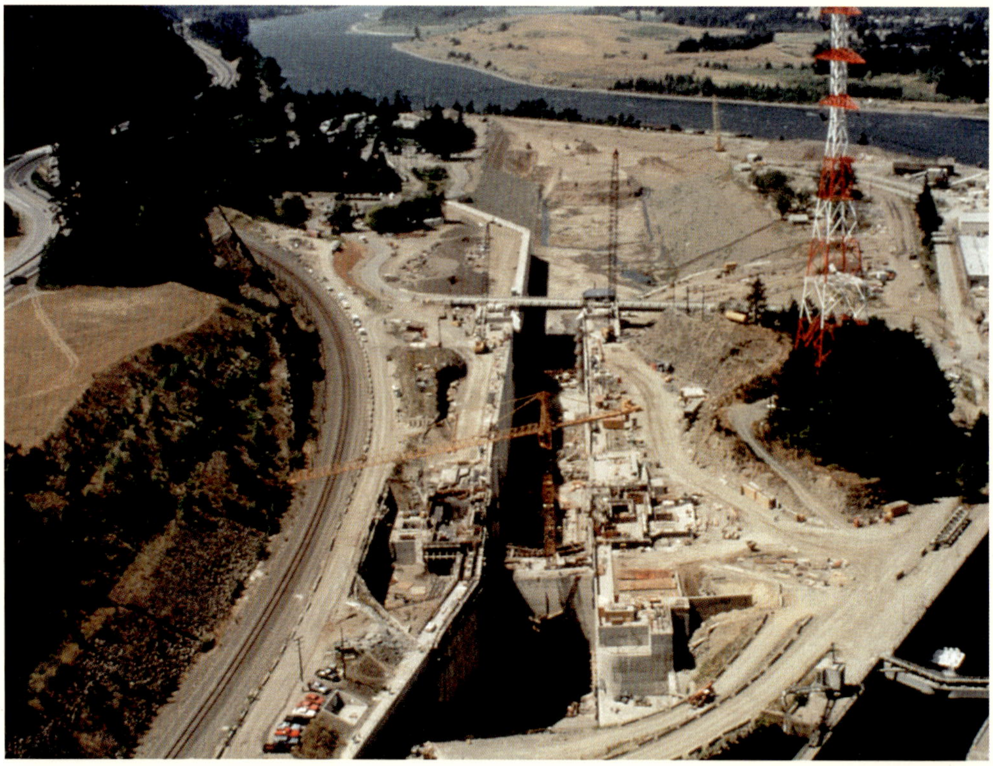

Ground was officially broken on June 7, 1993; the new, 58,000-square-foot building and renovation was completed seventeen months later and opened to the public on Saturday, November 19, 1994.

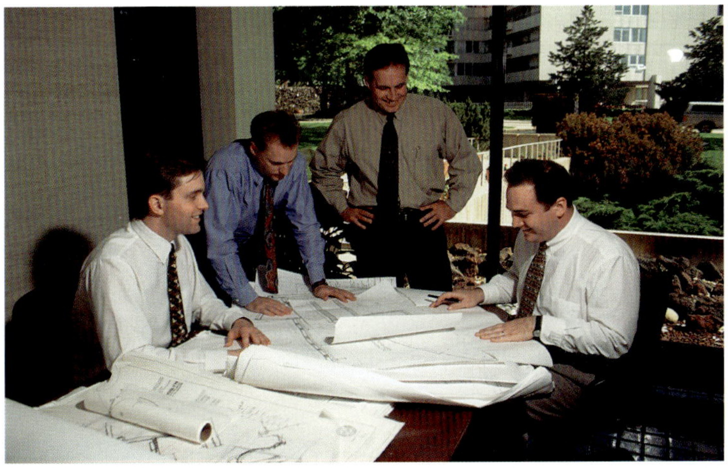

Completing the building team alongside Foster, Kiewit, and Joslyn was HDR, Inc., an Omaha-based architecture/engineering company with extensive experience in public building projects. Left to right: Patrick Leahy, Jeff Cramer, Bruce Carpenter, and Doug Wignall.

adversarial sequence of events by having all aspects of the design/build process represented on a single team from the early planning stages. Kiewit Construction Company (a division of the now vastly expanded Peter Kiewit Sons', Inc.) was appointed to coordinate this process and carry out construction. Joining the team at the London end were the quantity surveyors, Davis Langdon & Everest. A peculiarly British phenomenon, quantity surveyors are nominally responsible for accurate estimates of the various construction methods under consideration. But, under the right circumstances, an imaginative Q.S. is able to suggest material options to the design architects and contribute to the planning process far beyond the limits usually suggested in the more passive estimating process.

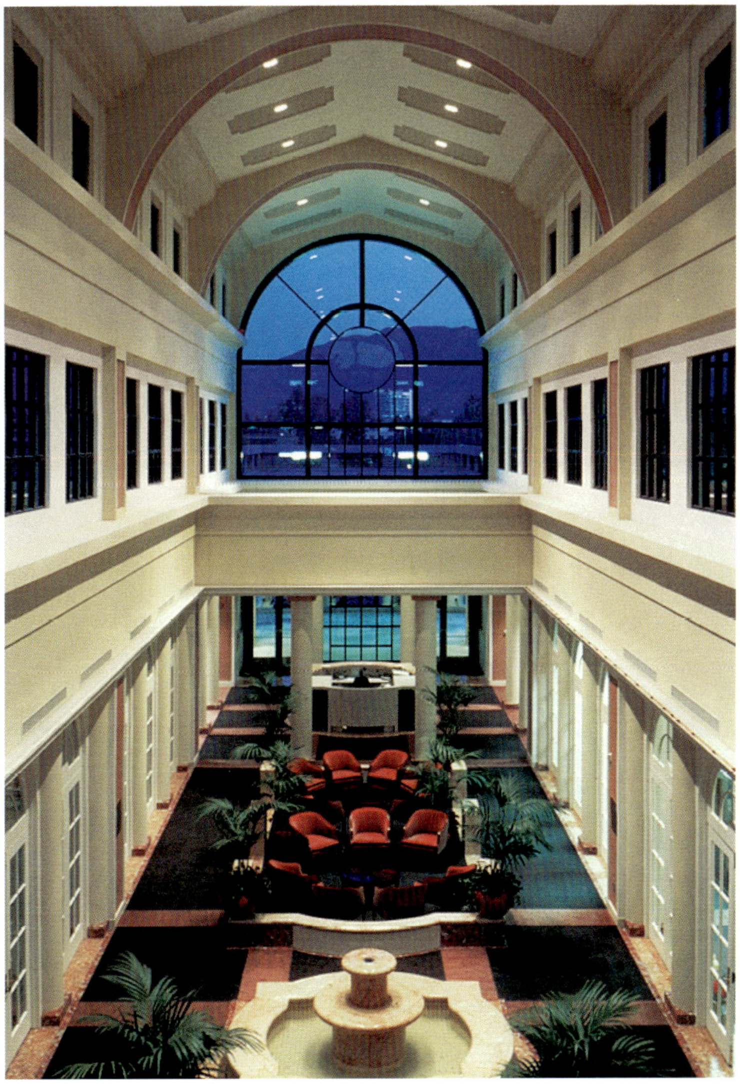

The entrance lobby to HDR's Huntington Memorial Hospital in Pasadena, California. (Photo courtesy HDR, Inc.)

The final, crucial decision was to combine the collaborative approach with a "fast track" schedule, designing the building in components ("packages") within an overall scheme as the construction progresses. The main advantages are accelerated dead-lines and earlier completion that, in theory, bring savings associated with reduced time projections. The risks lie in each decision having implications for subsequent design and planning components not yet worked out in detail. In this regard it is especially critical that the partnering process work to identify all requirements at the appropriate time. By a nice historical irony, in opting for a partnering/fast track approach, the late-twentieth-century team was duplicating the hectic pace that tested the young Herschel Elarth in the Art Deco redesign of the Memorial building.

the EVOLUTION *of a* SCHEME

The Museum's original letter to architects, inviting their interest in its capital expansion project, identified three interrelated characteristics as lying at the core of the design challenge: the need for functional, secure spaces specific to an art museum; the provision of public-service features, notably retail store and catering facility, insulated from galleries and "back room" museum activities; and respect for the architectural character and integrity of the original building.

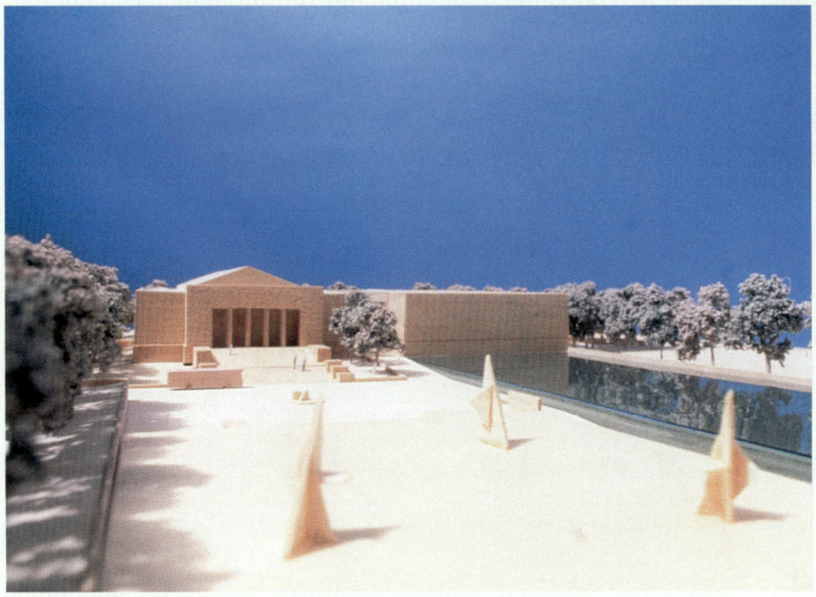

Other subsidiary, but essential, concerns were: the requirement for public access in accordance with the 1990 Americans with Disabilities Act; maintaining parking volume and convenience for museum visitors; and retaining the essential area of the 1983 sculpture garden for outdoor events.

From his analysis of the original competition brief, Foster devised a comprehensive plan that embraced not only the Museum's stated needs but posited a revised traffic system complete with a covered, multi-story parking garage below a remodeled sculpture garden. Although funding was inadequate to carry out the complete scheme, the final concept incorporated its main features and allows for its completion, if desired, at a later date.

Foster's thorough analysis of the original brief led him to propose a simple block to the north of the Memorial building with a parking garage to the east, under a sculpture garden.

In the meantime, the architects were asked to re-examine all of the options available to the Museum in its efforts to gain more space; notably that of extensively remodeling the Memorial building to take advantage of the spacious attics above the galleries and the high-ceilinged offices in the lower level. Analysis of these spaces quickly revealed that, once allowance had been made for the installation of air-conditioning and other functional requirements, they were not nearly as promising as they appeared. To use the attics as galleries would require raising the roofs above them and thereby alter the profile of the original building; the discovery of differing ceiling heights on the lower level indicated that these spaces, if converted, would yield only mediocre galleries. But such considerations paled into relative insignificance alongside other consequences of converting these private areas to public and office spaces.

As with everything else, safety codes had changed greatly since the 1920s, and the beautiful, virtually hand-crafted Joslyn Memorial contains many features no longer acceptable. Any extensive remodeling would have triggered requirements for full compliance with modern safety codes. The attics, reached either by obscure staircases or a small elevator installed in 1983, presented particular problems of access that could only be solved by inserting sizable staircases and elevators in multiple locations, the provision of which inevitably would have impinged upon the spaces below – the

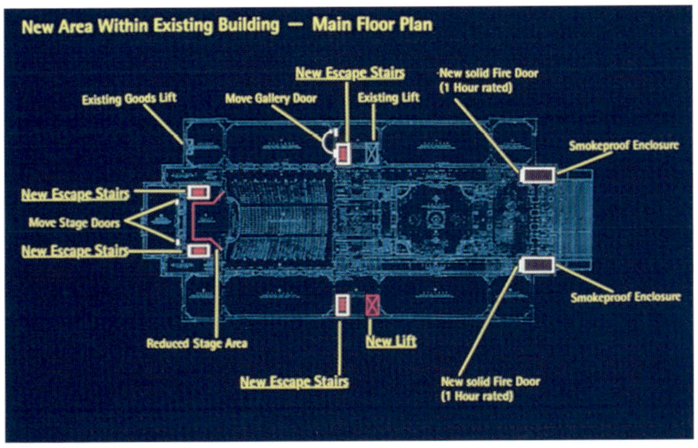

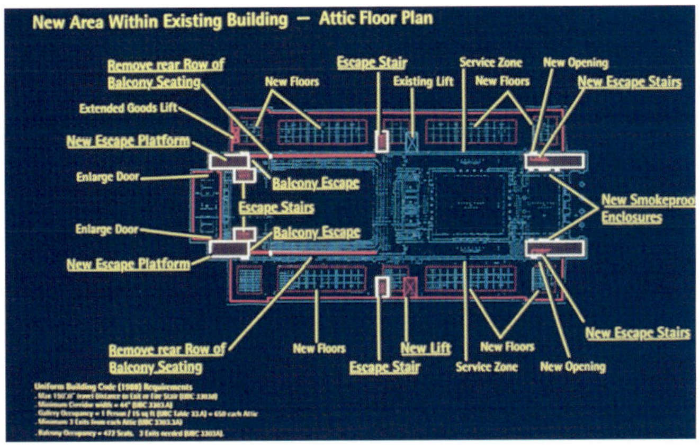

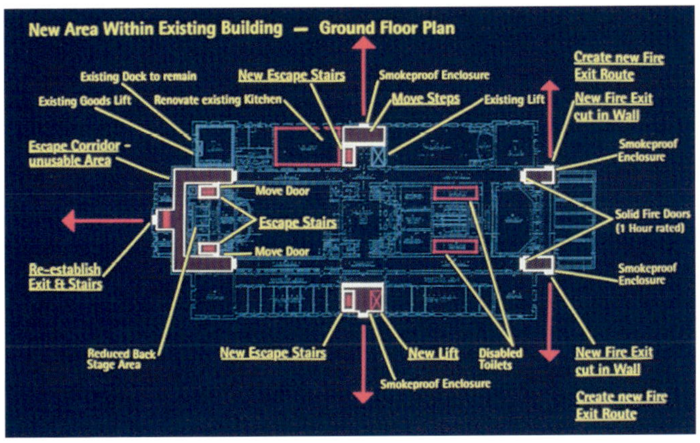

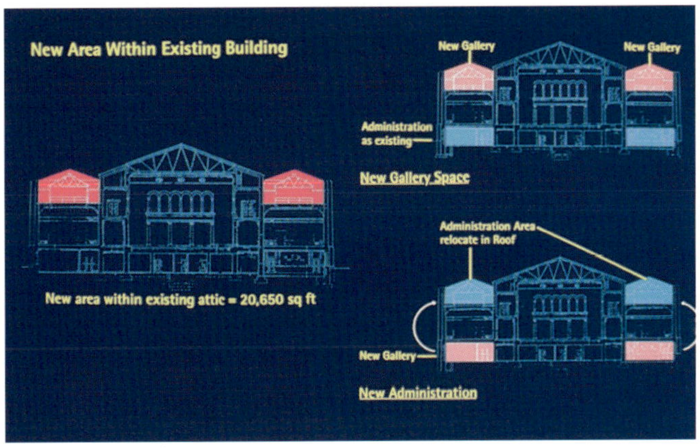

original galleries! Fire safety regulations also would have required the enclosing of the interior stairwells at each side of the east end of the building. While it would have been possible to achieve this using glazing, the appearance of the hallways on the lower and main levels would have been marred, and that of the arcades on the balconies to an even greater extent. And, not only would this remodeling have disrupted the original character of the building, it would still have left half of the Museum's requirements – shipping and receiving facilities, kitchen, dining, art storage, and expanded education and library facilities – comprising some 30,000 square feet, to be accommodated.

Finally, everything known about the extreme durability of the Memorial building's fabric (in the 1950s, dynamite was used to create a doorway in one of the lower level corridor walls) reinforced the notion that extensive remodeling was likely to have a cost quite disproportional to the gains.

With emphasis redirected toward new construction, the various locations for an addition were re-examined. There being no realistic possibility of building to the south or west, any new addition would have to go on the Museum's own land to the north, northeast, or east. The oft-suggested notion of building an underground wing – attractive to many because it left the Memorial building's exterior untouched – was abandoned for problems similar to those besetting remodeling: how to provide adequate public and working access between the old and new facilities without turning some of Joslyn's existing functional space into yet more transitional areas.

Before proceeding to design extensive new facilities, the team examined possible remodeling of the considerable unused space in the attics as well as alternative use of offices on the lower level as art galleries. Detailed analysis soon revealed that such remodeling would require intrusive public-access structures throughout the main level, while still leaving the need for about 30,000 square feet of new construction for badly needed functional facilities: loading dock, kitchen, restaurant, library, and art storage. Finally, the fortresslike construction of the Memorial building indicated that remodeling was unlikely to be even remotely cost-effective.

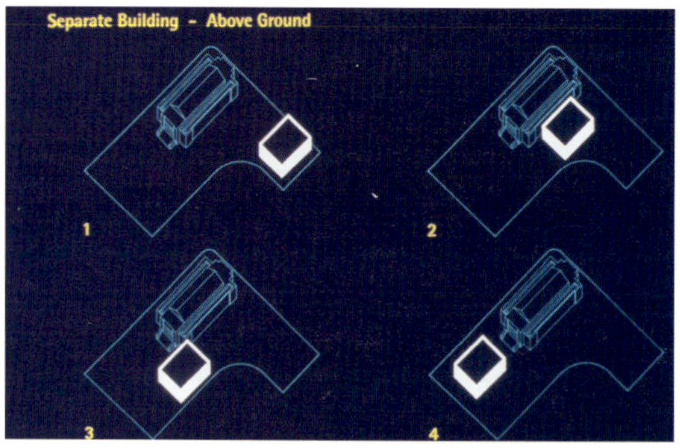

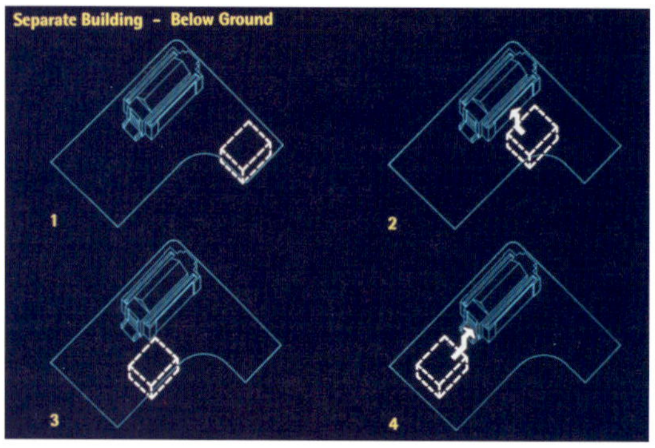

ABOVE: The shape of Joslyn's grounds suggested four basic possibilities, above and below ground, each with their own limitations. The underground approach was abandoned because of the difficulty of making easy public access from the new building to the old without disrupting functional lower level spaces. Also, a serious lack of documentation on the site's history made extensive excavation something of a gamble.

Also, an underground building would have to be linked to the Memorial by at least two tunnels; probably, as at the National Gallery in Washington, D.C., one for the public and the other for service. Finally, there were no reliable records of the surrounding property owned by Joslyn – land that used to be a residential area intersected by Capitol Avenue and 22nd Street. There was no knowing for certain what network of utilities, functioning or abandoned, and old structures lay beneath the ground.

Moving fully above ground, the relationship of the new structure both in terms of form and function became paramount. A detached building would necessarily duplicate many of the features of the existing structure – entry lobbies, security points, and so on – while still leave unaddressed the problem of access from one to the other. Prior feasibility studies had favored a building set off to the northeast, toward Central High School, and linked to the existing building by a glass walkway that penetrated at the northeastern-most gallery; a solution that had the net effect of turning precious gallery space into yet another lobby. A second free-standing building also highlighted the distinct architectural context that had to be addressed; with two historic and much-loved structures in the vicinity – the Beaux-Arts school and the Art Deco museum – the style of a third building became of paramount consideration. What exactly should it look like and how would it relate to the other two? To contrive a building that somehow resembled the original Joslyn Memorial ran the risk of diluting its distinctive character; anything very modern could be jarring.

Foster and his team returned to their original analysis of the brief. For over a decade visitors had been directed to approach the building from the west by car, park, and

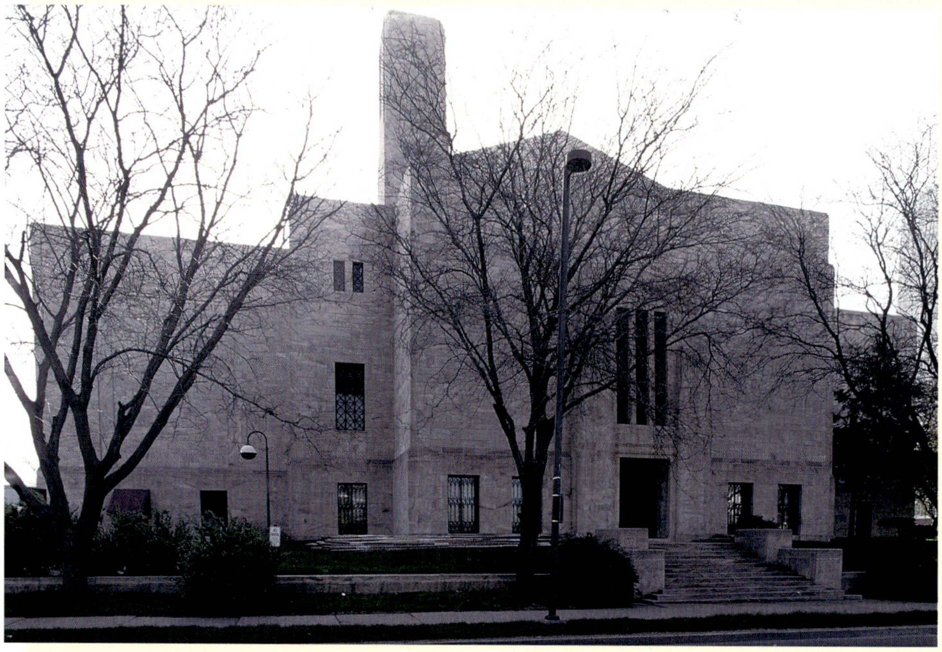

Foster realized early on that the northwest corner of the building (left area of photo), with its long history of utilitarian use and the more domestic scale of the west facade, offered a chink in the otherwise monumental, apparently seamless architecture of the Memorial building.

enter through the north door that led directly to the lower level. Foster wished to give back to the grand east entrance its original emphasis. By the same token, they had realized that the seamless-looking temple structure was open to manipulation at the west end – especially the north corner. Three of the four facades are characterized by imposing formal elements: a massive portico on the east; long, assertively blank walls on the north and south. The west end is curiously different in both scale and detail. In plan, the wall plane breaks in and out several times, creating a small-scale, domestic feeling. Years before, a loading dock had been added and trees planted to obscure the service nature of this corner of the building. In short, this was the fulcrum on which the addition turned. By starting the design in this area with such functional facilities as loading docks, it was possible to take advantage of the busy (and sometimes untidy) aspects of the architecture and activity without unduly disrupting the integrity and history of the original structure. Other back-room facilities – kitchen, art storage, staff offices – as well as such public facilities as restrooms and coat check, could be added at the lower level as the new building progressed east, and spacious galleries could be placed on the floor above.

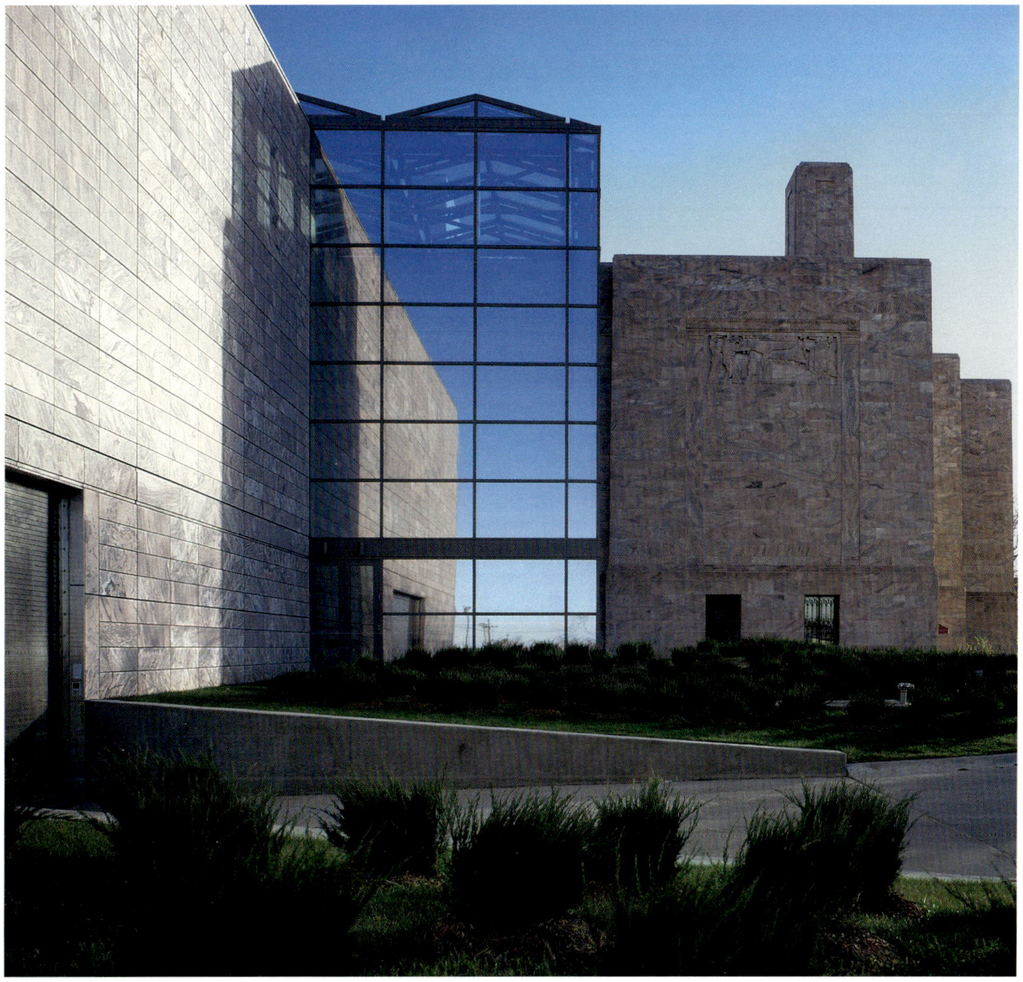

The north and west faces of the glass atrium and the new building continue the rhythm of the Memorial's west facade.

By building forward from the northwest corner, traditionally a service area, and linking the new structure to the old with a long atrium, Foster created a compact and respectful solution that, functionally as well as stylistically, seemed to defer to the original building.

From the beginning Foster was convinced that, were it still available, the only sensible material to use for an addition was the same Etowah Fleuri marble used on the Memorial building. In a radical departure from his signature high-tech style, and building on his experience at the Royal Academy, he had proposed a solid rectangular form, minimally articulated but similarly proportioned, and parallel – a shadow, as it were – to the original building, to which it would be linked by a great glass room, or atrium, running almost the full length of the old north facade. The new wing deferred to the spirit of the original design, upstaging it, if at all, by taking its monumental simplicity several modernistic steps further.

The glass atrium solved several problems. On the aesthetic level it firmly but sensitively united the two buildings without causing undue alteration to the essential profile of the older one. On a functional level it provided a bright, potentially lively space for a café and public circulation at the very heart of the design and, very importantly, gave direct, unimpeded access to both buildings from the parking lot.

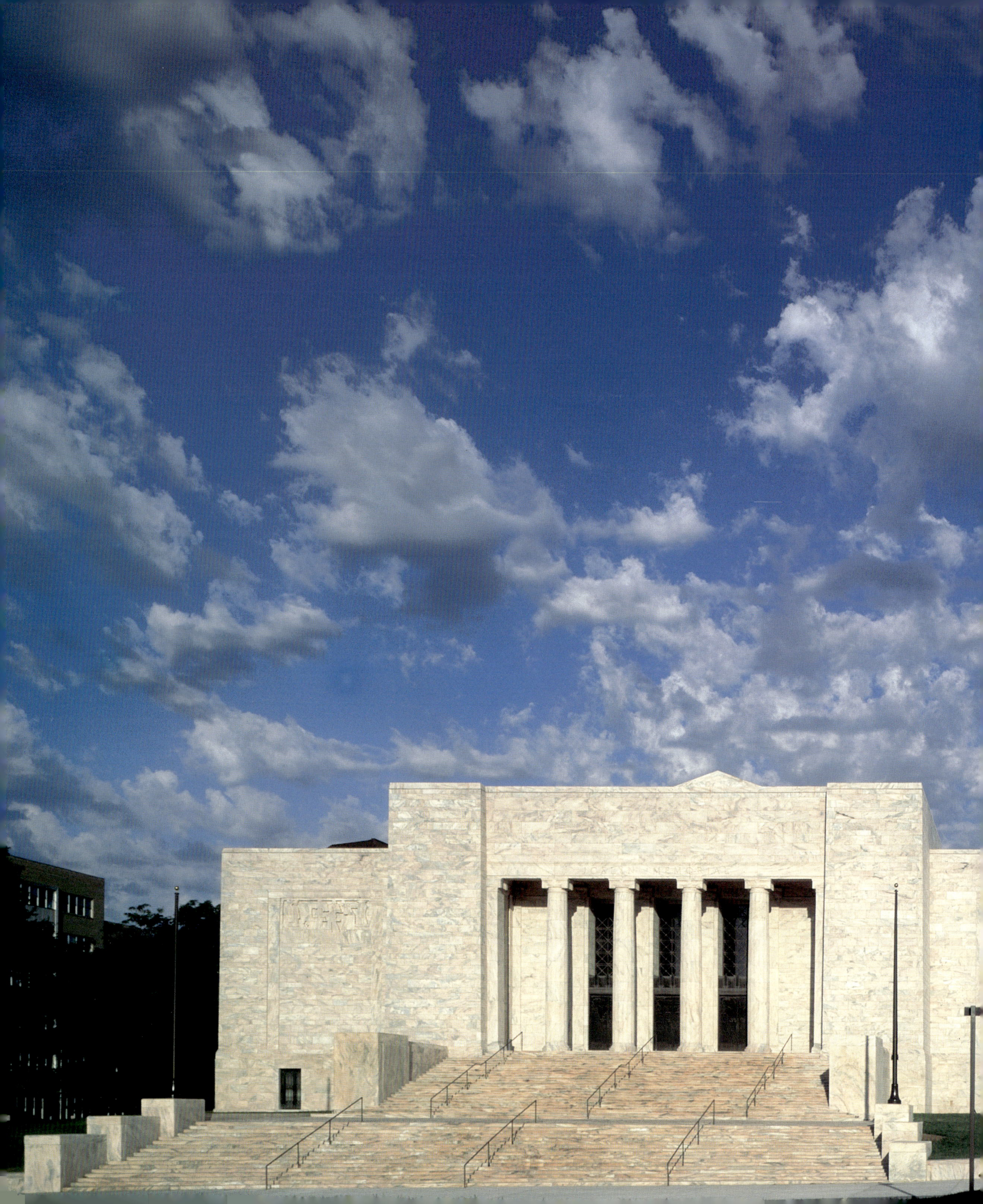

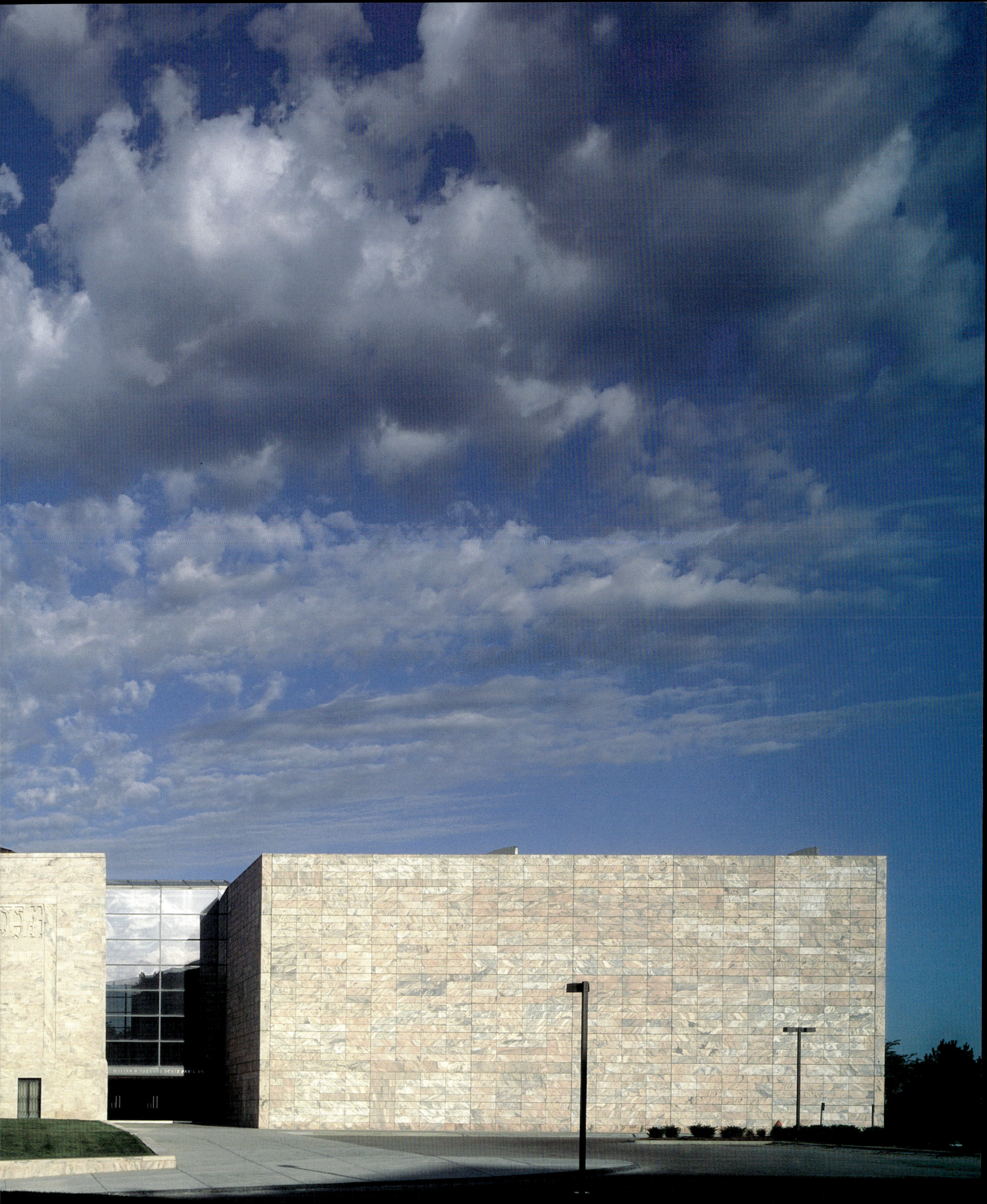

the DEVELOPMENT *of a* DESIGN

In commencing the detailed design, the first decision involved the size and proportions of the addition, a decision very much driven by features of the Memorial building and the configuration of the site.

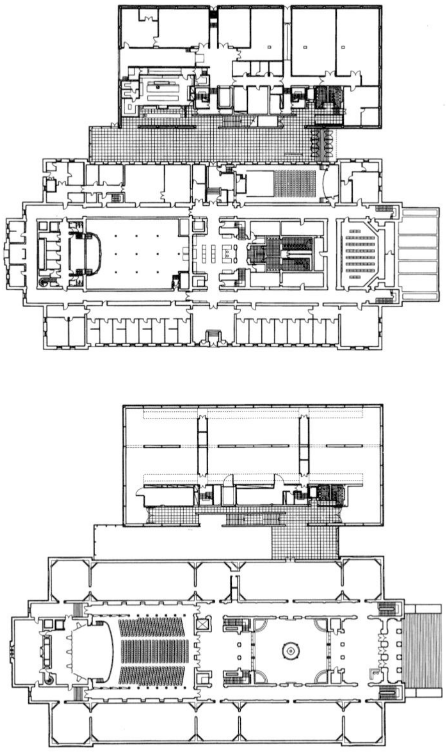

ABOVE: The newly configured Joslyn Art Museum lower and main levels. The site plan (BELOW) shows the relation of the building to the new parking lots to the north and east, linked by a service road, as well as the reshaped lawn to the east of the original building.

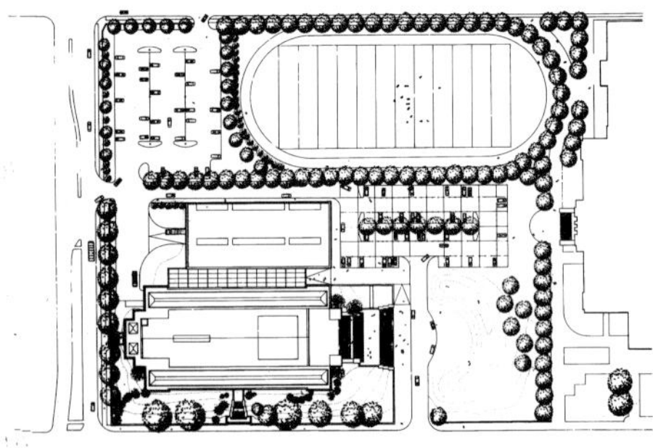

Never under serious question was the relationship of the new building's east facade to that of the old one – set back from the plane of the portico at the location of the side pylons. The length of the atrium, too, was a given, determined by the length of the Memorial building's north wall. The break forward at each end of the long wall, where it meets the pylons, constituted the only logical place to insert the atrium's glass walls.

Two footprints for the addition were explored. One, longer and narrower, yielded a more symmetrical plan, with the new building capturing the atrium completely; the other, shorter and wider, allowed the glass atrium to project beyond the western end of the new marble structure. The adoption of the second solution was partly driven by the increased efficiencies known to derive from rectangular plans, whereby the more a plan approaches a square, the better its use of space is likely to be. Of equal significance was the sense that, in visual terms, a more interesting west end was likely to result with the breaking back of the atrium to meet the west end of the addition, echoing the faceting of the Memorial building's west facade. The glass would also reflect the surfaces of both buildings while, at the same time, provide glimpses of the same materials on the interior.

The requirement for a road to link the proposed new east parking lot to the overflow lot on the north effectively dictated the northern boundary of the building (experiments with a tunnel were quickly abandoned for reasons of cost as well as the architectural incongruities they caused); the need for an atrium wide enough to accommodate large social gatherings roughly set the southern boundary. Even so, the final dimensions of the atrium reflected Foster's determination to create a space with something of the dramatic tension of the light well at the Royal Academy.

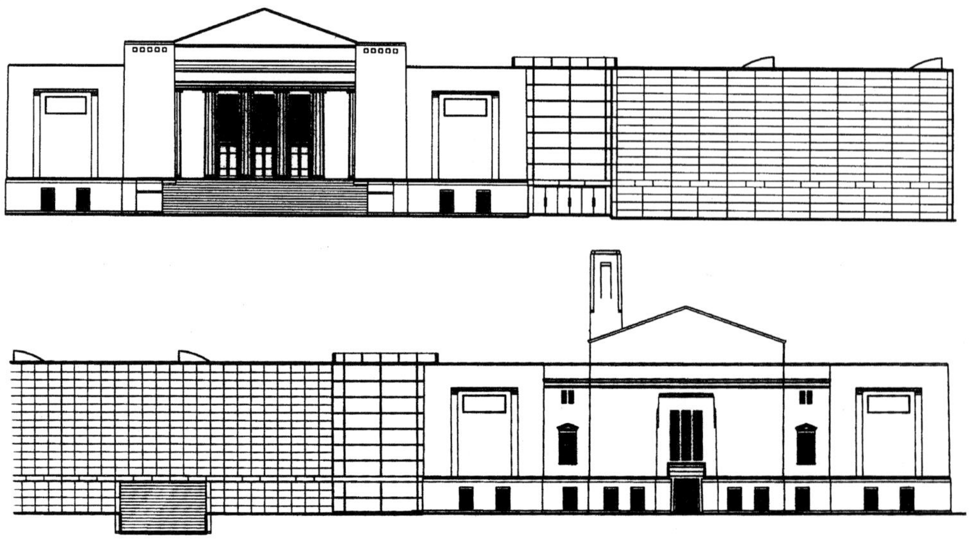

East and west elevations of the new complex. Skylight segments peek over the curtain wall of the addition, hinting at the art galleries below. The abstract, gridlike pattern of the new walls contrast distinctly with the historicizing, almost geological nature of the Joslyn Memorial's facades.

THE LOWER LEVEL

The decision to put the new galleries at the same level as the existing ones, also something of a given, demanded that the lower level of the new building be below grade – again echoing the Memorial. Fortunately, the headroom in the lower level of the McDonalds' building was ample, so there was no need to excavate any deeper than they had in order to meet the practical requirements of those working with the often oversized art of the late twentieth century.

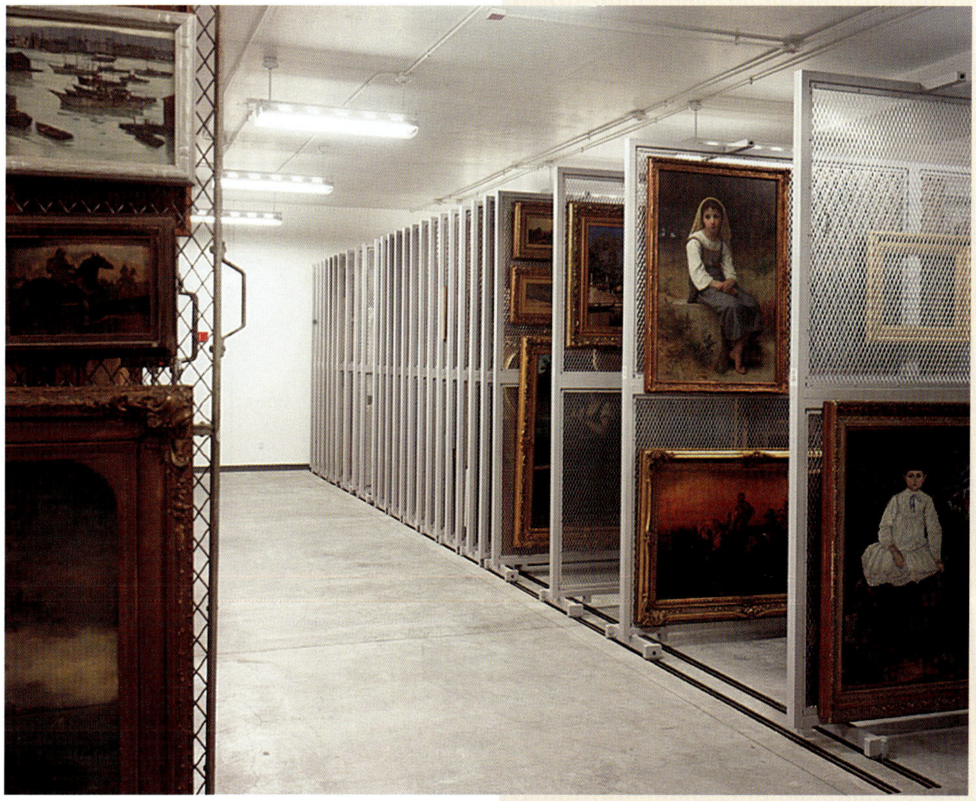

The storage area for two-dimensional works is one of two equally sized art vaults in the addition. On the right are new "moving aisle" painting racks. Those on the left are recycled from the original vault.

Storage

On the lower level is storage for the Museum's collections: two similarly proportioned rooms, each approximately 2,100 square feet. Next to the art storage rooms is the Collections and Exhibitions Department office suite. (Two additional storage areas – one for large, generally twentieth-century works of art, the other for exhibition furniture – are located on the main level adjacent to the galleries.)

Loading Dock

No amount of renovation in the original building could accommodate up-to-date facilities for the handling and storage of art – that of Joslyn's own collections as well as those objects borrowed for special exhibitions – and the emphasis on new construction was constantly reinforced by practical requirements and modern professional standards. In the finished plan, an interior loading dock, capable of accommodating the largest standard tractor-trailer, is immediately adjacent to large rooms for receiving (unpacking and crating), temporary storage, and exhibition preparation, as well as the art elevator. Access to each of these facilities is under the direct surveillance of a security booth.

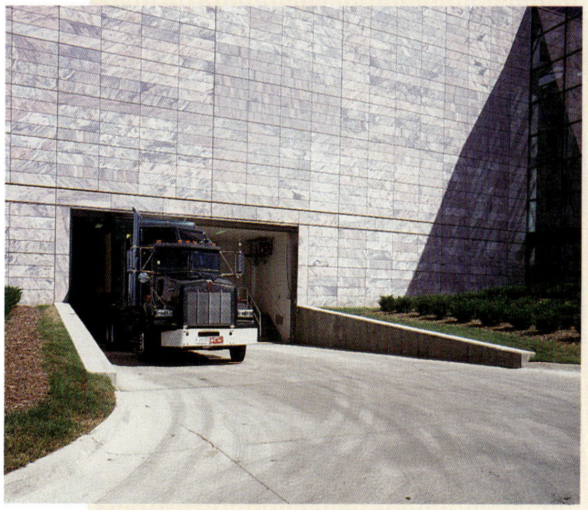

The covered loading dock affords full protection to works of art, whatever the season.

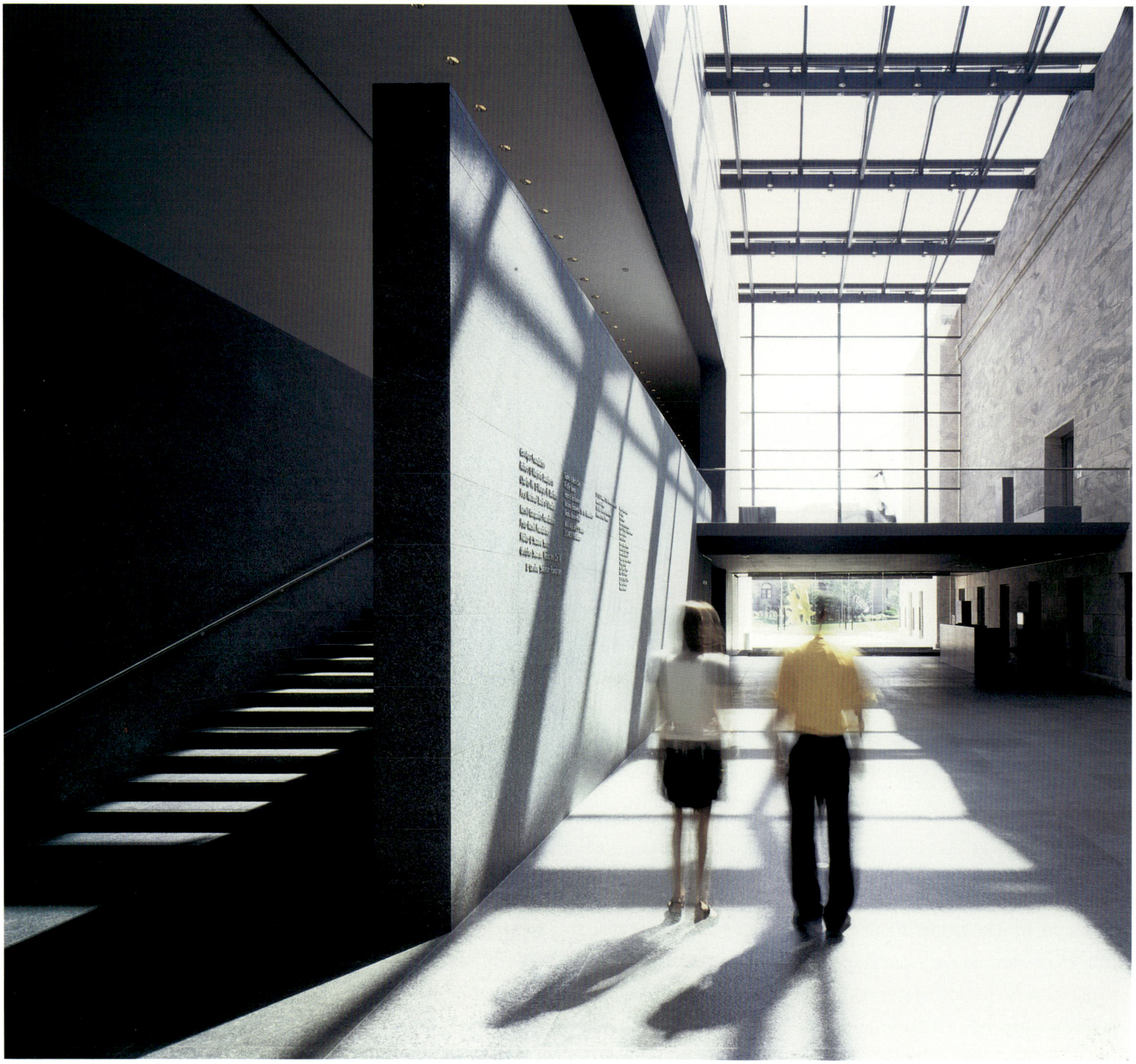

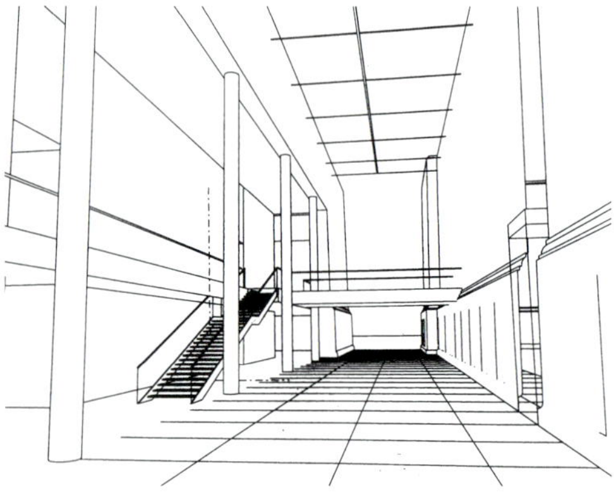

The final appearance of the atrium was only arrived at after exploring a wide range of possibilities, including a variety of staircase configurations and placing the floor at the same grade as the lower level of the Memorial building. The solid stone staircase with its high rectilinear walls was preferred as being more in keeping with the monumental quality of the two main buildings, as well as more clearly separating social and artistic spaces. The atrium floor was left at the existing level to retain the proportions of the McDonalds' design of the north facade.

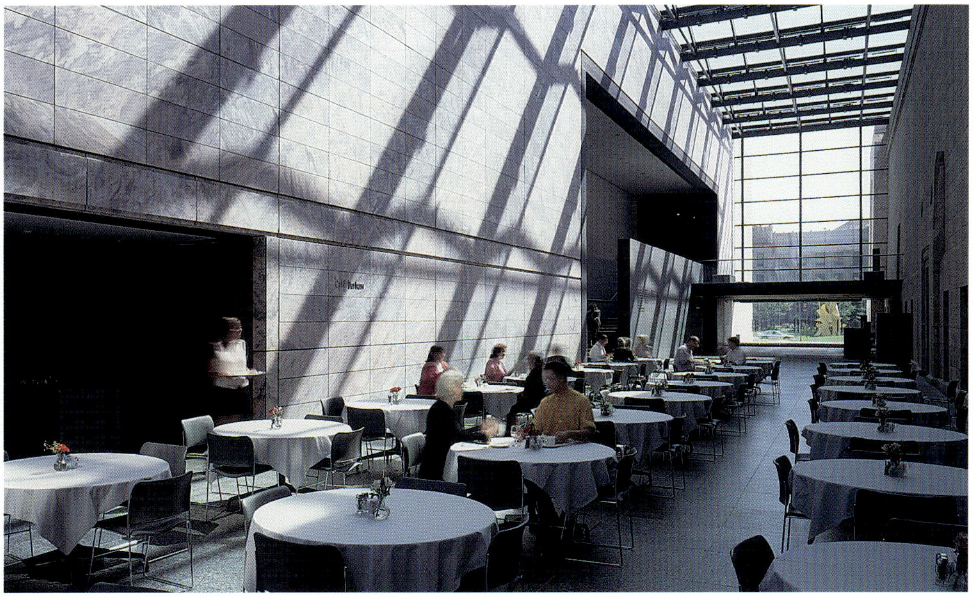

The atrium, featuring the café, is designed as a "main street" and functions as a public area, providing ample space for social functions as well as a departure point for the art galleries to the north and south.

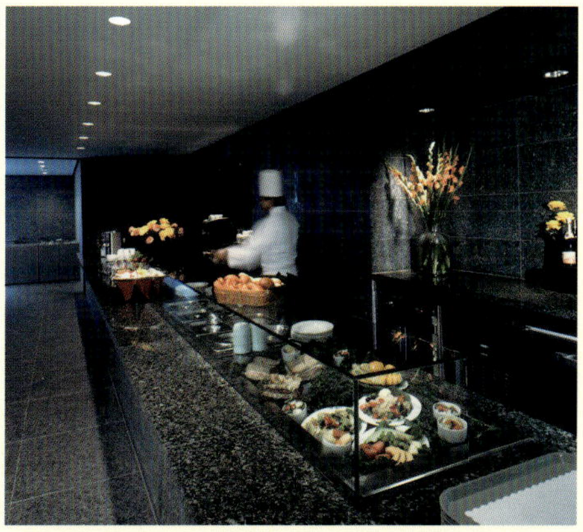

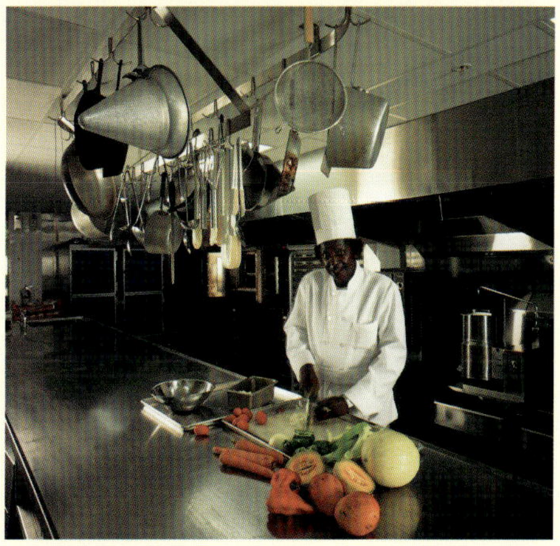

Providing buffet service at lunch, the enclosed servery (TOP) also is used as a staging area for more formal events. Behind it is a fully equipped kitchen (ABOVE) with its own loading dock.

THE ATRIUM

Conceived of as a transparent link between the old and new buildings, the atrium fulfills the functions of entrance, meeting place, and crossroads; a grand and light-filled social space leading to the more contemplative galleries on each side. At the west end of the atrium is the café, seating 120 people, alongside which, in the new building, is the kitchen. An early notion that the museum shop might be placed in the center of the atrium was abandoned because of the need for space for additional seating during the many social functions held at the Museum. The shop is situated immediately through the door in the south wall of the atrium (the "old" north door of the Joslyn Memorial).

The Bridge

As well as providing a bird's-eye view of the atrium, the bridge fulfills a number of crucial functions. Most obviously, it links, on one level, the old and new galleries; a feature greatly to the advantage of the visitor, who would otherwise be obliged to follow complicated directions from one building to the other. Although not an easy decision, the practical benefits outweighed reservations over cutting into the north wall of the Memorial building. Set into this wall on axis with the fountain, a double glass door provides a view from the bridge through the fountain court to the south wall of the original galleries. By running the bridge all the way to the east curtain wall, the architects were able to conceal the airlock double doors of the atrium's entrance and also create a compressed entry space in dramatic contrast with the main body of the atrium. The bridge also serves as a reception space, as well as an auxiliary dining area.

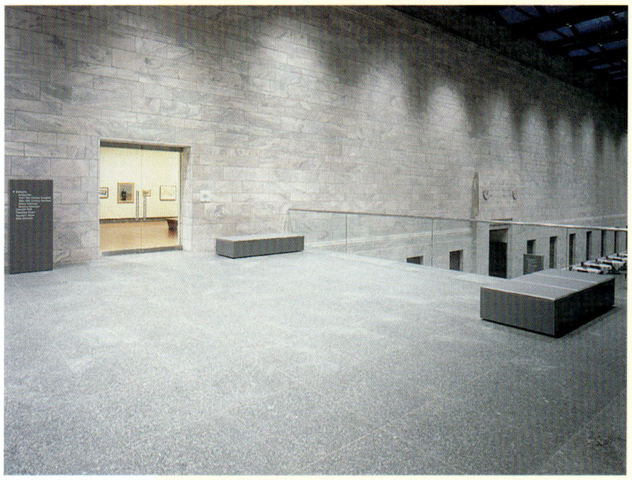

The bridge fulfills many functions: a convenient connection between the old and the new galleries; part of a dramatic north/south vista; a secondary reception or dining area.

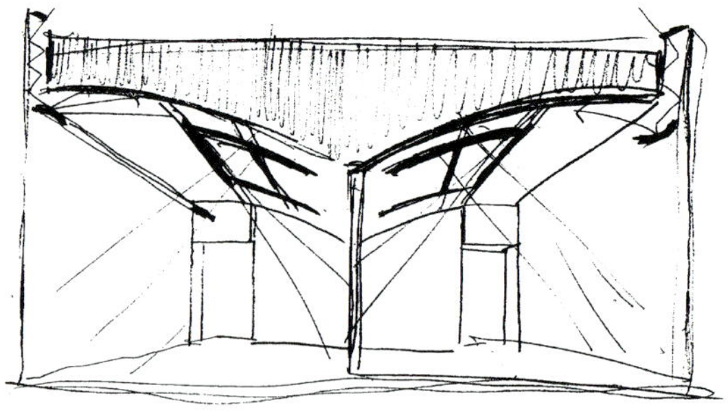

Initial gallery designs (ABOVE) proposed a shallow cove roof, deriving from Foster's earlier work at the Royal Academy. The desire for something more expressive led to the soaring "gull-wing" configuration of the final designs (BELOW).

THE MAIN LEVEL

Very early designs showed the galleries occupying the eastern two-thirds of the main floor, with the western third given over to utilitarian spaces. As the floor plan developed in coordination with the atrium, the logic of running functional – that is to say, non-display – spaces along the southern third of the new building became apparent. By placing the heating, ventilating, and air conditioning on a mezzanine high above the main floor, both atrium and art galleries could be serviced from the same space. Below, a narrower "spine" containing a variety of functional spaces (including spacious storage areas for exhibition furniture and large works of art) would also act as a sound and light trap separating the lively, general-purpose atrium from the contemplative, specialized art galleries.

To accommodate Joslyn's collection of contemporary art, as well as the variable needs of special exhibitions, the architects were asked to provide tall, flexible gallery spaces. Early designs proposed symmetrical rooms with shallow, coved ceilings split down the center by skylights. In the process of establishing the general character of the galleries

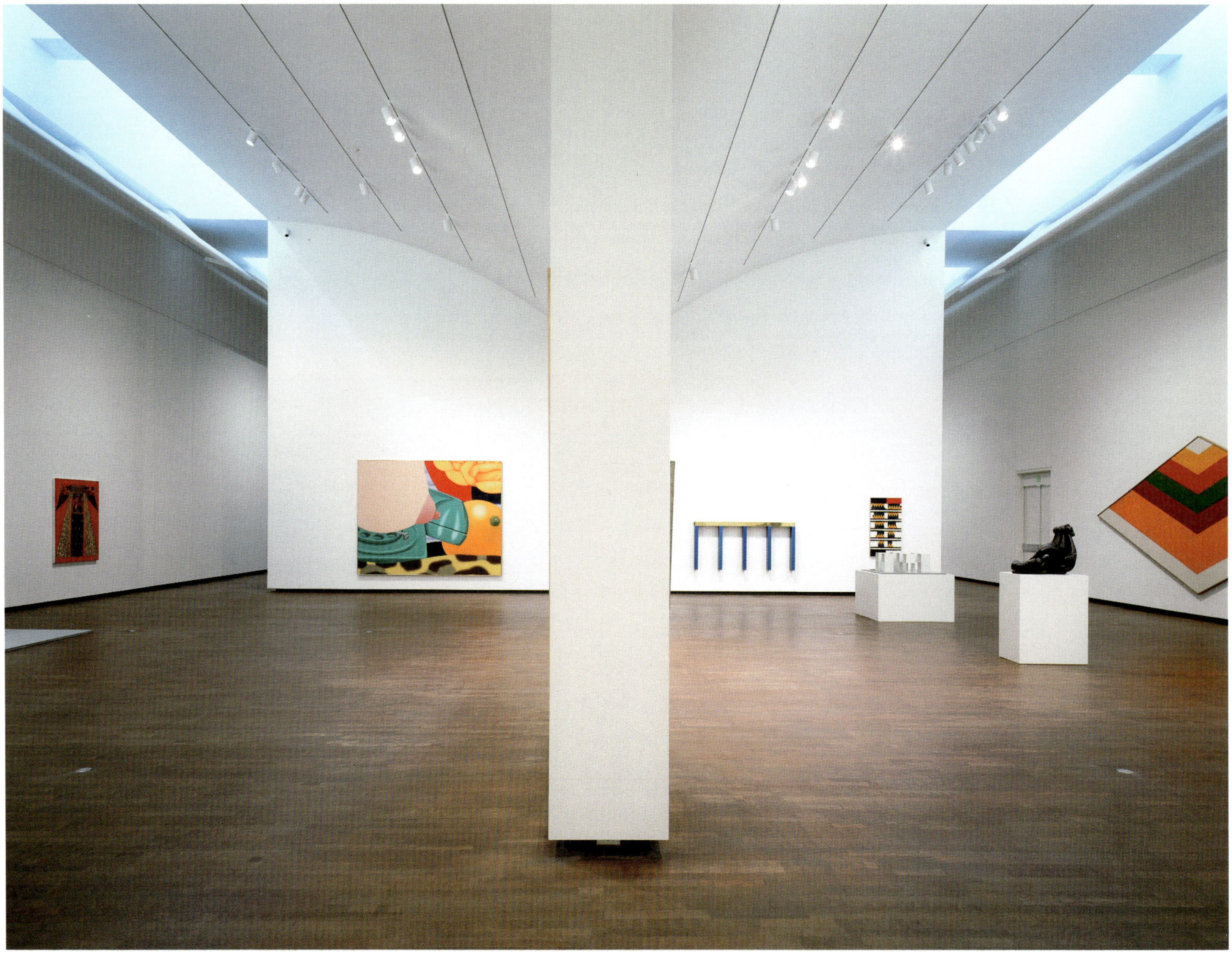

and how they would be serviced, form and function combined to determine the final configuration and exact appearance.

The desire to have the exhibition walls as uncluttered with utilitarian features – notably outlets and vents – as possible led to the decision to have a reveal running all the way around the base of the walls, where much of the heating, cooling, and power-related fittings could be concealed. Originally, the air was to be conditioned from vents in the wide walls separating the galleries on the north/south axis but, as the logic of the hidden mezzanine developed, it became more economical to deliver air through the narrower, east/west walls. The wide walls, now hollow, became storage compartments for temporary walls and other exhibition furniture. At the same time the engineering problems were being addressed, the architects, dissatisfied with the somewhat straightforward gallery ceilings, were seeking something more expressive. In the final design, dynamic asymmetry is contained within symmetry. It is as if one suite of galleries had been split down the long axis, enlarged, and reversed into a "gull-wing" configuration with the skylights perched at the top extremity of each cove.

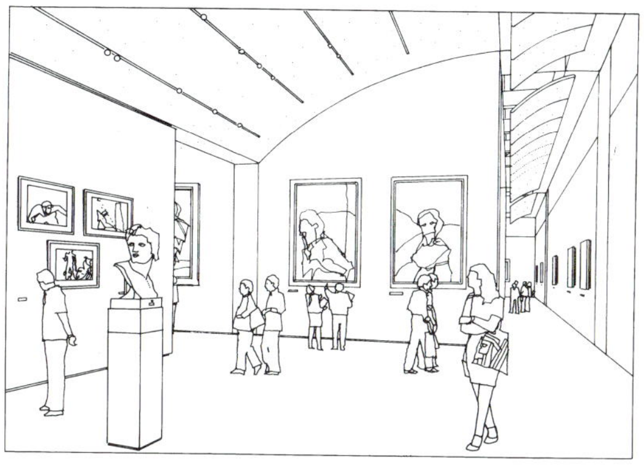

In the finished galleries, utilities are confined to narrow strips at ceiling level, as in the vent (UPPER LEFT AREA OF PHOTO BELOW) or the reveals at floor level. Wall and floor surfaces are virtually unencumbered for anything but the display of art.

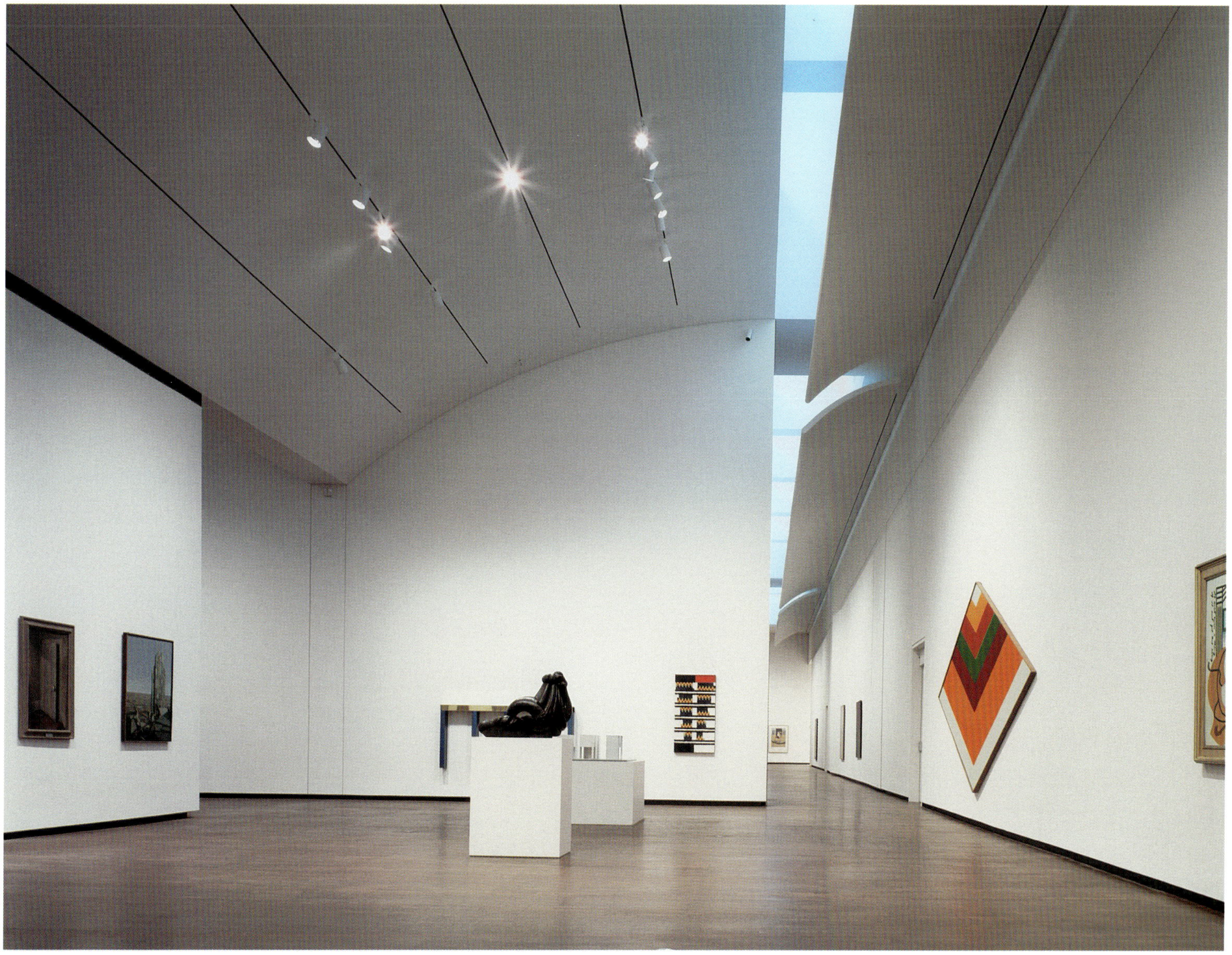

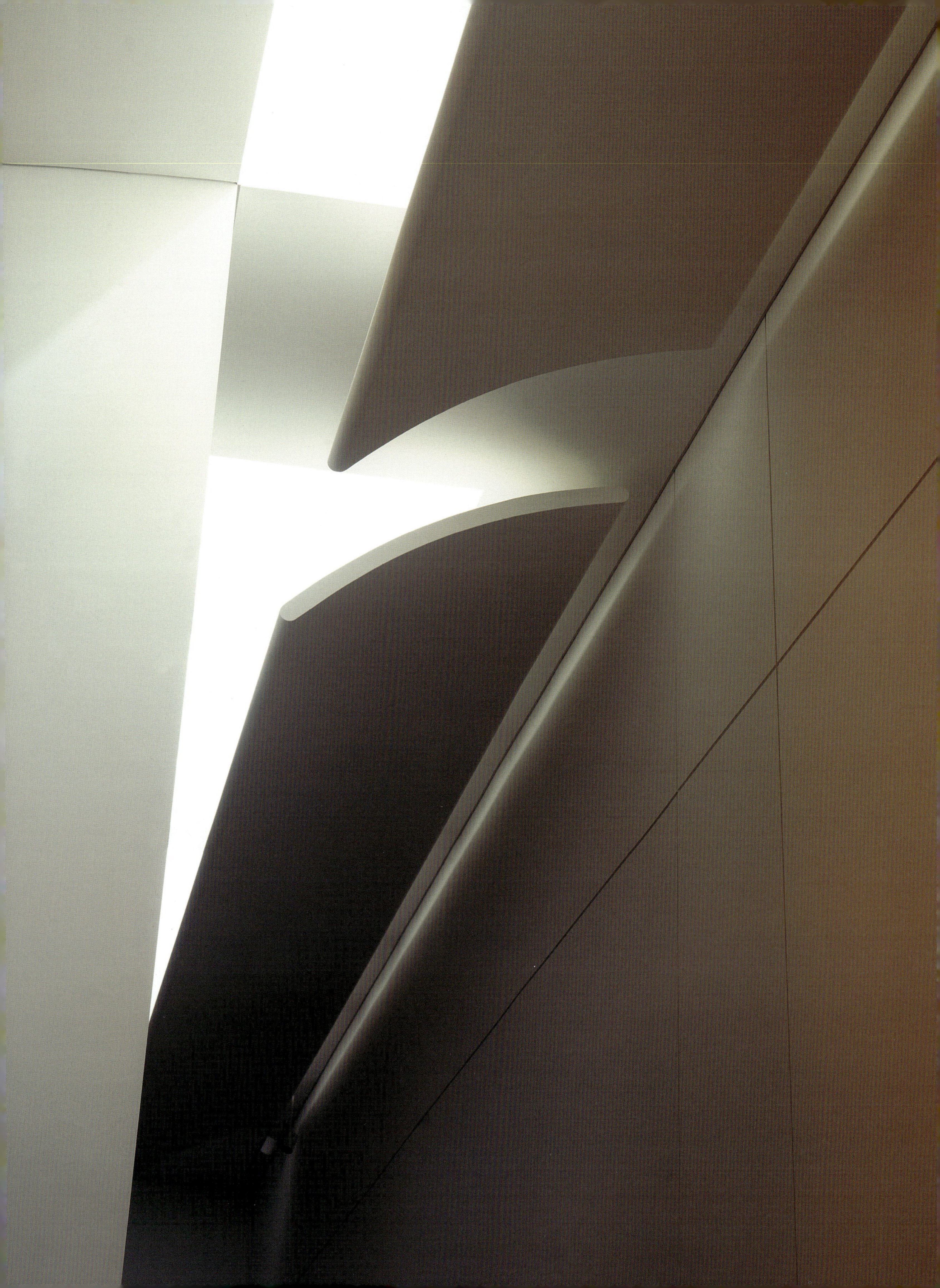

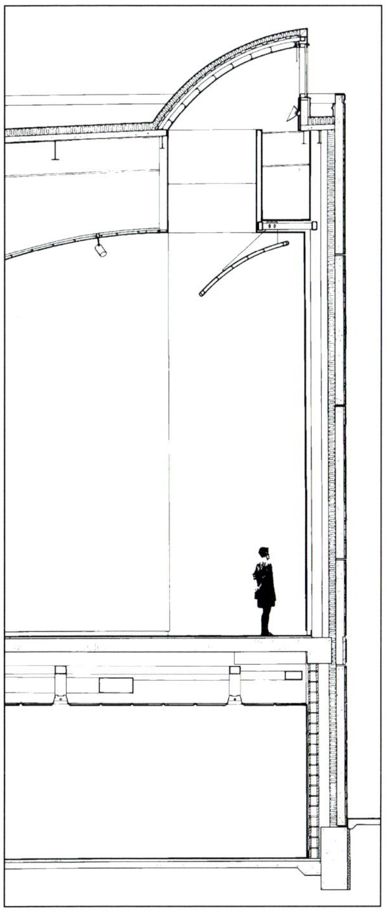

The Skylights

The skylights face north on top of a twelve-foot-deep well. Light coming in bounces two or three times before reflecting off a long aerofoil form onto the curved ceiling and infusing the gallery space. Should exhibition conditions demand minimal light levels, the area of the skylights can be reduced or eliminated by manually closing blinds from a catwalk built into the light well. Exhibition lighting is provided from tracks running parallel to the long axes of the galleries. At night, or when the blinds are closed, the ceiling can be washed by fluorescent lights concealed in the catwalks.

While it is a sad fact that, for conservation reasons, daylight is often conspicuous by its absence in exhibitions of art, Foster found the idea of designing galleries without at least the possibility of daylight unpalatable. Art, he pointed out, is ultimately about light; to exclude it altogether would have an unhappy symbolism.

THE MATERIALS

The Marble

Although there was no shortage of Etowah Fleuri marble from the same quarry that had supplied the original building, selecting the finish posed its own problems. The sixty-year-old Memorial had weathered considerably, long ago losing the crystalline white of its hand-hammered finish in favor of its natural burnished pink, mellowed by the impurities found in the air of every major urban area. It was possible to imitate the original finish mechanically, but a new, whitish building would have looked unconvincing and incongruous to an admiring public accustomed to the soft, warm tones of the older building. Furthermore, the aged marble changes color depending on the ambient light and humidity and, while a more highly polished new marble would sparkle with the saturated colors of wet stone, it would age more slowly (if at all) in these less industrially polluted times. Inside the atrium, there would be no comparable aging process at all. A compromise finish, known as 120 grit, was selected: a surface polished enough to share coloristic and textural qualities with the older marble yet porous enough to age sooner rather than later.

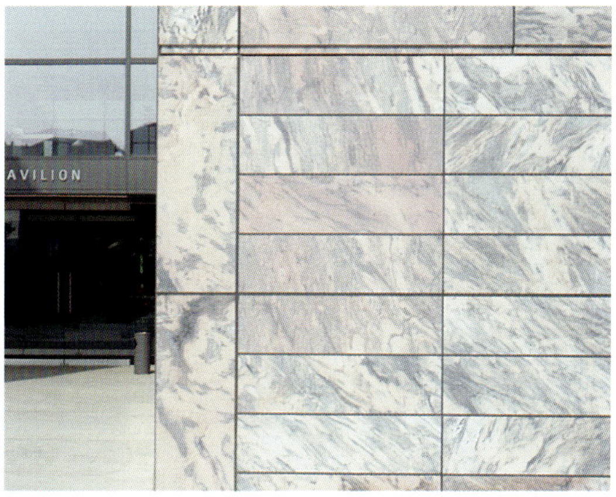

The extremely variegated color of the Etowah Fleuri marble from Georgia – the same material used in the 1931 Memorial – proved to be a nice foil to Foster's rectilinear style.

The exterior of the Memorial building consists of a thick veneer of marble blocks laid like masonry over massively thick brick walls, a building technique as old as the monuments of Egypt (which the structure so poetically evokes) and owing little or

OPPOSITE: Back-lit by the skylights some ten feet above them, the gently curved, light-deflecting baffles seem to hover in place.

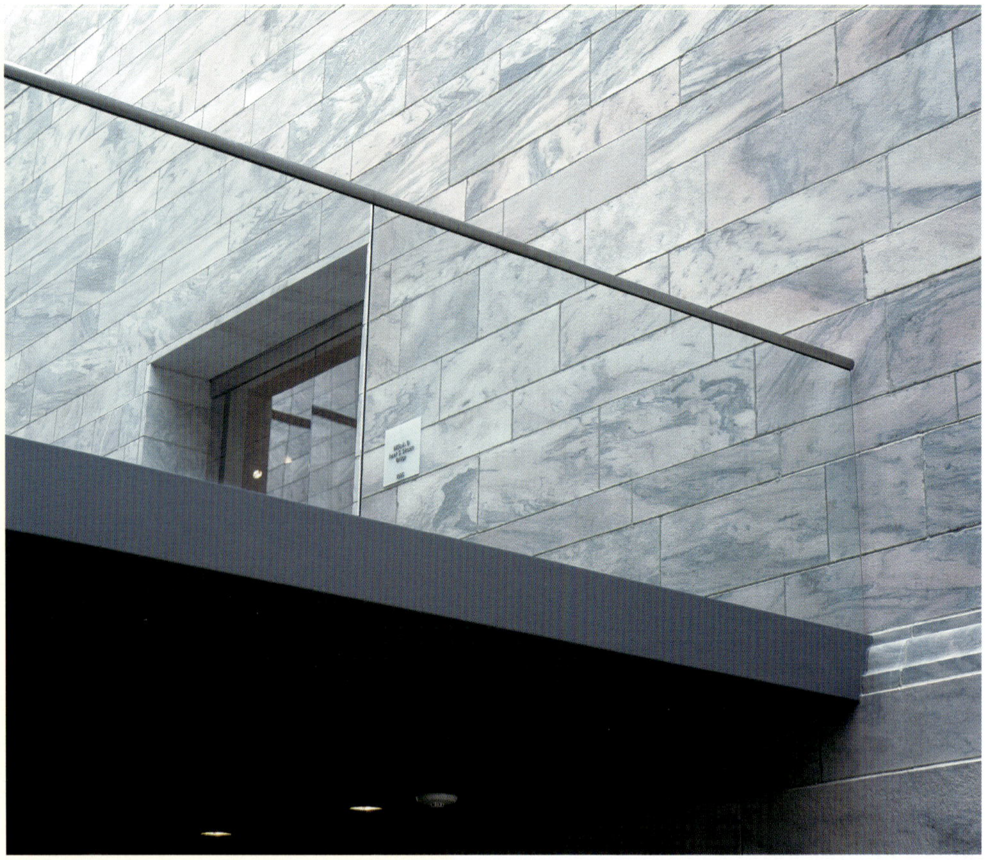

nothing to the innovations of nineteenth- or twentieth-century engineering. Even Brcin's relief carving reinforces the notion that the Memorial is virtually hewn out of the living rock. The new building, by contrast, is a marble skin stretched over a steel framework, and Foster designed the minimal articulation of its exterior to reflect the bare bones of its construction. Relying upon the idiosyncratic pink marble to create a coat of many colors, and echoing the string-course on the original building, the architect drew a horizontal band around the new building to denote the location of the main floor. Surfaces above and below were divided into a grid of intersecting vertical and horizontal lines that, as anyone who has played with bricks as a child knows, cannot be structural. The vertical intervals on the band signifying the main floor are different from those of the wall panels above and below; where they coincide indicates the location of structural steel columns. (See elevations, page 83.)

Thin steel tubes on top of vertical glass panels make up the barriers on the bridge and above the west end of the grand staircase.

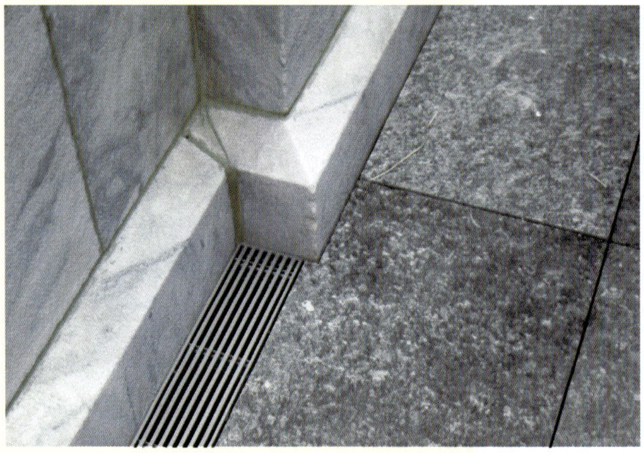

The Steel

Steel is among the most noticeable materials used in the atrium, where its structural purpose is also apparent. Equally important in the new building, its use there is concealed by the pink marble skin. To express the crucial role played by steel, the architects framed the great aperture in the south wall of the addition with a post and lintel made from an I-beam of giant proportions. (See pages 85 and 86.)

The Granite

Vermont Green slate is featured in the foyer floors of the original building, and a similar material was selected for the atrium floors as well as for the secondary walls in the addition. The barely perceptible green cast of this Brazilian Verde Lavras granite sets up a subtle contrast with the pink of the marble while, at the same time, complementing the flat gray of the painted steel.

Verde Lavras, a green granite from Brazil, was chosen for the atrium floor and grand staircase as a gentle contrast to the pink marble of the walls; it also echoes the green Vermont slate used in the Memorial building.

The Galleries

The walls in the gallery are finished in plasterboard, to be treated – usually painted – in accordance with the art on exhibition. Pairs of three-quarter-inch reveals defining the display surface of the walls create narrow vertical transitional zones for signs and security equipment. Doors are similarly defined, including the enormous panels that give direct access from the freight elevator and two large storage areas.

The floors are finished in a birch wood cross-grain "factory" surface, a forgiving and durable material ideal for the heavy wear and tear common to galleries constantly rearranged for changing exhibitions. The wood is stained walnut, a dark hue that blends into the shadowy reveal, making the walls appear to float.

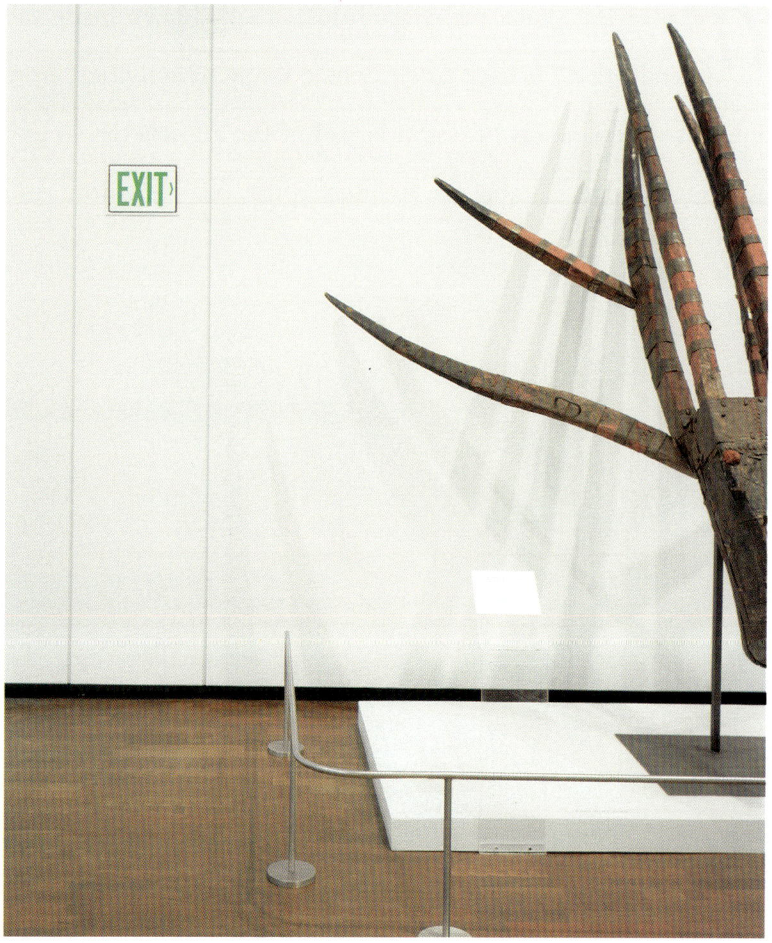

Delicate vertical reveals punctuate the white plaster skin of the gallery walls. In some cases they serve as subliminal boundaries for individual galleries, in others they incorporate functional features ranging from small exit signs (RIGHT) to twenty-foot-high storage and elevator doors. (Special exhibition: *Animals in African Art: From the Familiar to the Marvelous.)*

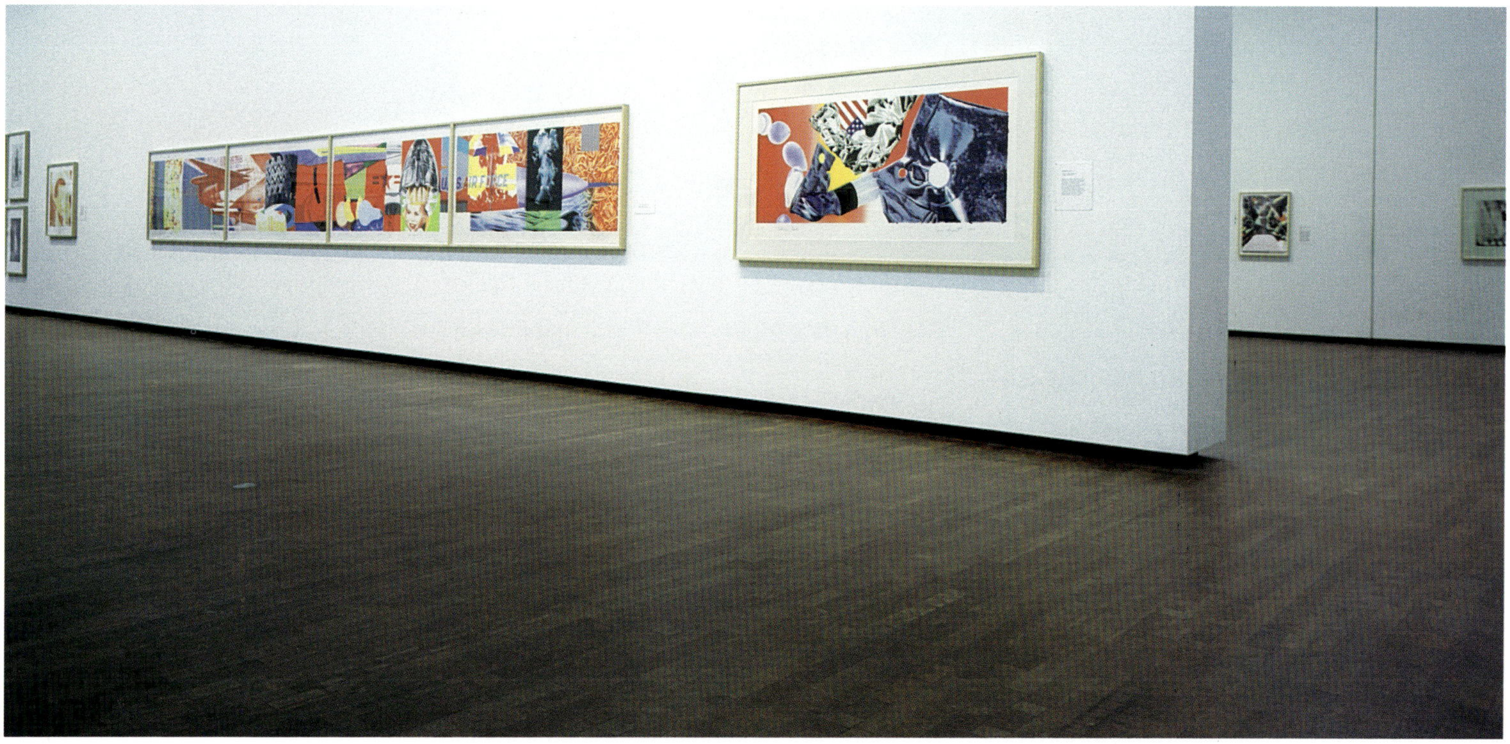

The floor surface of the galleries is end-cut birch, stained walnut. Commonly used for factory flooring in the United States, it is a durable and forgiving surface, easily repaired and kind to visitors' feet. (Special exhibition: *James Rosenquist: Time Dust, Complete Graphics 1962-1992.*)

As, over the years, many modifications had been made to the fabric and spaces of the Joslyn Memorial, the term "renovation" is used to describe a range of activities: from modernizing the grand concert hall and the distinctly less impressive rest rooms to restoring half of the art galleries to their original proportions. As the central public spaces had been well maintained, notably the fountain court, relatively little restoration work had to be done.

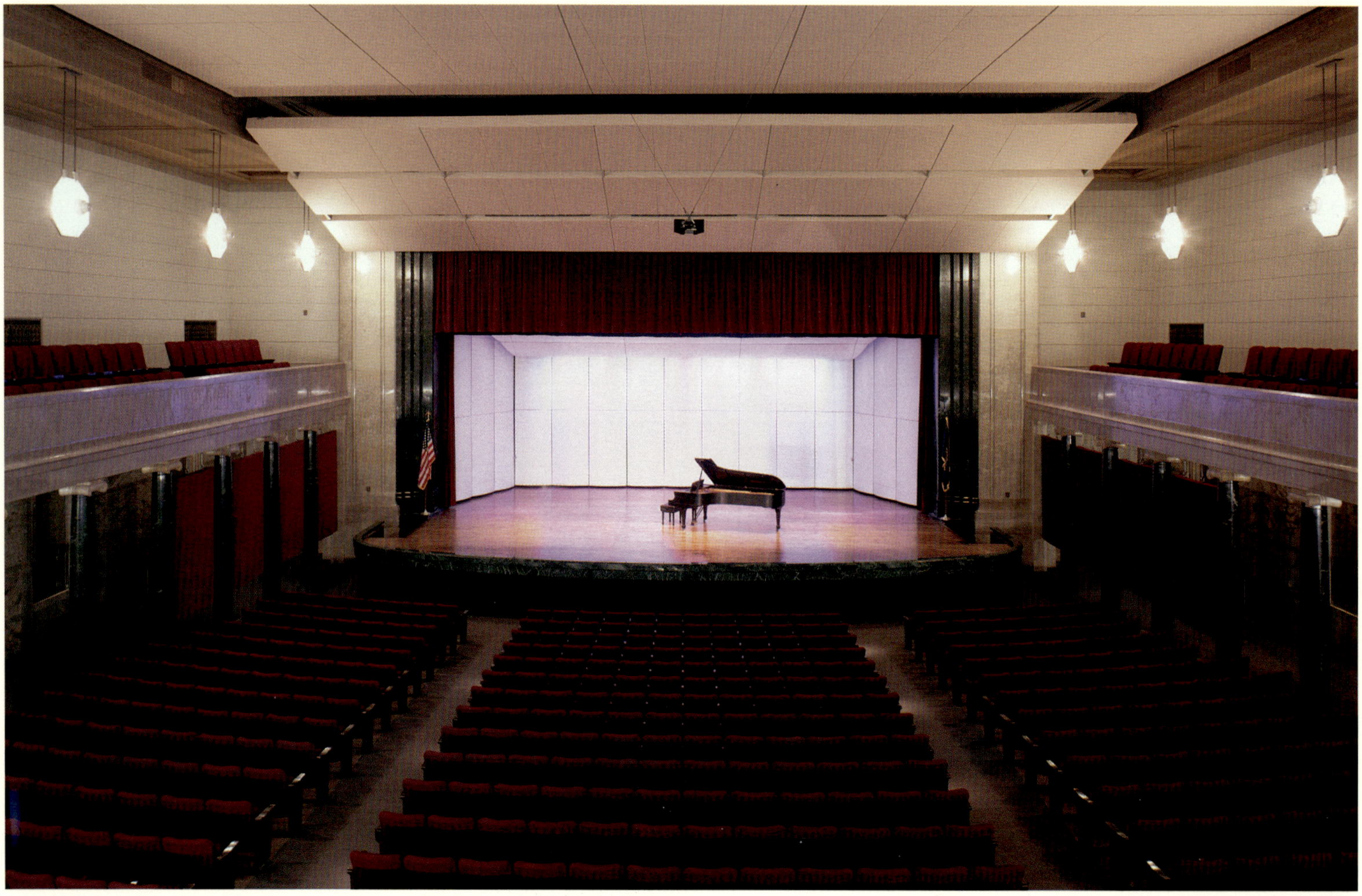

To provide balance to the concert hall's outmoded acoustics, the upper sound-absorbing wall surfaces were encased with plasterboard, and the lower marble walls were muffled with demountable panels. The stage was extended by nearly twenty feet and a portable orchestra shell was fabricated; to this was added an adjustable acoustical panel, suspended from the ceiling.

THE MAIN LEVEL

The Concert Hall

At the time of its design in 1928, the concert hall reflected the current acoustical preference for halls that evoked sound qualities associated with open-air performances. The Guastavino Akoustolith tile was a commercial product designed to simulate the rapid sound decay occurring *en plein air.* On the other hand, in keeping with the rest of the Memorial building, the lower part of the hall was lavishly adorned with some nine different marbles and relief bronze doors that reflect sound and give rise to a curious visual as well as acoustical bifurcation. The hall's distinctive sound qualities were further hampered by the low proscenium arch which, being only seventeen feet high, effectively placed the stage in a different room; no great impediment for theatrical performances, but highly undesirable for concertizing.

In undertaking modernization of this facility, two concerns were paramount: one, that the hall continue to be adaptable to a wide range of activities – from chamber music concerts and dramatic productions to lectures, films, and convocation ceremonies; two, that its original distinctive design characteristics be retained as far as possible.

The unusually low proscenium arch, which the McDonalds disguised by the *tromp l'oeil* device of running an elegant black marble frame up close to the ceiling and hanging a velvet valance beneath, was the result of two factors: the need to provide fly space (vertical storage for scenery) without distorting the templelike exterior of the whole building; and to hide a solid, seven-foot girder running across the building.

While raising the girder in the course of renovation was deemed structurally feasible, the loss of fly space was not, and the decision was made to extend the stage into the house, taking out 164 seats. The provision of a two-part shell – the rear, portable section on stage; the forward pieces lowered from the ceiling – effectively converted the old, two-part hall into the single space required for music concerts without drastically altering its original configuration. Other acoustic treatment included covering the sound-absorbing tiles with plasterboard and the provision of demountable, sound-diffusing panels to cover the rear marble walls during concert performances. A cloth-covered frame suspended below the Akoustolith ceiling presents a seamless surface with the orchestra shell when in its retracted position.

The projection booth was enlarged and a long, sectioned window substituted for the five asymmetrical apertures in the upper east wall. Lighting slots were inserted into the ceiling (to the east of the original slots that had accommodated the organ pipes) and an elevator installed at the back of the stage, permitting the removal of a service elevator that had been constructed in a nearby gallery in 1958.

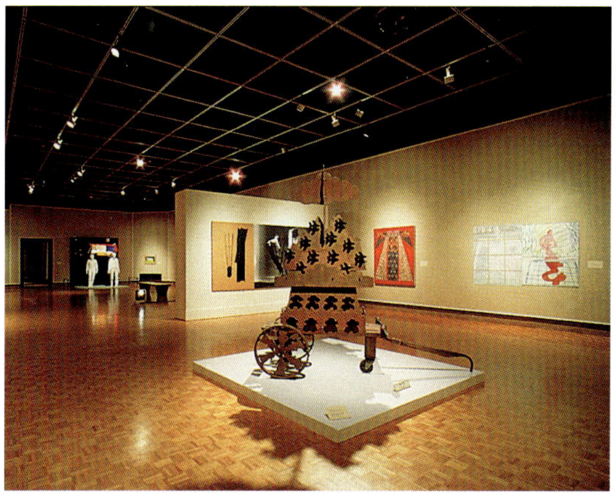

The suspended lighting grid (ABOVE) was removed from the north galleries and the ceilings finished (BELOW) to match the south galleries. The lighting system employed in the addition was also installed throughout the Memorial galleries on the main level.

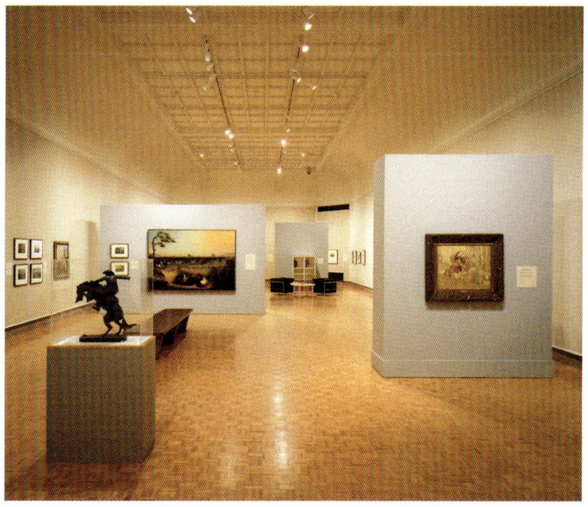

The Galleries

In the early 1970s, lighting conditions in the galleries were extensively modified. Responding to heightened awareness of the need to control light levels, as well as a sudden increase in energy costs, the skylights were closed and insulation installed above the laylights. In the north galleries, where special exhibitions were regularly featured, a lighting grid was suspended below the cove of the ceiling and the area above painted black, creating the anonymous, boxlike spaces generally thought desirable at the time.

As part of the 1983 redesign of the north entrance, an elevator was inserted into a north gallery to give easy access to all floors of the Museum open to the public. Although the long east-west vista was interrupted, this ingenious solution solved so many public and service access problems that it was left undisturbed in the renovation.

In the 1994 remodeling, the suspended grid was removed and light track installed in the mullions of the skylights. Coving and skylights were painted off-white to reclaim something of the flavor of the original design.

THE LOWER LEVEL

The extraordinary nature of the construction of the lower level, with its massive brick walls and duplicated circulation systems, rendered moot the idea of extensive remodeling of most spaces. On the other hand, much tinkering and the wear and tear of six decades had left many areas badly distressed. The northwest wing had undergone the most changes, through the installation of a kitchen, and offered the greatest flexibility in relocating museum functions. In the interests of cost, comfort, and efficiency, it was decided to modernize the lower level without extensive reconfiguration of walls, the notable exception being the public rest rooms which, having been considerably modified in the 1950s, were gutted and refitted to match those in the addition.

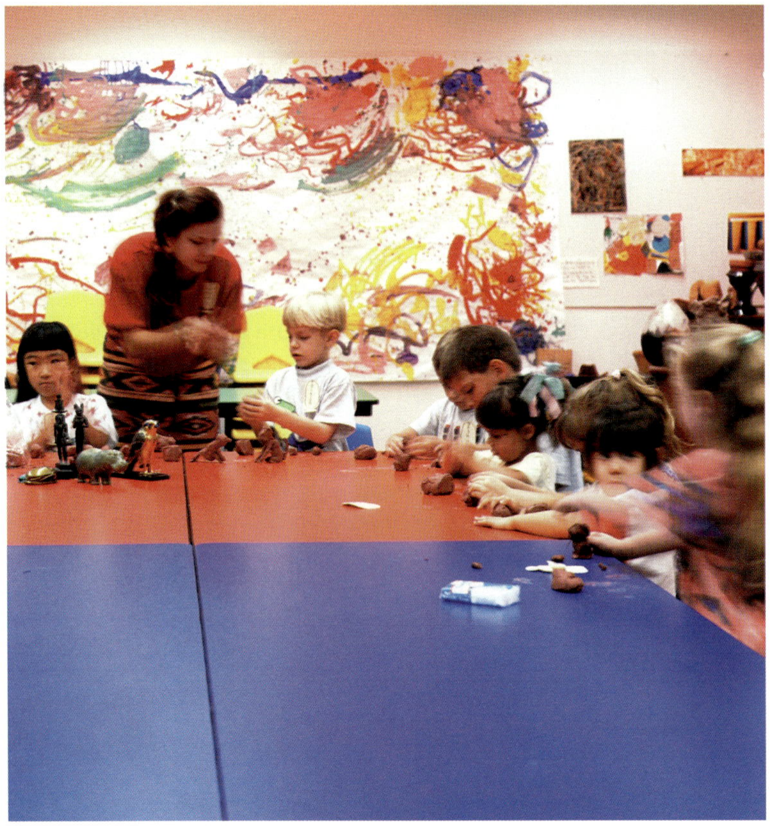

The old art packing and shipping area was remodeled into a classroom for art making and children's activities. The original floor, which was retained, is the same end-cut wood surface used in the new galleries.

The Education Center

Hitherto a combination of offices, receiving room, staff room, kitchen, and (in the public corridor) art display, the northwest area was converted into a continuous suite for the Education Department consisting of two classrooms, a resource room, and exhibition space. Education offices were relocated to rooms at the west end and the capacious corridors redesigned for storage and display of outreach material. As the lecture hall and Center for Western Studies were left in place, the entire west and north sides of the lower level comprise an educational and research facility. Rounding out this function is the northeast corridor and adjoining room, now a gallery dedicated to educationally oriented exhibitions.

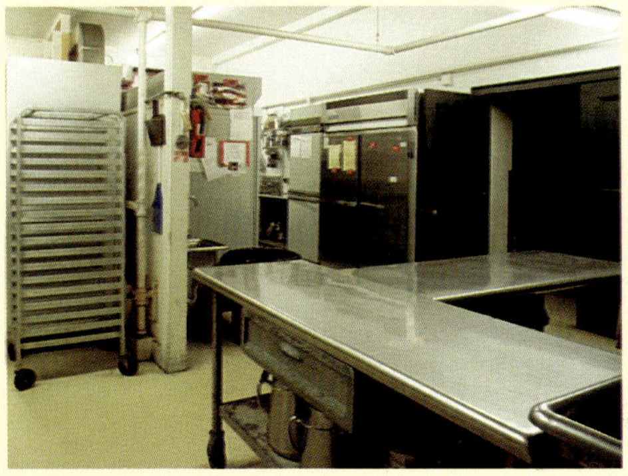

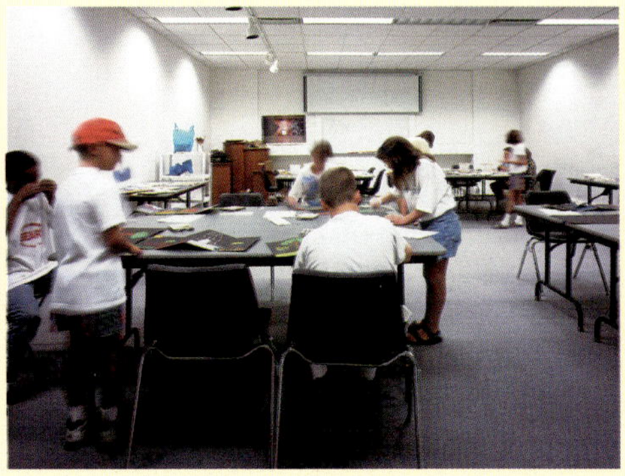

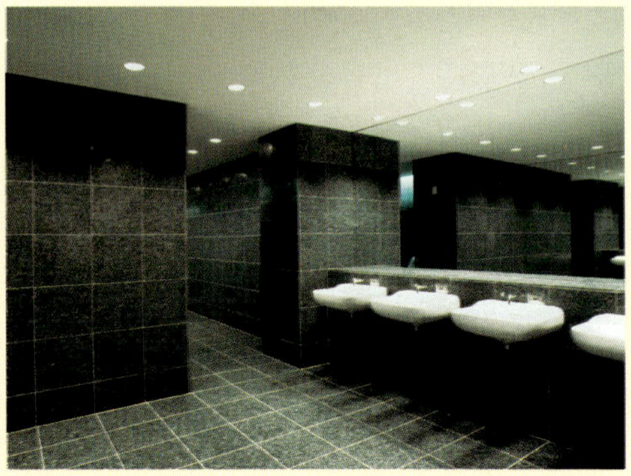

The space occupied by the kitchen (LEFT) was converted into a room for classes and conferences (CENTER) as part of the Education Center. The rest rooms, much altered over the years, were completely remodeled (RIGHT) to match those of the pavilion.

The Art Reference Library

Originally conceived of as occupying the southeast wing of the lower level, over the years the library had actually been confined to the original reading room and one adjacent office. As the book collection grew, shelves filled up the reading room, invaded the southeast office corridor, and took over a storage room below the east steps. In the renovation, new book stacks were placed in the former art vault and two rooms off the public corridor were converted to library use. The east end of the staff corridor and two offices were also remodeled for library office and work space.

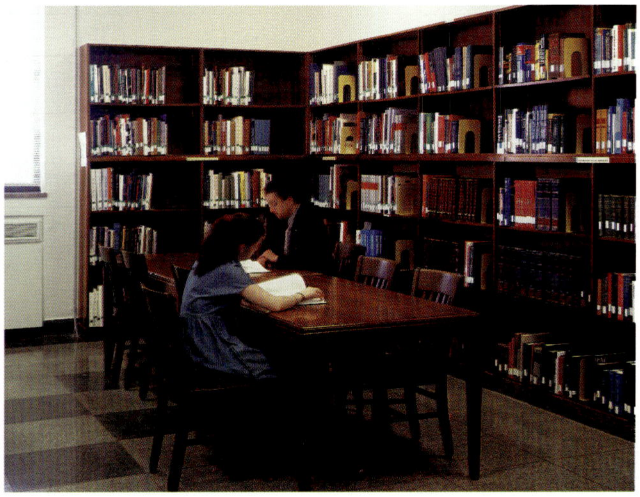

Although the library (ABOVE) and the museum shop (BELOW) were two of three functions not to be relocated, they both expanded into adjacent areas.

The Museum Shop

Because of its central location in the original building, as well as its proximity to the atrium, the museum shop was one of the few departments not to be relocated. Instead, in an extensive redesign, it was expanded to the north and south, and additional office and storage space was provided nearby.

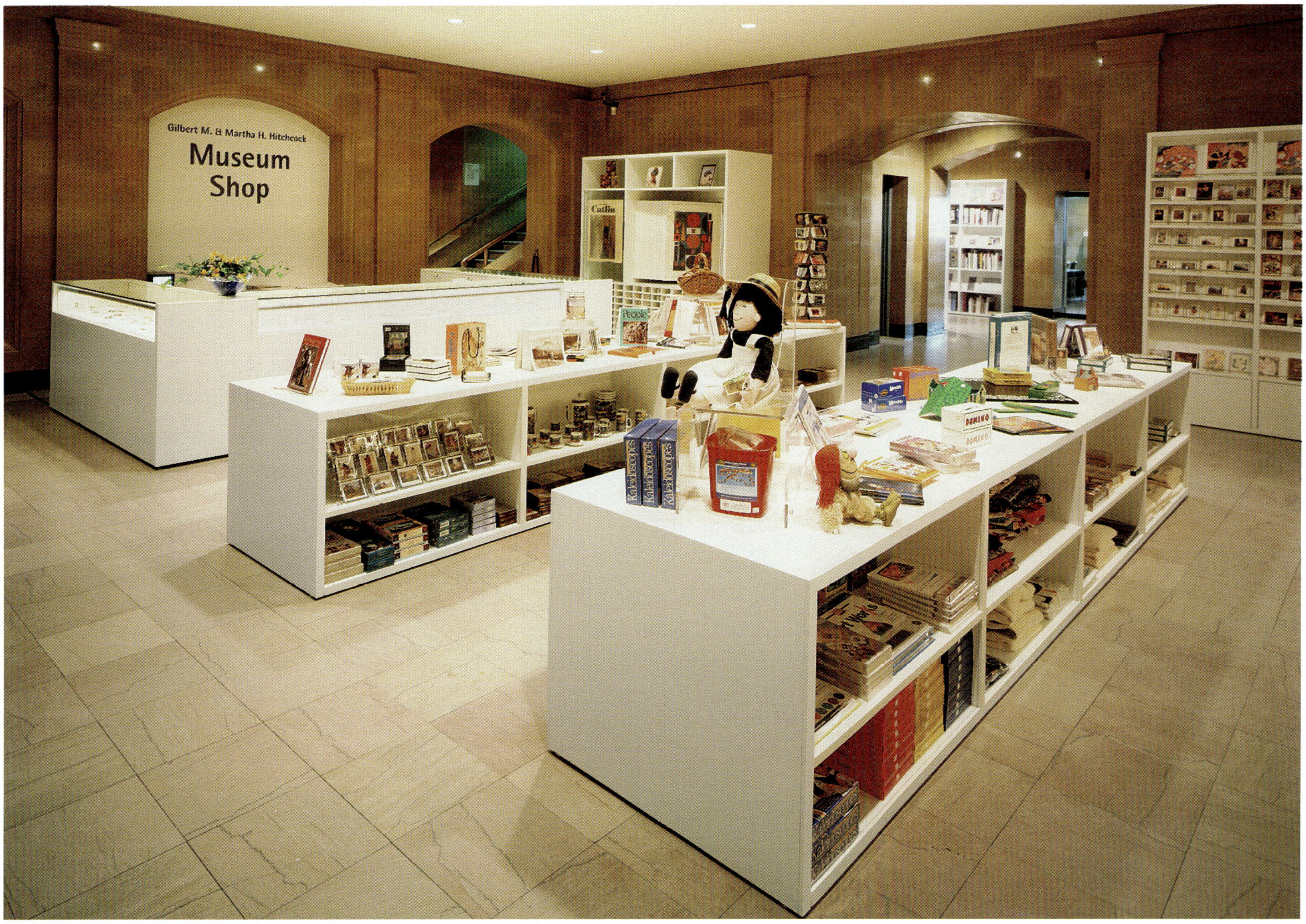

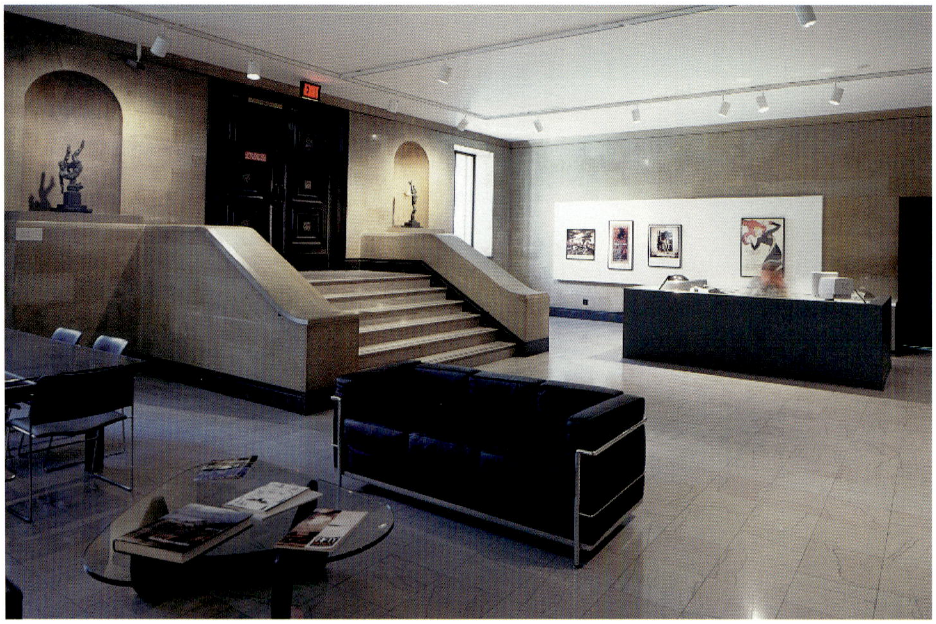

The Curatorial and Administration Offices

Offices for the curatorial staff, previously in two separate areas of the lower level, were relocated in a single suite next to the art reference library in the southeast wing.

At the other end, in what had been the education department's single classroom, are offices for the director and deputy director. The various administrative departments were brought together in the southwest wing.

The original lobby area for the south door (from 1980 to 1994, a café) was developed into a reception, waiting, and conference area.

Originally the main entrance off Dodge Street, and for many years the Museum's café, the lower level lobby on the south now functions as a reception, waiting, and conference area.

The Lecture Hall

Although on a much reduced scale from the concert hall on the main level, the lecture hall is also a rich combination of marbles. The wainscot is of Regal Blue trimmed with Belgian Black, the floors are terrazzo, and the walls were covered with Akoustolith tiles. Its original appearance had been much modified by the addition of a projection booth and partial redecoration in the late 1970s. Renovation of this room was not part of the 1994 plan; however, as the project wound down, it became clear that there were sufficient resources to update this much-used room as well. The marble was refurbished and, for purely aesthetic reasons, the functional Akoustolith tiles were covered with sound-absorbing white cloth panels similar to those at the entrances to the galleries in the addition. The ceiling was reworked to replace the general lighting with a flexible system designed to cope with the varied needs of art history lectures and other classes, as well as with musical and theatrical events.

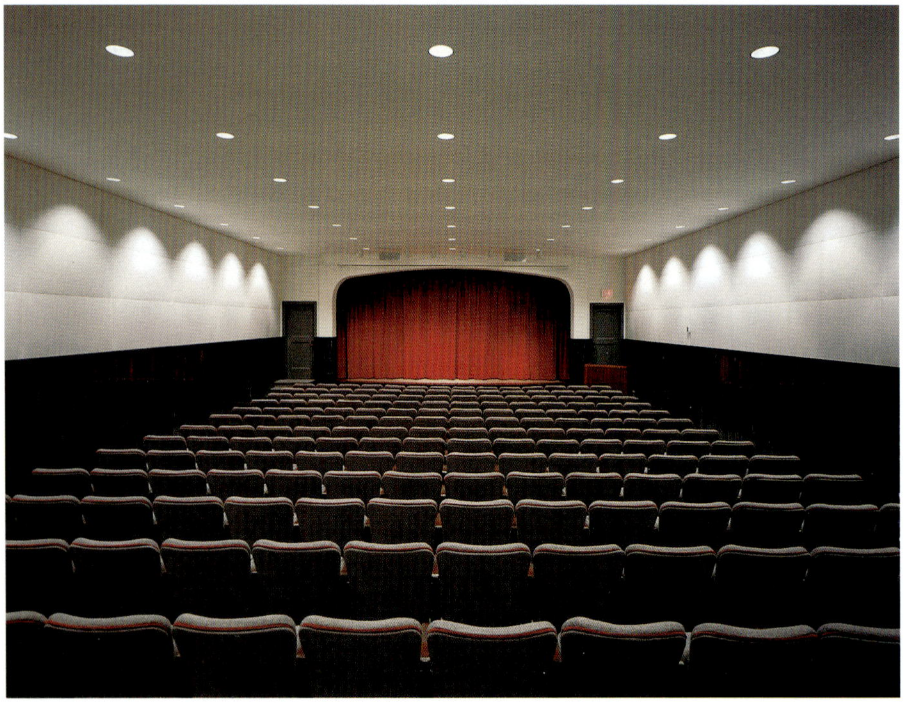

Not part of the original plan, the lecture hall was renovated in the summer of 1995.

The new, improved, and enlarged Joslyn Art Museum was complete in all essentials when it opened to the public on November 19, 1994.

Every aspect of the original program of new construction and renovation had been accomplished, and the work remaining to be done was limited to details in the staff areas. What started as an ambitious project to renew the Joslyn Memorial building as a serious art museum ended by restoring all aspects of the program originally deemed important by the founder, Sarah H. Joslyn: the visual arts, music, and education.

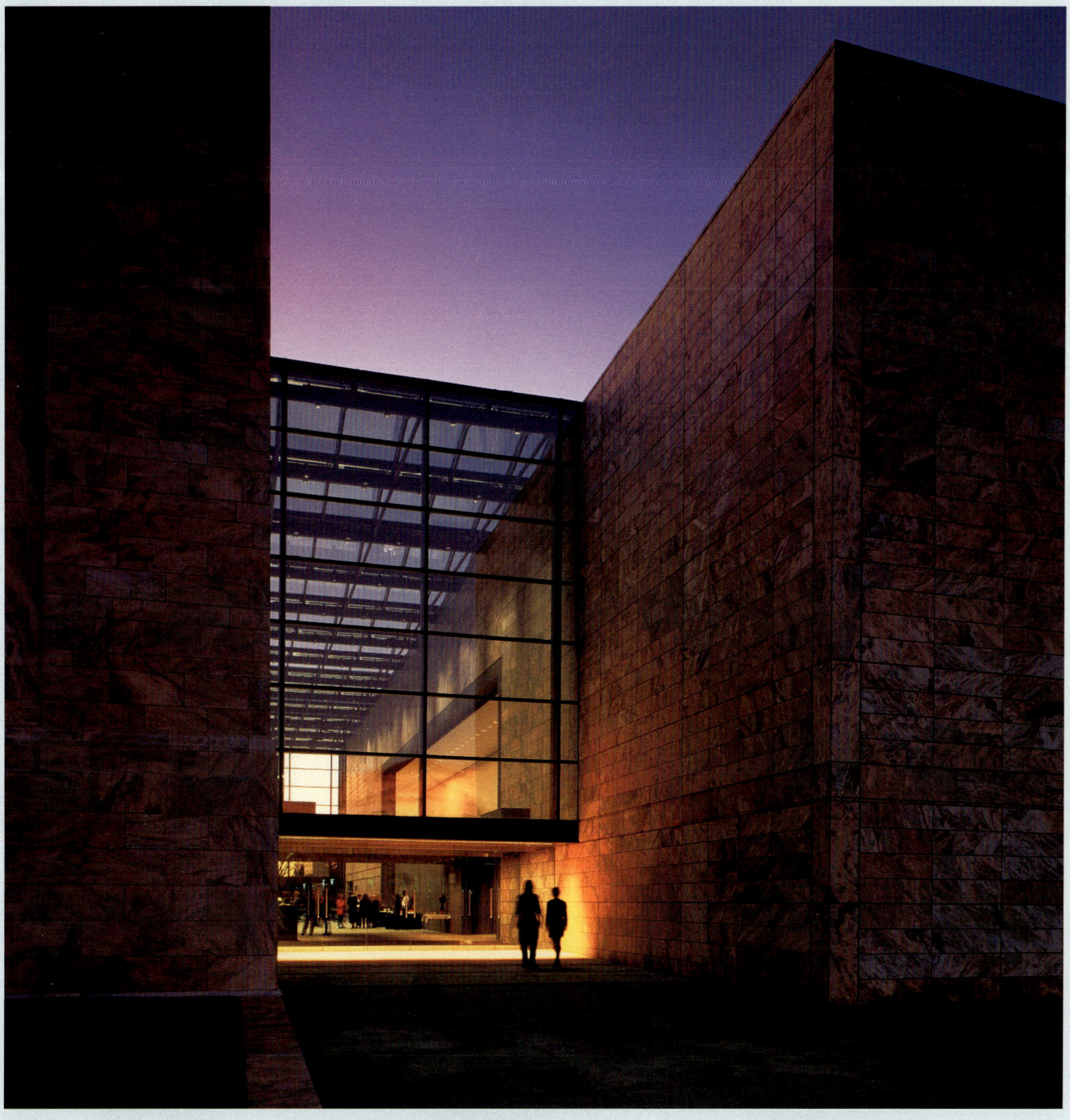

A diaphanous steel and glass membrane, the atrium links the old and new with the most delicate of touches. In daylight, a bright and busy public space; in the evening and at night, visitors are drawn toward it by the glowing light that emanates from between the solid bulk of the original Memorial building and the sheer-sided walls of the addition.

AFTERWORD

Mrs. Joslyn's gift to Omaha was enthusiastically recognized by an appreciative public and, as this narrative shows, throughout the six decades of its existence, her Memorial building fulfilled many roles: from concert hall and art museum to history museum and education center. Its original design gave powerful expression to the deep-seated need in any community for a Temple of Culture, a need that never diminishes, no matter what changes may occur in general attitude or particular terminology. It was this very perceived need that led to the dramatic capital expansions and modifications of 1994 – all designed to further Sarah Joslyn's own hope, expressed at the 1931 opening ceremony, "that it will go on and on."

With the addition of the Walter and Suzanne Scott Pavilion, Joslyn Art Museum has been transformed from a beautiful, but inflexible, general-purpose cultural center into a specialist facility, equipped to accommodate the full spectrum of activity associated with today's art museum: from presentation of the full range of its permanent collections and an ambitious schedule of special exhibitions to extensive education programs; from music concerts and film screenings to banquet-sized social events.

Building an art museum is often said to be the modern equivalent of building a cathedral and, certainly, it represents a special challenge to architects: how to design a building that has its own character but does not, in the end, overshadow the art it is supposed to accommodate. There are many more cautionary lessons to be found in the museum architecture of the late twentieth century than there are useful precedents, and in planning the Scott Pavilion, Norman Foster and the team – fellow architects, engineers, construction company, and client – were frequently thrown back on their own experience. The primary concern was to create a new Joslyn Art Museum that embodied and respected the history of the original structure. Secondarily, there was an awareness that, if everything came together into this "new whole," the Joslyn expansion would become part of the history of art museum architecture, a place that future museum designers could look to for ideas and inspiration.

Writing two years after the opening of the Pavilion, it seems fairly safe to claim that the project was successful. Critical comment in the professional architectural press was uniformly enthusiastic, praising Foster for his restraint with regard to the original structure and for the drama of the new interior spaces, notably the galleries and the atrium. How it will be viewed in the future, what lessons will be drawn, and what new demands accommodated is, of course, impossible to say. As Sarah Joslyn declared in 1931, when questioned about her intentions for her husband's memorial: "That's up to them."

A NOTE ON SOURCES

As this book is intended to be more of a guide to Joslyn Art Museum than any kind of full historical analysis, no attempt has been made here to supply such scholarly scaffolding as footnotes and appendices. All of the material referred to – the correspondence among artist, architect, and philosopher, correspondence with Herschel Elarth, newspaper articles, accounts of gossip – can be found in the archives and libraries of Joslyn Art Museum, the Douglas County Historical Society in Omaha, and the Nebraska State Historical Society in Lincoln. In shaping my narrative, I owe a considerable debt to Ellen Simak, Curator of American Art at Joslyn from 1985 to 1988, who gathered much of the material cited here regarding the construction of the original building and drafted an unpublished essay on the subject. Two recent publications, in particular, provide a wealth of related information: Richard Guy Wilson, et al., *The Machine Age in America, 1918-1941* (New York: 1986); and Frederick C. Luebke, ed., *A Harmony of the Arts: The Nebraska State Capitol* (Lincoln: 1990).

GWJB

Memorial Building

Ethel S. Abbott Lecture Hall
Milton R. & Pauline S. Abrahams Library
The Cooper Foundation Classroom
Drew Gallery
Gerald E. & Paula J. Hazelrigg Gallery
Gilbert M. & Martha H. Hitchcock Gallery
Gilbert M. & Martha H. Hitchcock Museum Shop
Peter Kiewit Gallery
John & Elizabeth Lauritzen Gallery
John F. Merriam Gallery
Omaha Steaks Office Reception
The Doug Riley Family Education Gallery
Carolyn J. Scott Gallery
Robert H. & Mildred T. Storz Fountain Court
Witherspoon Concert Hall

Walter & Suzanne Scott Pavilion

ConAgra Atrium
Café Durham
FirsTier Bank, NA and FirsTier Financial, Inc. Gallery
Omaha World-Herald Gallery
Willis A. & Janet S. Strauss Bridge
Carl A. & Caroline Swanson Foundation and Gretchen Swanson Velde Galleries
Benjamin D. & Anna E. Wiesman Promenade

JOSLYN ART MUSEUM BOARD OF TRUSTEES (1928-1987)
BOARD OF GOVERNORS (1987-PRESENT)

■ Presidents/Chairmen of Joslyn Art Museum's Board of Trustees/Governors

Original Board Members

■ Sarah H. Joslyn, 1928-40
Coit L. Farnsworth, 1928-37
Herbert H. Fish, 1928-30
Charles F. Harding, 1928-31
John McDonald, 1928-56
William A. Redick, 1928-36
Charles W. Russell, 1928-33

Subsequent Board Members

Alexander H. Richardson, 1931-40
■ Roy Page, 1934-48
Fred A. Wright, 1936-42
William R. Watson, 1936-55
W. Dale Clark, 1938-74
■ Frank T. B. Martin, 1941-52
■ Casper Y. Offutt, 1943-74
W. A. Cassidy, 1946-74
Irving Benolken, 1949-54
■ John F. Merriam, 1952-73
Jasper L. Hall, 1952-53
■ Laurance R. Hoagland, 1952-63, 1967-76
J. Dewey Bisgard, 1953-72
Francis T. B. Martin, 1954-75
Willard D. Hosford, Jr., 1955-74
Jay Cherniack, 1956-73
A. F. Jacobson, 1958-74
■ Drexel J. Sibbernsen, Jr., 1958-75
Milo Bail, 1959-71
■ N. Phillips Dodge, Jr., 1959-75, 1977-78
■ E. Stanton Miller II, 1959-74
Peter Kiewit, 1960-74
V. J. Skutt, 1961-74
Gilbert C. Swanson, 1961-68
John F. Davis, 1961-67
Edward W. Lyman, 1961-74
Eugene Kingman, 1961-69
I. W. Carpenter, 1962-70
Leo A. Daly, 1962-73
Morris E. Jacobs, 1962-70
Frank Latenser, 1962-70
A. V. Sorensen, 1962-70
Robert H. Storz, 1962-74
Kenneth C. Holland, 1963-66
Carl Jonas, 1964-74
Thomas C. Woods, Jr., 1964-74
H. C. Young, 1964-74
Edd H. Bailey, 1967-71
Lawrence R. James, 1967-75
J. Alec Merriam, 1967-72
Dale Ball, 1968-75
John R. Lauritzen, 1968-74
John L. Offutt, 1968-77
Jay F. Swanson, 1969-72
D. J. Witherspoon, 1970-74
Jerome I. Cohn, 1971-75
■ Stanley J. How, 1971-76
Thomas S. Nurnberger, 1971-75
Willis A. Strauss, 1971-74, 1977-81, 1987-94
Beatrice Utley, 1972-76
Gretchen Swanson Pullen Velde, 1972-78, 1992-present
Edgar M. Morsman, Jr., 1974-77
■ Michael B. Yanney, 1974-76, 1987-present
■ Mary Landen, 1974-80, 1984-87, 1992-present
■ Sydney L. Cate, 1974-79
Earle A. Clark, 1974-78
■ Charles A. Monasee, 1974-79, 1992-present

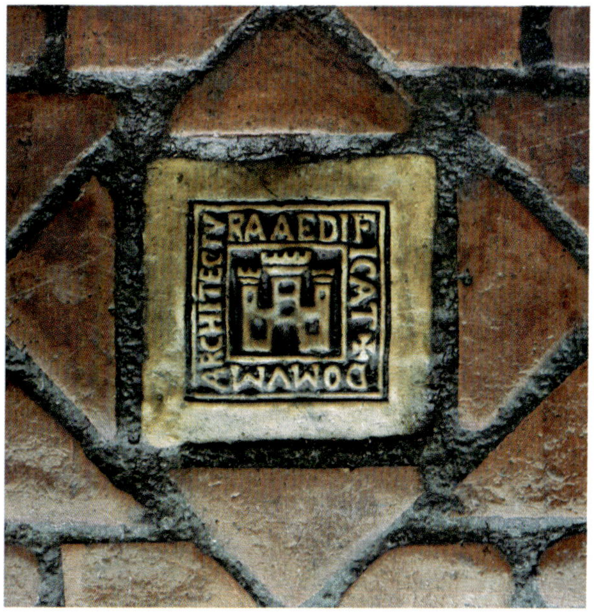

JOSLYN ART MUSEUM BOARD OF TRUSTEES (1928-1987)
BOARD OF GOVERNORS (1987-PRESENT)

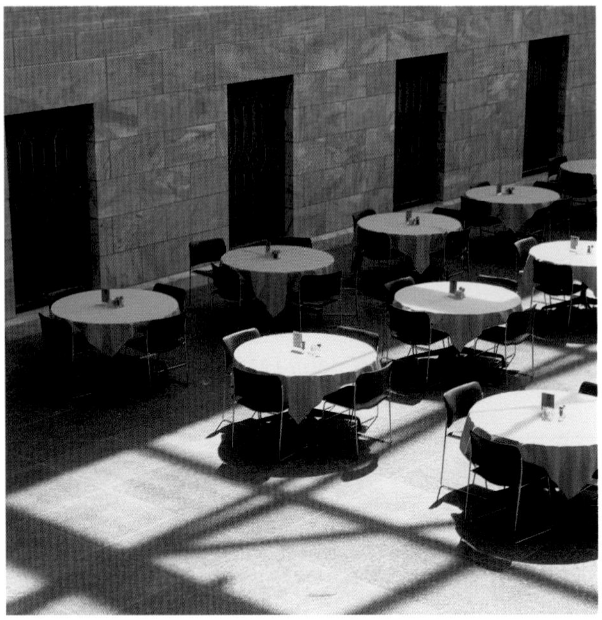

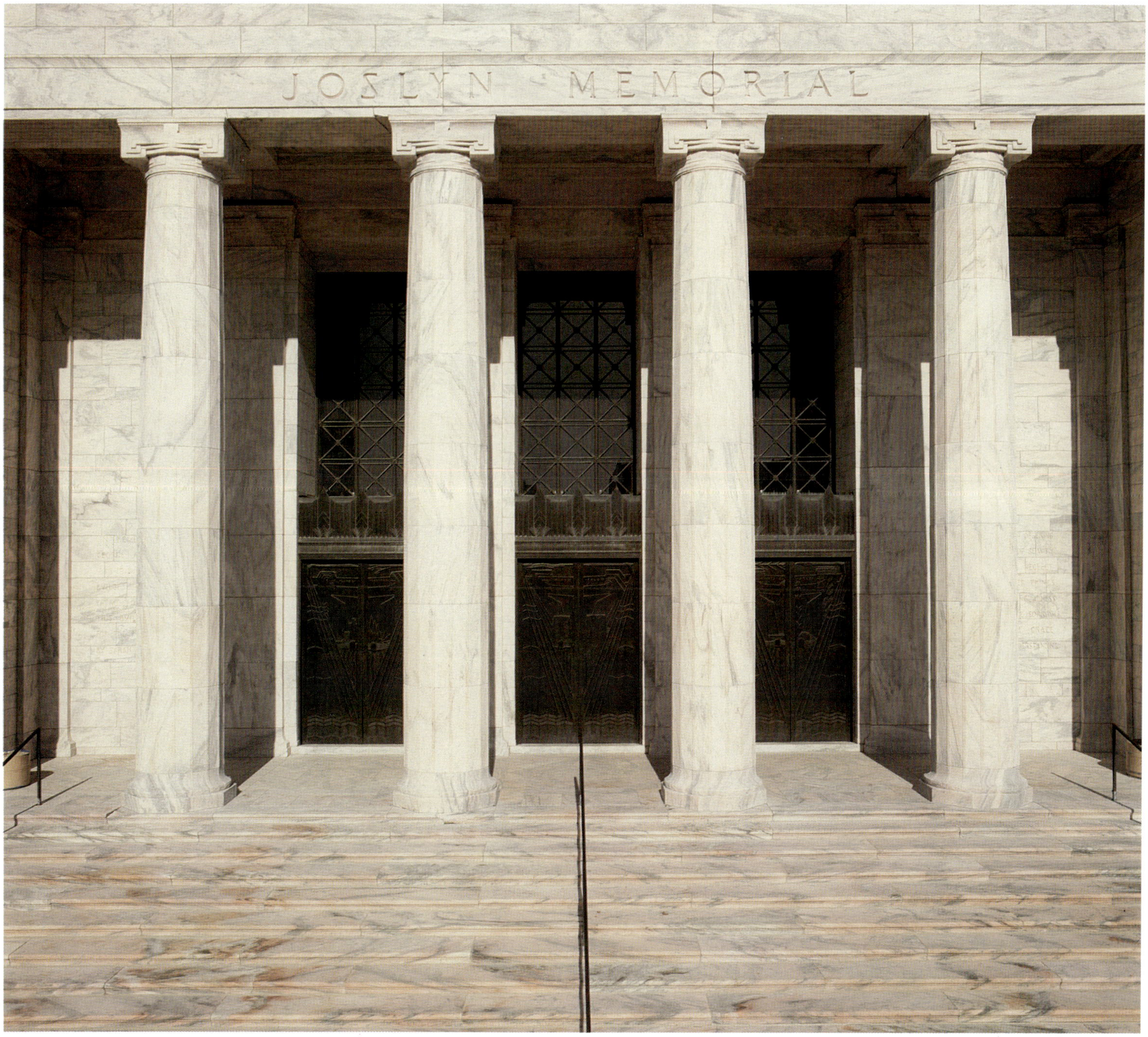

David A. Rismiller, 1992-present

Anne Rismiller, 1992-present

Suzanne Scott, 1992-present

Jackie Vrana, 1992-present

Susan Buffett, 1994-present

Sue Fletcher, 1994-present

Dianne Seeman Lozier, 1994-present

Robert Masterson, 1994

Lois Roskens, 1994-96

David Sokol, 1994-present

Janyce Hunt, 1995-present

Frederick J. Simon, 1995-present

Charles Heider, 1996-present

John Gottschalk, 1997-present

Joanne Harrell, 1997

Richard Jaros, 1997-present

David Wiesman, 1997-present

Paul H. Grummann, Ph.D. (1931-47)

Eugene Kingman (1947-69)

Richard N. Gregg (1969-71)

William A. McGonagle (1972-74)

Laurance R. Hoagland (1975-76)

Fredrick Schmid (1976-79)

Henry Flood Robert, Jr. (1979-88)

Graham W. J. Beal (1989-96)

John E. Schloder, Ph.D. (1997-present)

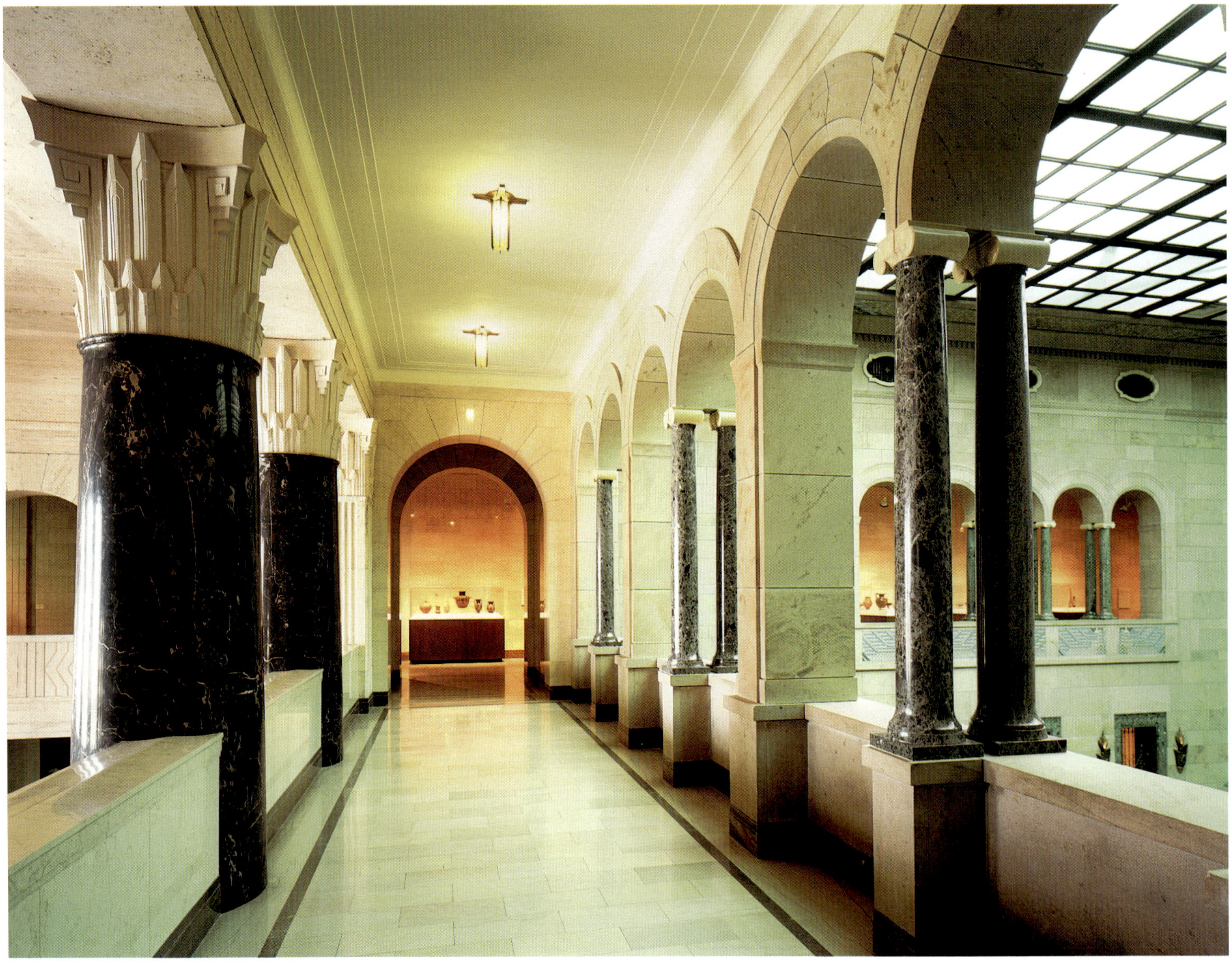

Sir Norman Foster & Partners

Sir Norman Foster, Architect
David Nelson, Partner in Charge (of project)
Ken Shuttleworth, Partner
Nigel Dancey, Project Architect
Tom Leslie, Architect
Lulie Fisher, Architect
Nigel Greenhill, Architect
Justin Nichols, Architect

Kiewit Construction Company

Bruce A. Tresslar, Vice President
Mark Nienhueser, Project Manager
Charles Sachs, Superintendent
Kevin Murray, Superintendent
Charlie Ring, Superintendent
Joe Lempka, Project Engineer
Kevin Gigax, Field Engineer
Darrel Frisch, Business Manager
Cliff Kern, General Foreman
Charlie Nelson, Laborer Foreman
Don Buboltz, Carpenter Foreman

Henningson Durham & Richardson, Inc.

Patrick McDermott, Project Principal
Bruce Carpenter, Project Manager/Architect
Douglas Wignall, Architect
Jeff Cramer, Architect
Patrick Leahy, Architect
Greg Gensler, Architect
Steve Eavens, Architect
Dan Hahn, Structural Engineer
Randy Kumm, Structural Engineer
Brian Green, Structural Technician
Jerry Holmes, Structural Technician
Lynn Werman, Mechanical Engineer
X. Hoffman, Mechanical Engineer
James Nowak, Mechanical Technician
Garry Richardson, Mechanical Technician
Joe Sather, Electrical Engineer
Dick Raven, Electrical Technician
Steve Dyrstad, Electrical Technician
Paul Lage, Specification Architect
Bruce Maine, Specification Architect
Jill Peterson, Specification Technician
Kevin Bailey, Construction Administrator
Tim McDonnell, Construction Administrator
Jeff Pauba, Construction Administrator
Frank Fauble, Interior Designer
Mary McCawley, Landscape Architect

Consultants to Project

Davis Langdon & Everest, Quantity Surveyors
Claude Engle, Lighting
R. F. Mahoney & Associates, Acoustic
Paul Morrell, Consultant
Thomas Morrow Associates Inc., Food Service

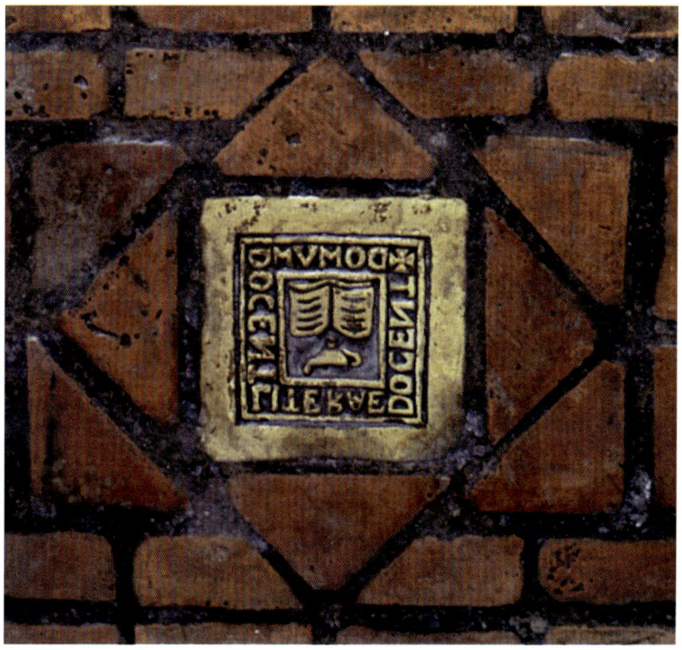